Performing
Revolutionary

First published in the UK in 2018 by
Intellect, The Mill, Parnall Road, Fishponds, Bristol, BS16 3JG, UK

First published in the USA in 2018 by
Intellect, University of Chicago Press,
1427 E. 60th Street, Chicago, IL 60637, USA

Copy-editor: MPS Technologies
Cover image: UPRISING #8. Photo by Tara Malik
Design: Aleksandra Szumlas
Production manager: Amy Rollason
Typesetting: Contentra Technologies

A catalogue record for this book is available from the British Library

ISBN: 978-1-78320-794-7
ePUB ISBN: 978-1-78320-891-3
ePDF ISBN: 978-1-78320-795-4

Printed and bound by Hobbs

This is a peer-reviewed publication.

Performing Revolutionary

ART, ACTION, ACTIVISM

By Nicole Garneau
Edited by Anne Cushwa

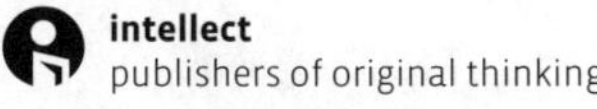

intellect
publishers of original thinking

For my parents, Bonnie and Mo. Endless gratitude!

– Nicole Garneau

Contents

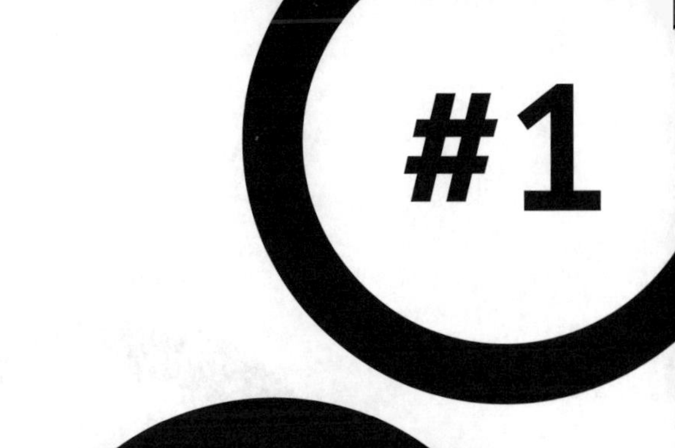
#1

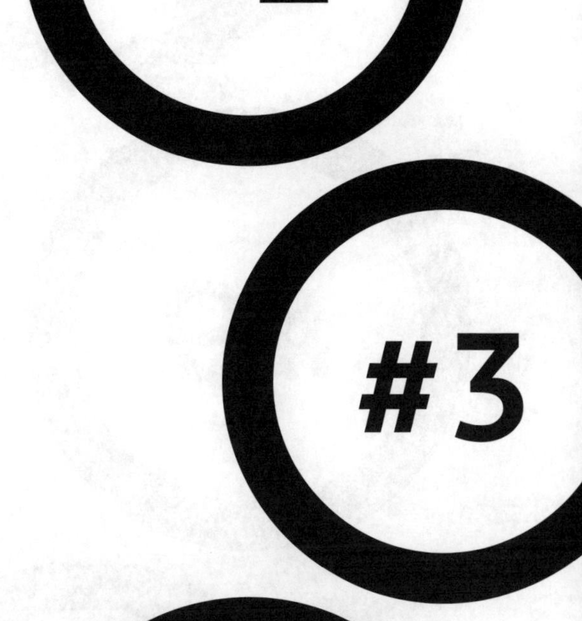
#2
#3
#4

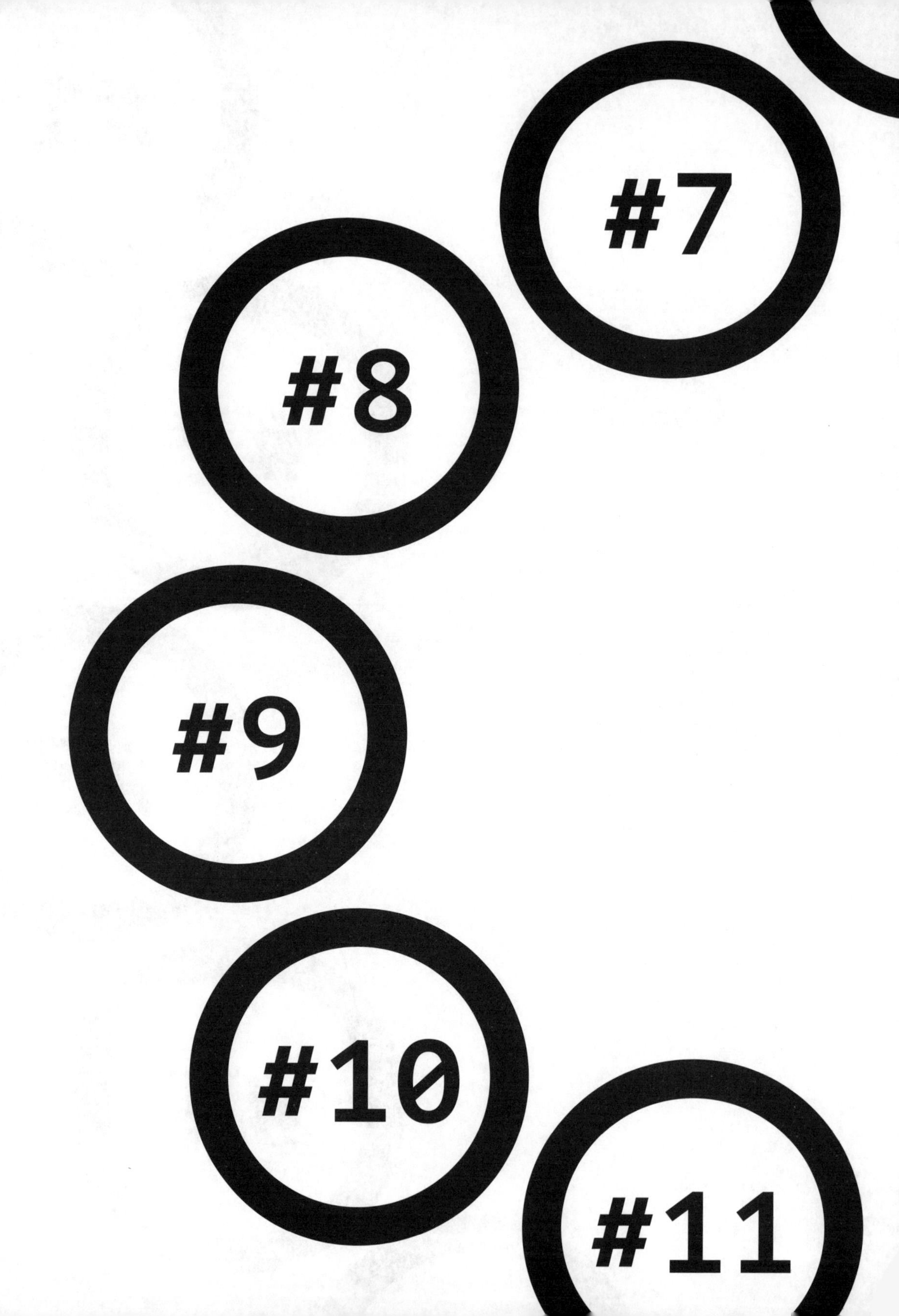

#7
#8
#9
#10
#11

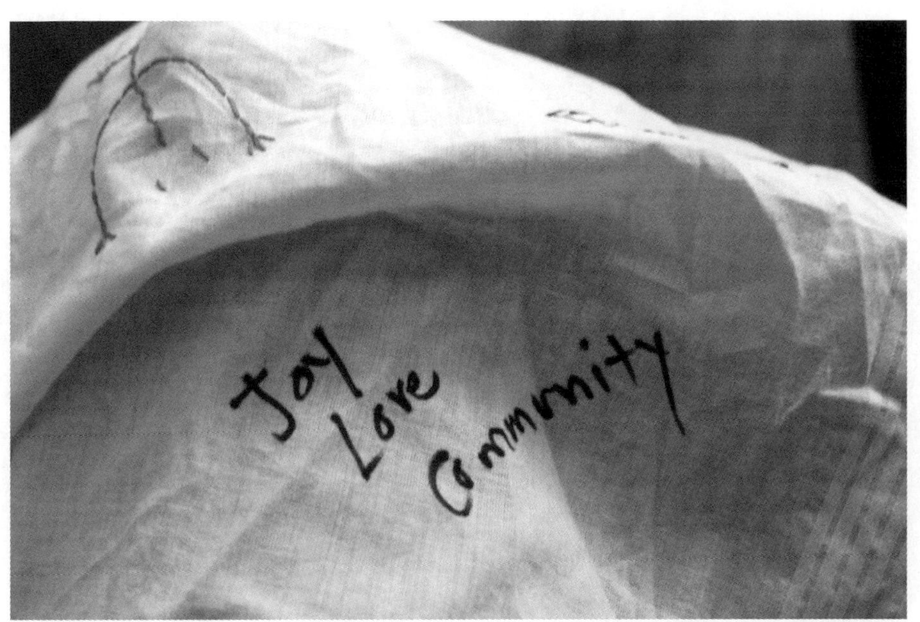

Figure 1: A vision of liberation on an embroidered handkerchief in UPRISING #9. Photo by Tara Malik.

Acknowledgements

First and foremost, this book would not exist without UPRISING participants: the volunteer performers, writers, theorists, artists, activists, and random strangers who crossed our paths. This book is my way of discovering what UPRISING meant for me and the community of folks who made it happen. It is my hope that all of the people who participated in UPRISING can receive this book as an expression of genuine gratitude for the ways their bodies and souls fed the work.

The economy of the UPRISING tour and years of book-making were partially supported by my loving parents Bonnie and Emile Garneau, who allow me to store things in their basement, sleep in their guest room, and eat from their fridge in Central Illinois between performances, residencies, and gigs. I received an Artistic Assistance grant from Alternate ROOTS and a Critical Fierceness grant from Chances Dances to support the printing of color images in this book.

As of this writing, I have been someone's houseguest for most of the last four years. This book was written in Catapult Studios in New Orleans where I lived in the home of MK Wegmann; on a month-long residency at Crosshatch Center for Art & Ecology in northern Michigan; in the Rogers Park condo of Anne Cushwa; looking out at my parents' backyard pond in Normal, Illinois; while serving as Fairy Worker in Residence with Bob Martin and Carrie Brunk on Clear Creek in Rockcastle County, Kentucky; in Sarah Stigler and Amber Miller's bunker in Humboldt Park; in Lisa Mount's artist bunkhouse in Sautee Nacoochee, Georgia; in the Tarburtons' cabin in Estill County, Kentucky; and on the Collins' Farm in Printer, Kentucky. The UPRISING project is fueled by economies of generosity.

For several years of UPRISING, I was in a relationship with the artist Ruth Robbins, an excellent photographer who captured many of the UPRISINGs beautifully, and for free. Like many artists, my lovers are drawn into my work. When I think of how the ideas for the UPRISING project came together, before it was even called UPRISING, I remember driving in a rental car with Ruth from Atlanta to New Orleans, on that long, hot strip of Highway 65 that traverses Alabama on the way to Louisiana. As the UPRISING project continued, Ruth's participation was significant. Having a lover of such artistic brilliance, intellectual depth, conceptual sophistication, and spiritual wisdom inspired me to make UPRISING as ambitious and high quality as I could.

This book also features wonderful images by Carlton Turner, Melisa Cardona, Nick Slie, Uncle Bear, Bailey Ferguson, and Tara Malik.

A positive pressure on the planning/dreaming for UPRISING was the genuine curiosity and gentle support of C.J. Mitchell, then Executive Director of Links Hall, a space for contemporary performance in Chicago. (C.J. is now Director of the Live Art Development Agency in the United Kingdom.) In the fall of 2007, I came to C.J. with an idea about a five-year project of mostly outdoor performances, and Links Hall offered to be the fiscal agent and administrative support for the project. Links Hall contributed significantly to me believing that an UPRISING book was possible. Links Hall staff members Roell Schmidt, Erica Mott, and Marie Casimir have helped me over the years by distributing EVIDENCE postcards, brainstorming marketing and fundraising, and cheering me on through the years of UPRISING and the making of this book.

In the spring of 2013, I received the first critical feedback and encouragement on a draft of this book from Bonnie Fortune. Since then, drafts of the book, proposals, chapters, and essays have been generously reviewed by Jeff Abell, Ann Russo, Craig Harshaw, Daniel Tucker, Terri Griffith, Nick Slie, Bob Martin, Carrie Brunk, Leah Mayers, and the DePaul University Center for Writing-Based Learning. Special gratitude to my guides, ancestors, and angels, as well as Saint Expedite!

A crowdsourced fundraiser through USA Projects (now Hatchfund) for the UPRISING book raised over $9,000 from 144 donations. Supporters included Aaron Richmond-Havel, Abigail Satinsky, Adam Young, Alex Fullerton, Alice Lowenstein, Alisha Tonsic, Amanda Stefanski, Amber Miller, Amy and Vince DeGeorge, Anita Evans, Anne Adams, Anne Statton, Ariel Luckey, Arnie Malina, Ashley Sparks, Ben Weinberg and Lisa Morrow, Benjamin Rosenthal, Beth and Ken Ferris, Bill Van Berschot, lark Ábout, Brooks Hall, Cam Mangham, Carla Perlo, Carlotta Figliulo, Carlton Turner, Carol O'Brien, Carolyn Boucher, Carrie Lydon, Christine Thom, Christopher Mitchell, Claire Pentecost, Clark Baim, Clay Thomas, Craig Harshaw, D'LocoKid, Dan Paz, David Granskog, Deborah Bryer, Denise Karczewski, Devra Breslow, Elizabeth Doud, Elizabeth Wuerffel, Emile and Bonnie Garneau, Erik Roldan, Erin Barnard, Francis Tobin, FT, Gail Soave, Hannah Davey, Heidi S. Howard, Iveliz Orellano, Jamie Royce, Janine Hoft, Jeannette Perkal, Jeff Abell, Jennifer Fite, Jessica Halem, Jill Bruellman, Jennifer Mefford, Joanna Quealy, Joanna Russo, Joanne Vena, John Ruby, Jordan Peimer, Joseph Hulbert, Joseph Varisco, Judi Jennings, Kate Drabinski, Uncle Bear, Kathie deNobriga, Kent Garneau, Kim Nicholson-Messmer, Kristen Cox, Kristina Wong, Lani Montreal, Lara Oppenheimer, Latham Zearfoss, Laurie Jo Reynolds, Leslie Wallin, Linda Wagner, Lisa Barcy, Lisa D'Amour, Lisa Mount, Lisa Samra, Lise Kloeppel, Lois Huminiak, Lois Remeikis, Louisa Sargent, Maria and Jørn Eichhorn, Maria Gray, Marie

Casimir, Marion Preez, Mark Jeffrey, Mark Valdez, Mary Coble, Mary Patten, Meg Leary, Megan Carney, Megan Whiteford, Melinda Rueden, Melissa Turner, Morgan Jenness, Nance Klehm, Nick Slie, Nora Dunlop, Peter Carpenter, Philip Cramer, Rachel Damon, Rami George, RAQUEFELLA, Robert Martin, Sarah Andrew, Sarah Haas, Sarah Jackson, Scarlet Rivera, Scott Noren, Searah Deysach, Seth Thompson, Shannon Turner, Stephanie Elizondo Griest, Stephen Bailey, Stephen Clapp, Susan Ganem, Suzanne Weiss, Tamale Sepp, Tamara Alvarado, Tanya Mote, Tara Malik, Therese Quinn, Topher McCulloch, Trey Hartt, Valerie Chang, Vallejo Gantner, and Vicki Meek.

There is one particularly steadfast friend and collaborator who made this book possible: Anne Cushwa. Anne Cushwa is an independent art historian who I met in New Orleans in the spring of 2005. Our friendship was born in collaboration: she was a participant in that year's project of daily performances. When Anne offered to work with me on the UPRISING book, I was intimidated. She's so smart and knows so much about art! I thought she would review it once and move on, but she became committed to the project. Anne read and edited multiple drafts. She wrestled with me on questions of structure. She came to the cabin in Kentucky for an intensive book retreat after a couple days sprawled on her floor in Brooklyn proved insufficient. She wrote three beautiful pieces for this book. She helped me choose images. But her most important gift was years of faith in the project, despite all of my doubts and unrelenting self-sabotage. I can't imagine completing it without her. She compassionately listened to my insecurities, and just kept repeating some version of encouragement: 'You are a good artist and writer. This book is worthwhile. Keep going.'

Introduction

Nicole Garneau

IT BEGINS IN CHICAGO

Lake Michigan in winter delivers an endlessly varying drama that might feature slushy ice chunks clanking musically against one another; blue-grey vistas that barely delineate between water and sky; or giant sculptural waves that have frozen before breaking against the edges of the city of Chicago. One may never grow tired of walking, biking, or driving along the lake to see the show. One January evening in 2006, my brother Kent and I cruised up Lake Shore Drive. The United States had invaded Iraq. I still couldn't believe that a global anti-war movement had not stopped the Bush administration in its tracks. The larger meaning of this failure was articulated by Judith Butler, who wrote that

> the raw public mockery of the peace movement, and the characterization of anti-war demonstrations as anachronistic or nostalgic, work to produce a consensus of public opinion that profoundly marginalizes anti-war sentiment and analysis, putting into question in a very strong way the very value of dissent as part of contemporary US democratic culture. (2004: 4)

There was no discussion of a draft, so unlike the US Gulf War of the early 1990s, I was not consumed by fear that one of my brothers would be sent to shed his blood for oil. I was trying to find sense in the stew of US hyper-militarization and the fantastical revenge narratives that followed the terrorist attacks of September 11, 2001.

As the stunning Chicago skyline smoothed into parks and apartment buildings, we sat riveted by a public radio broadcast by Chris Hedges (*War is a Force that Gives Us Meaning*, 2006). Hedges told a story from the Serbo-Croatian war in the city of Goražde, where many Serbs were attacking their Muslim neighbors. A Muslim farmer brought milk to a non-Muslim Bosnian Serb woman who had recently given birth, but was not able to nurse her newborn. The farmer, facing constant scorn from family and neighbors, delivered milk for the baby every day for 442 days during the war. He always refused offers of money. Against the backdrop of accounts of the horrors of war, Hedges also asserted, 'here was the power of love. What this illiterate farmer did would color the life of another human being, who might never meet him, long after he was gone. In his act lay an ocean of hope' (Hedges 2002).

I became fixated on the conceptual problem of quantifying acts of love in relation to acts of atrocity. What is the measure of compassionate gestures that would help us cross a tipping point into deeper humanity? As a politically engaged performance artist, how could I undertake this research question in earnest?

WHAT IS THIS BOOK?

The book is the result of the UPRISING performance project, five years of practice-based creative research into the embodiment of hope-filled, connective art actions that allow us to practice the skills we need in order to build a better world. It is the story of how thousands of participants in eight US and five international locations worked together to manifest the loving and visionary community we need for revolutionary times. The book illustrates methodologies for engaging a diverse public in political struggles in ways that are pleasurable, interactive, and concrete. This book is the result of many years of exploration into how performance can be used to create public demonstrations of the possibilities for a more loving, just, and humane present and future. It offers strategies for participatory artmaking in service of social justice. It is part idealistic instruction manual, part artistic memoir, and part love letter to the sacred work of making radical change.

Beginning in January 2008, and continuing once a month for five years, I put on white clothes, took my body out on the street, met up with volunteers, and created a performance I called an UPRISING. There were 60 UPRISINGs in all, involving easily thousands of people in Chicago, Berkeley, New Orleans, Brooklyn, San Francisco, Asheville, NC, Rockcastle, KY, Oshkosh, WI, Russia, Denmark, the United Kingdom, and Portugal.

I used my performance practice to train myself to be a more revolutionary person and invited other folks to join me in this research. I wrote about what happened in each UPRISING and I asked participants to reflect on their experiences. After the five years were over, I took several more years to write about what I learned, study reflections from volunteer performers, and consider these performances in relation to social justice activism, stewardship of the earth, and healing for individuals and communities. This book explores the multiple meanings of these gestures when they are deployed in a creative context, outside of traditional activism and art institutions. These goals and methods place the UPRISING project in the realm of 'activist art,' about which Greg Sholette writes:

Activist art is the opposite of those aesthetic practices that, however well-intentioned or overtly political in content, remain dependent on the space of the museum for their meaning.

To produce activist art is therefore to put one's political commitment to the test, first through non-institutional forms of cultural distribution and interaction – art for demonstrations and picket lines, mail art, on city walls or on the sides of buses, art in the middle of shopping malls and crowded plazas – and second to use that form of dissemination to speak about social injustices with an audience who presumably has little patience for refined aestheticism but does care about war, inequality, political freedom and protecting the environment. (1999: n.pag.)

ROOTS OF ART ACTIVISM

I had the tremendous good fortune to be able to study dance and theater from a young age. I was never a great ballerina, but I loved the part where we dressed up in sparkly costumes and moved around under bright lights in an auditorium full of people. I trained and performed as an actor for about twenty years before I decided that performance art was the most accurate term for the kind of work I wanted to make: content-rich, politically engaged, physically rigorous, self-written/directed, openly critical of the standards of beauty to which female actors are subject, and not necessarily bound to the confines of institutional performance spaces.

There are a number of groups in Chicago that have been important political and artistic homes for me: the Women's Action Coalition (WAC); The WAC Drum Core; Randolph Street Gallery; Big Smith Performance Ensemble; The Color Triangle; Queer White Allies Against Racism; AREA: Chicago Arts, Research, Education, and Activism; Sissy Butch Brothers' Gurlesque Burlesque; Girlie-Q Variety Hour; Chances Dances; and Northern Lights Queer Performance and Dance Party.

In the mid-1990s I became part of Insight Arts, a Chicago-based organization dedicated to increasing access to cultural work that supports progressive social change. I was active with Insight Arts as a resident artist, staff teacher, ensemble member, event producer, and board member between 1994 and 2010. The influence of Insight Arts on my work as an artist cannot be understated. Insight Arts collaborators like Craig Harshaw, Aislinn Sol, karen g. williams, and Davida Ingram are some of my most important teachers on art and activism. For most of its existence, Insight Arts was based in the United Church of Rogers Park, where we had access to dusty old church halls with wooden floors, peeling plaster, drafty windows, and no light or sound infrastructure. I lived within walking distance of our space, and I knew the children enrolled in our programs from the neighborhood. Those years were paramount to helping me see the ways that cultural workers are essential to political/social movements. Six years of co-producing Insight Arts' annual Women's Performance Jam laid an essential groundwork for me as a cultural worker who not only creates and performs, but also makes space for the presentation of other artists who are making challenging work. The final UPRISING performance was on 2 December 2012 in New Orleans, but it felt important to honor my Chicago lineage by bringing the project to a spiritual close at a Winter Solstice ceremony three weeks later at Insight Arts.

Another group that helped inform my practice as an art activist is the incredible community of righteous artists and presenters that make up the National Performance Network (NPN). Through NPN, I connected with Alternate ROOTS, an organization of artists and activists who center their work and lives in the US South. Alternate ROOTS calls for social and economic justice and is working to dismantle all forms of oppression – everywhere. Although I started UPRISING before I went to my first ROOTS meeting, the mission of ROOTS helped me feel like I had found an artistic and political home. Ten UPRISING performances took place in the US South, all connected to people and organizations I met through ROOTS.

WHAT MAKES AN UPRISING?

I define an UPRISING as a public demonstration of revolutionary practices. What do I mean by revolutionary practices? I mean a commitment to my community to work diligently on world-envisioning and world-building. I mean developing expertise I imagine we need for revolutionary times. I mean setting up some performative structures to embody our desired relationships with each other. UPRISINGs are experimental ways of practicing the skills we need in order to achieve a global culture of justice and compassion. They are attempts at making a slice of a world in which we want to live, and then inviting people directly and immediately inside it. I believe that if we can grow more comfortable with our post-revolutionary selves and social relations, we will be better equipped to recognize even momentarily liberated spaces. We will feel less shocked when we actually manifest a radically loving revolutionary culture. These are some of the consistent features of an UPRISING:

- I always wore white, and I tried to encourage others to wear white, too. I like white as a uniform because most of us have something white in our closet, and a group of people all dressed in white are clearly 'doing something.'

- All UPRISINGs explored ideas and histories of revolution.
- UPRISINGs incorporated gestures of world-building.
- An UPRISING was often an attempt to transform violent images into something hopeful.
- UPRISINGs were site-specific and consciously responsive to their geographical and historical contexts.
- UPRISING decisions were made quickly and the works were generally short, operating from the conviction that more time spent does not necessarily equal better art.
- UPRISINGs all included some volunteer or audience participation.
- Participants and I maintained a sense of humor and self-awareness.
- Structures were flexible to the extent required by the event, weather, people, and other circumstances.
- The five-year structure created a monthly imperative.
- UPRISINGs were documented in photos and writing (always) and video (mostly). Documentation was shared online.

UPRISING resists categorization, but has been called performance; actions; events; ceremonies; projects; demonstrations; rituals; interventions; live art; visual art; social practice; party tricks; entertainment; and social sculpture. It might even be an intergenerational dinner party at the home of former members of The Weather Underground (UPRISING #41). Abstract Expressionist Allan Kaprow coined the term 'Happening' in the 1950s to describe an art experience in which 'rather than being passive observers, the audience were participants – invitations to the event said *you will become part of the happenings; you will simultaneously experience them*' (Beaven 2012: n.pag., original emphasis). I never described UPRISINGs in this way, but I have said 'yes' when someone asked, 'is it like a Happening?' There are a number of similarities between UPRISINGs and Happenings, mainly that UPRISINGs engaged people who don't necessarily identify as artists in the creation of the work. In her book *Participation,* Claire Bishop shares this excerpt from Allan Kaprow's *Notes on the Elimination of an Audience*: 'The best participants have been persons not normally engaged in art or performance, but who are moved to take part in an activity that is at once meaningful to them in its ideas yet natural in its methods' (2006: 103).

I am trained as an artist, so when I make projects that are the creative manifestations of my hopes and dreams for the world, I call them Art. In fact, I prefer the term Cultural Work, as I think it more accurately describes the many ways of actively engaging in the cultural realm, and it more explicitly names the labor processes involved. From other perspectives, UPRISING could reasonably be called political activism, healing, or spiritual work. Someone on a grant panel once declared UPRISING to be more activism than art.

What I think this critique means is that in certain circles of the contemporary art world, if the work explores war or sweatshop labor or elderly people dying in heat waves, then it can cease to be art. I suspect that words like 'revolution' scream so loudly that some folks are unable to look at the work as artwork, because the content somehow overwhelms the form.

Most UPRISING performance plans emerged from one of three points of origin: (1) a necessity or desire to make work in a specific location; (2) a particular day of the month when an event was taking place or which was the best day in my calendar on which to work; or (3) a group of people who were available as participants. I did a lot of research about places and days in relation to revolutionary history or current activism. I distilled that research down to information that needed to be shared with volunteers or participants to help them care. Then I let images, gestures, and ideas bubble up.

The earliest UPRISINGs have well-documented (read: typed and saved) performance plans and texts. As the years progressed, and I felt more comfortable making UPRISINGs, I felt less of a need to script everything out. I became less interested in my own words, and more interested in the creation of ceremonial actions. UPRISING #3 is a good illustration of how I planned in the early months of the project:

UPRISING #3 PERFORMANCE PLAN

1. Enter from Experimental Station
2. Walk in street arm in arm
3. Turn corner, stand in a line at the south of the garden
4. Watch for a while
5. Nicole takes hands and starts leading others through the garden
6. If people are working, stop and say hi, ask them about what they are doing
7. Walk up and down the paths, Nicole leads people off: Nance, would you like to work here?
8. Continue talking to/helping gardeners as necessary
9. If no one to talk to, stand, wait, watch, try to learn
10. When talking starts: find a place to kneel
11. Roll up sleeves, dig a hole in the earth
12. Work hands inside the hole
13. Stay that way until Nicole asks if anyone has anything to add
14. When Nicole gets to you, extract hands, be helped up
15. Stand, thank the gardener(s)
16. Walk paths out of the garden (clockwise)

17.   Stand in a line, hands up and facing garden
18.   Arm in arm, exit the way we came

Before many UPRISING performances, I put out a call for volunteers, and then communicated with them in the days and weeks before the event. This is an example of my communication with volunteers for UPRISING #7 at the Bijou Theater:

> Bring/wear white clothes. I always do this but for UPRISING #7 I'd like to go for more of a sexy/costume thing. So if you have white ties, belts, accessories, underwear, hot pants, hats, etc. think about that. DO NOT STRESS if you don't have a whole white outfit because I will bring a bunch of whites too, including some slips/lingerie. Feel free to genderfuck.

> Bring ONE book that has meant something to you in the realm of radical sexuality, feminism, gender, queer/trans* politics, etc. You should have a personal connection to this book – it needs to have meant something to you. We will carry them and I think we will create intimate interactions with people at the party where we read to them from these books.

> Please consider what your personal boundaries are with regard to kissing acquaintances and/or strangers. I AM NOT FORCING YOU TO VIOLATE YOUR BOUNDARIES. This is me exploring the idea of intimate contact with strangers (it is a sex club!) and wondering what other people think. If you are not comfortable with this idea please don't quit the performance – just articulate your boundaries. Sexual boundaries are an explicitly feminist and revolutionary idea, so it is great to have them be part of the content!

I chose the name 'UPRISING' for a performance project because it referenced revolution, but also because the literal meaning – rising up – indicated uplift, positivity, and hope. Since there currently is no word that combines 'public demonstration of revolutionary practices, enacted in relation to sites and communities, with strong ties to ceremony and ritual,' UPRISING is the closest descriptor I have. UPRISING's alchemy is a starting place + research + creative energy + site + humans + chance. Now that I understand UPRISING as a form, I propose that I am not the only person who could make UPRISINGs. Through sharing this praxis, I hope to make a genuine contribution to the field of cultural activism.

UPRISING AS ART ACTIVISM OR ACTIVIST ART

> We are facing terrifying ecological challenges, ever-more-deeply entrenched economic inequality, huge and ingrained structures of systematic racism [...] Individuals or even small groups engaging in creative projects simply do not have the metaphorical generators or earth movers to turn these things around, and until the tide is turned activists and artists alike are going to be fighting an ever-increasing number of battles in ever more embattled circumstances.
>
> One of the useful things about [a Social Practice] approach is that it helps reframe the vexed debate over efficacy, which is for me perhaps better thought of in negative rather than positive terms. Building a culture of creative activism has value, as a base where ideas about social change can be fostered and, as Rick Lowe says of the Project Row Houses, as an example that can inspire bigger things, even if it doesn't actually solve everything itself. An art project needn't have any measurable immediate positive effect, as far as I am concerned. (Davis 2013b: n.pag.)

Applied to UPRISING, the dichotomy between art and activism is false. In the blog post above, Ben Davis relieves art projects of the responsibility to 'have any measurable immediate positive effect,' although I would argue that UPRISING's effect of building revolutionary skills is an outcome of the project. UPRISING had lofty goals such as 'building a more loving, just and humane present and future,' but the achievement of that goal is an ongoing concern. In her essay 'Participatory art: A paradigm shift from objects to subjects,' Suzana Milevska points out the contradictions in holding artists accountable for revolutionary goals:

> There is another problem with participatory art in activist circles, when art is understood as a call for revolution and its success or failure is measured according to its revolutionary prerogatives. The interpretation of art as an agency that should circumvent the main societal and ideological obstacles that artists face [...] is prescriptive and expects too big an impact from art activism projects.
>
> Finally, I would argue that art has yet to find a position that would reconcile the contradictions between these two radical ends:

between 'critique for critique's sake' and art that can be turned into a revolutionary instrument. (2006: n.pag.)

I approached both the content and the form of UPRISING as activism. By choosing to make the performances free, public, participatory, and interactive, I was drawing on a lineage of formal activist art practices. I articulated a vision for the kind of world I am trying to build and from what forces of oppression I am working to liberate myself, my communities, and the earth. I felt strongly motivated to work in 'new forms buried in social energies not yet recognized as art,' as identified by Lucy Lippard (1995: 126). Lippard calls for these new forms to 'change power relations inherent in the way art is now made and distributed,' but I seek to transform much more than the art world. I see UPRISING as participating in what Belgian theorist Chantal Mouffe (2012: n.pag.) calls the 'counter-hegemonic move against the capitalist appropriation of aesthetics,' which Mouffe claims can be achieved by 'putting aesthetic means at the service of political activism.'

DID IT WORK?

Sometimes I was able to quiet the demon of self-judgment about whether or not the work is good art by reminding myself of the endurance aspect of the project. First of all, UPRISING was 60 actions that made up one project, and until all 60 were done, there was no rush to assess success or failure. Individual works accumulated and gained meaning from the relationships to the UPRISINGs that came before, and the ones that came after, as parts of a larger whole. I thought of each UPRISING as a step along a path – an attempt to practice some kind of revolutionary strategy with other folks, and then find meaning in the wholeness of these strategies taken together. UPRISING was one long five-year performance with monthly breaks for life and integration of lessons.

Thoughtful dialogue about an artwork constitutes its own assessment tool: to what extent does the project provoke discourse? Chicago artist/educator Craig Harshaw launched a multiday Facebook conversation with several contributors after the UPRISING Winter Solstice ceremony at Insight Arts in December 2012 by posting the following comment:

> Nicole Garneau mentioned last night at Insight Arts that there is a distinction between a performance and a ritual which if I remember correctly was that the expectation for an audience member at a performance is to watch/experience the work of the artist whilst the expectation of people attending a ritual is collective participation.

> True enough. However, I wonder if one might begin to think about performances (art in general) as containing a delayed step of participation that is related to discourse. A performance of any kind actually takes on life after it ends – it is the afterlife of a performance that matters the most. How does the work get worked on by the audience after they leave the space? How do they remake the work in ways that give the work an afterlife? (Harshaw 2012: n.pag.)

In this same spirit of fostering dialogue, Canadian artist Justin Langlois (n.d.) created a fascinating inquiry called *Methodologies of Failure: Evaluation Practices for Socially Engaged Art*. He raises relevant questions for critiquing work like UPRISING, many of which are addressed in this book:

> Are you uncomfortable with calling your artwork an artwork?

> Have you tried to explain at length the ways in which you are defining the terms 'involved' and 'other people' and 'community'?

> Are you painfully aware that there are unavoidable power imbalances at play in your project?

> Have you considered trying to present your project as a book, documentary, or play?

> How much pressure did you feel to defend the work as tackling political change?

> Did you assume that your project needed to continue indefinitely towards achieving some political end in order for it to be successful?

> Were you asked about success, measurable outcomes, attendance levels, or evidence of change?

> Did you expect there to be answers to those questions?

> Is your project illegible enough to likely never be printed in *Artforum* or your local newspaper?

> Were you asked to explain the reason you think your project is art?

While I was part of the Living Copenhagen Artist Residency in 2012, my colleague Joss Allen said my work reminded him of Hakim Bey's *Temporary Autonomous Zone* ([1991] 2003). Bey describes pop-up creative expression:

> History says the Revolution attains 'permanence', or at least duration, while the uprising is 'temporary'. In this sense an uprising is like a 'peak experience' as opposed to the standard of 'ordinary' consciousness and experience. But such moments of intensity give shape and meaning to the entirety of a life. ([1991] 2003: 98–99)

After five years of performance activism, I see how UPRISINGs created ephemeral glimpses into worlds that felt beautiful and connected.

When people ask me if I think the UPRISING project was a success, I answer that the only measure of success I understand is that it *happened:* 60 UPRISINGs took place once a month for five years. I made work and there were gestures, actions, and images that made me cry or produced delight in me and in other people. It was useful to build a structure of accountability based on time and the sharing of documentation as a way to keep working and not stop. It was helpful to have the imperative of a necessary monthly work, even if I was the only one who seemed to need it. It was just never an option not to do it.

UPRISING'S ECONOMY OF GENEROSITY

I made UPRISING actions live in public spaces for free, so that I could make them wherever and whenever I wanted, every month, without waiting for someone to give me a gig. I never refused a gig, but I also wanted to offer them as gifts in a spirit of generosity. There was no ticket revenue from an UPRISING. I am attracted to what Greg Sholette describes as the subversive possibilities of art as gift:

> Is the gift in other words, inherently apolitical? Or is it possible that the very act of generosity is itself a form of resistance in so far as absolute expenditure appears to contradict the very basis of a market economy: the buying and selling of commodities (including labor) using money as the medium of exchange? The concept of a post-scarcity economy of expenditure appears contrary to the logic of capitalism, and especially any system of exchange based on luxury merchandise (such as art). And yet art as gift has become increasingly popular in recent years. How then do we reconcile this fact with the simultaneous rise of the multi-million dollar, global art market? (2008: n.pag.)

I needed a way of supporting the work, so I sold subscriptions for postcards I called EVIDENCE. After each monthly UPRISING, I chose one photograph and wrote one paragraph describing the work, printed them, and sent them out to people who had purchased subscriptions at $120/year. The UPRISINGs themselves were autonomous, free, and not beholden to the subscribers of EVIDENCE. While the UPRISINGs were subject to so many chance elements, the EVIDENCE postcards were an opportunity for me to choose how to tell those stories. EVIDENCE postcards were a very personal communication between supporters and me. Once the postcards went out, I loved hearing about which pictures disturbed people, and which ones were taped to someone's computer monitor. In the face of ridiculously limited resources for experimental/political art and culture, EVIDENCE subscriptions were the single most important source of financial support for the UPRISING project, and sending the postcards every month was an act of gratitude. The postcards also formed the basis of this book.

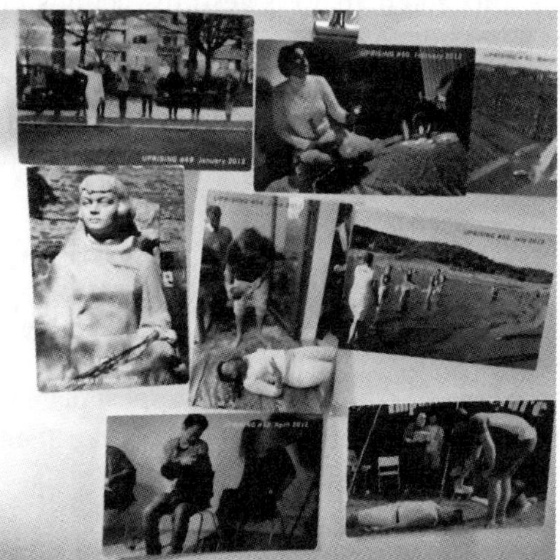

Figure 2: EVIDENCE postcards on Leah Mayers' refrigerator. Photo by Leah Mayers.

TIMING AND CONTEXT

As I was beginning to envision the UPRISING project, I had started studying and doing ceremony with Peruvian *maestro curandero* Oscar Miro-Quesada. I began to hear Oscar and other people talk about the year 2012, which according to some scholars marked the end of the Mayan Long Count Calendar. Daniel Pinchbeck offers a useful perspective on the contemporary necessity and utility of connecting with ancient healing philosophies and strategies in his book, *2012: The Return of Quetzalcoatl*:

> Developing the world view of a shaman, in contrast to that of our present society's achievement-oriented professional, helps one to become a healer in all one's activities, harmonizing the needs of the individual with the needs of the community, and bringing about a balanced relationship between inner and outer worlds. World healing, in this sense, begins with the individual who welcomes in the other. This lowering of the personal wall and expressing spontaneous empathy has not been highly valued in the dominator society, whose emphasis generally has been on separation, self-control, autonomy and mastery. (2006: 75)

Additionally, futurist Barbara Marx Hubbard heralded 2012 as a moment of planetary spiritual shift: 'if we can connect that which is loving, creative, and innovative in an expression of global coherence of the heart and of our creativity, we can effect the tipping point' (Miejan 2012: n.pag.). Beginning UPRISING in 2008 allowed me to complete monthly actions for five years, culminating with Winter Solstice 2012.

The UPRISING performance project was born during a time of great political optimism in the United States. During the campaign and election of Barack Obama, many of us (especially Chicagoans) believed deeply in his message of hope. We understood the incredible significance of electing a person of African descent to be President of the United States. I will never forget the joy that electrified downtown Chicago on election night 2008, and the radiance in the faces of my black Chicago siblings on the train the next morning.

By the end of 2009, many Obama supporters were angry at the escalation of US wars and were feeling disenchanted with the ability of electoral politics to create real progressive change. We were also witness to the violent and irrational racism in the US government that prevented Obama from accomplishing even simple things. As part of that year's Winter Solstice ceremony (UPRISING #24), we shared a message from the scholar and activist Starhawk:

> This year the darkness is intense. The bright hopes of last year are worn and tattered from obstructions and betrayals and compromise. Our personal health and the health of all the life support systems of the planet hang in balance, and how can we tell whether we've inched forwards or been sucked back into deals and appeasements worse than what went before? Last year we hoped for an end to war – this year we see war escalate. But the message of Solstice is this: hope does not come once into the world and fulfill itself. Hope and light must constantly be reborn, over and over again. They wax and wane, and must be renewed. (2009: n.pag.)

Halfway through the UPRISING project, in the winter of 2010, a revolutionary wave of violent and nonviolent demonstrations swept across the Arab world. Protests in Tunisia, Egypt, Libya, Yemen, and many other countries meant that words like 'uprising' and 'revolution' started appearing in the newspaper describing real political events, and shaped UPRISING #38. In the fall of 2010, the Occupy movement began in the United States, inspiring UPRISING #46 and positioning the project in the context of a huge revolutionary social movement, which provided gravity and momentum to the rest of the UPRISING performances.

By contrast, this book was written in 2015–16 while Hillary Clinton and Donald Trump were campaigning, and it was finished shortly after Trump won the 2016 US presidential election. The day that Trump was elected, I sat in a cabin in Kentucky (one of the first states called for Trump) and experienced genuine political despair. I understand that for many Americans who voted, Trump was delivering a message of some kind of hope, but I was devastated and afraid.

Yet this book needed finishing, even though all I wanted to do was call my mother and cry. I could not afford to take a day off from writing and editing, so I pulled myself together as much as possible and got back to work. I felt tremendous gratitude to be able to dig in and remember that world-building is a long game. Revolutionary Practice #50 particularly resonated with me on 9 November 2016: 'Recall moments when you believed the world might actually change for the better.'

At the time of this writing in 2017, when white nationalism is on the rise in the United States and neo-fascist movements are gaining traction around the globe, activists must continue to expand our working methods to enliven our communities. We must use cultural work to grapple with difficulty, complexity, and genuine wonder. This book audaciously defines UPRISING performances as 'public demonstrations of revolutionary practices.' To create positive change, we must discover fresh perspectives on moving from critique to possibility, maintaining hope in light of the numbing negativity of contemporary political discourse.

PRACTICING OUR REVOLUTIONARY SELVES

As someone who comes out of the world of theater, I am committed to the notion of *practice.* In theater, we rehearse. We know that there is no alternative to rehearsal. There is no substitute for practice. We plot points in space with our bodies. We create neural pathways that help us remember our lines based on where we are on stage and what our bodies are doing. We practice listening to other characters. We try to refine it all in rehearsal because we have the notion in theater that in the moment of performance, with the pressures of audience and adrenaline, we can only hope to do it as well as we did in our best practice run. Sometimes we might be able to access new stores of energy, but all we can count on is doing it the way we did in rehearsal. Some of us who are movement-based artists train ourselves and our bodies as a lifelong process. Well into my forties, I am still training as a performer, using techniques that were developed by the Polish Theatre practitioners Jerzy Grotowski, Rena Mirecka, and Double Edge Theatre, as well as the pedagogy of Guillermo Gómez-Peña and La Pocha Nostra. I am in my second decade of yoga practice, and it is precisely the yogic principle that the fruit is in the effort that is most meaningful to me, physically and spiritually.

I believe we can practice for revolution, and we can use performance as a way of practicing to become our most revolutionary selves. UPRISING performances are an answer to Italian Marxist theorist and activist Franco Berardi's concern that we need to do more than participate in demonstrations of negativity if we want to re-craft a humane society. As British theorist Mark Fisher expressed, in a conversation with Berardi:

> We need to be both more patient and more confident than we have been. We need to reclaim the future whose disappearance you mourn, and that means recovering a *prospective* time, where we are not endlessly protesting against or obstructing capital, but thinking ahead of it. Here is the space for art to reinvent itself – as the site for a multiplicity of visions of a post-capitalist future. (2013: n.pag., original emphasis)

HOW TO READ THIS BOOK

This book is organized around 60 Revolutionary Practices stated as urgent imperatives. These imperatives are each followed by a section called 'In Action,' which illustrates the Revolutionary Practice used in an UPRISING performance. Interspersed throughout the text are essays by scholars who were engaged with the project: Anne Cushwa, Ph.D.; Daniel Tucker, MFA; and Nicole Coffineau, MA. I've also included short reflections from UPRISING participants, most of which are responses to e-mails I sent out after performances with a prompt like, 'How was that for you? What was surprising or touching?' The book is organized chronologically, but readers are encouraged to jump around the text as they see fit, taking in UPRISING stories and Revolutionary Practices that seem most relevant to their current interests and desires.

I purposely reject both the notion of the disembodied genius artist and the idea that 'good art' should be appreciated without knowing or caring anything about its creator. I am a person in the world, subject to American capitalism, heteropatriarchy, and white supremacy. I do not pretend that my subject positions and identities are absent from the work. For me, this choice is aligned with an activist approach to making work related to social justice, in which messy and complicated relationships to power and privilege are part of the process and acknowledged openly. The book embodies the spirit of full engagement with revolutionary practices, including moments of despair, doubt, vulnerability, and joy.

When I was struggling to name this book, I took to social media, where friends and colleagues suggested titles. The tenderness and creativity of these proposals (listed below) tell me what folks desire and expect. I hope that this book honors the many people who shared their aspirations for positive social transformation by participating in creative experiments all over the world. Based on artistic investigation through UPRISING, I lovingly offer 60 proposals for ways to practice being our most revolutionary selves.

This Art: Revolutionary Uprising
UPRISING: Performance Art, Revolution, Connection
UPRISING: The Art of Fiercely Loving the World Through Performance
UPRISING: The Fierce Heart of Performance
The Heart of Fierce Love: Performing Revolution with Community
UPRISING: A Manifesto for Revolution Through Performance
DEFIANT: Sacred Revolutions
Visioning Humanity: Performing Possibility
Heart and Fierceness: A Visionary Performance Manifest
Performing Art: Revolution Made Manifest
Fierce Hearts: Concrete Actions for Resistance
UPRISING: Instructions on What to Do at the End of the World
Revolutionary Strategies for Loving, Art, and Activism
Performing ReLOVEutionary
UPRISING: Performing Social Transformations
Fierceness of the Heart: Transformational Performance
Armour Amour
UPRISING: Revolutionary Performances
Compassionate Rebellion: Bringing Your Fierce Heart to Art

– On a bed of nails,
– On the edge of the roof,
– Come, come, whoever you are:
Love, Performance and Revolution

#16

RECIPE FOR AN UPRISING.
START WITH ONE OF THESE INGREDIENTS:

3

specific place

specific day or event

specific community of people

Go to the space or location. Listen. Feel. Allow your intuition to speak. Visualize how something could happen. Respond to the needs of the space. Research the history of this place. What significant events have happened here? What does the space need in order to be activated for revolutionary purposes?

Does this day correspond with any significant events in history? What happened 10 years ago? 40 years ago? 100 years ago? What is the purpose of this event? What are the highest intentions of the organizers? What are the desired social relations within the event?

Who are the people? What is your relationship to them? How can our social relations be more open, honest, loving, friendly, thoughtful, and revolutionary? What are some individual expressions that could activate revolutionary relations among these people? What is a gentle, loving challenge that encourages participants to venture out of comfort or habit while preserving their ability to care for their needs?

#14

UPRISINGs do something. What is the desired action or transformation that is the result of this UPRISING? Enacting a social relation? Activating a space? Transforming an image? Commemorating revolutionary history? Changing the cells of our bodies?

UPRISINGs emphasize action first, and reflection later. How can people be engaged in an experience *before* they start analyzing and labeling it? What is an activity in which we can all participate before we comprehend why?

ACTIVATE RESEARCH INTO AN UPRISING

What are the materials of this revolutionary history, place, idea and practice? How can these materials create revolutionary gestures or images? How can these materials be recycled, repurposed, or released to the earth when the UPRISING is finished?

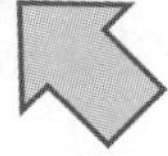

What is the gesture or task that helps us feel revolutionary practices in our bodies, hearts, and voices?

Figure 3: Recipe for an UPRISING infographic. Created by Nicole Garneau in collaboration with designer.

UPRISING: Encounters with Revolutionary Unity and Beauty (An Appreciation)

Anne Cushwa

Performance. Feminist Art. Queer Art. Conceptual Art. Happening. Site Specific. Site Intervention. Earth Art. Process Art. Post-Minimalism. New Genre Public Art. The work of Nicole Garneau, and especially UPRISING, defies neat categorization. Indeed, Garneau's Revolutionary Practice #41 is: 'Understand that we will never fit in one box.' If an individual will not fit in one box, then an individual's creative output is unlikely to fit in a tidy package. This refusal to create art any less complicated and beautiful than life is a position that I value. UPRISING is composed of individual pieces that make up the whole, like a symphony, tapestry, or parts of a tree. Its themes include history, solidarity, and independence. Garneau's art makes visible the complex sociopolitical networks that link us in striking, yet subtle ways.

What was/is UPRISING? UPRISING was conceived and organized by Garneau as a five-year project of monthly events that incorporated voluntary participants to help make the work, either by plan or by chance. Each piece was centered on a theme or concept, and these ideas were generated most frequently by site, history, or contemporary events. Some UPRISINGs took place during another organization's event, supplying a number of volunteers who were present for a different purpose; some UPRISINGs took place on city streets and in public parks, with volunteer passersby. An UPRISING could be summarized as a thematic event led by Garneau that utilized volunteers for various tasks (i.e., reading, singing, drawing, and/or speaking with strangers, among others) to create an ephemeral cultural product of conceptual and aesthetic beauty. Taken together, these events generated a template for others to build imaginative activist events. UPRISING allowed Garneau to experiment with the melding of disparate influences and motivations in service of her work.

Garneau's concentration during UPRISING was to offer people the chance to have a personal experience with art (something that can be rare for Americans), but one that would not alienate or facilitate passive consumption. Often, she asked individuals to share their experiences, dreams, hopes, or worries, but never compelled them to do so or to do it publicly – consent and freedom of choice were primary concerns. She introduced topics or historical events in nonthreatening ways, by singing, or reading, or tug-of-war. She encouraged people to look at the labels inside their clothing, revealing the names of the countries that manufacture it, highlighting at once events like the 1911 Triangle Shirtwaist Factory Fire and the 2013 factory disaster in Bangladesh, and our intimate interconnectedness through labor, capital, and apparel.

UPRISING developed over the five years, growing and changing through trial and error, shifting priorities and creating fewer material traces. The earlier UPRISINGs sometimes produced a physical artifact, and very quickly that process turned to re-using or creating ephemeral artifacts (chalk flowers on a sidewalk, beet stains in an intersection). By the end of UPRISING, each event left objects or traces that were predominately impermanent, with only digital documentation and memory. The motivations for these changes were as much practical as philosophical. During the period of UPRISING, Garneau traveled frequently, eventually moving out of her longtime home in Chicago, and the desire to manage fewer things in general fed the impulse to create fewer objects. In addition, Garneau's commitment to environmental stewardship contributed to the inclination to 'reduce, reuse, recycle' in her art production.

Performance has had a significant place in Garneau's art since the beginning of her career. By 'performance,' I mean using her body and/or words as the dominant feature of the work. She often included various materials as part of these pieces (notably, beet juice was/is a featured medium), as well as song and movement, but her physical body was the most prominent presence. A theatrical nature pervaded many pieces, with drama as part of their overall tone. As her work has matured, and as clearly demonstrated through UPRISING, Garneau's focus has moved outward, emphasizing the importance of others as participants, co-conspirators, students, and teachers. She has taken elements of the theatrical craft and dramatic tension to create inviting environments and scenarios in which strangers are welcomed to help make the art, to share an experience of beauty and communion. Garneau presents opportunities for people to use their voices and visions, to consider the past and its relationship to the present and future, and to learn about what it is to have a personal art experience. UPRISING encapsulates the evolution of Garneau's career to this point; it reveals her as an artist whose keen observation and passion for art and social justice speak to our contemporary culture in understandable and powerfully sensual ways.

Performance is only part of the equation, and the changes in the performative nature of the work reveal developing interests that overlap and expand its contexts. As Garneau discusses in the introduction and elsewhere, her study of cross-cultural healing arts encouraged the progressive ritual or sacred context of UPRISING. Her pursuit of anthropology, history, and social justice dovetails with the importance of community involvement and traditions inherent in indigenous spiritual and medicinal practices. Honoring the earth, its plants, and its animals, is a vital part of spiritual and healing arts and serves as the foundation for cultural ceremonies worldwide. While Garneau orchestrated UPRISING's possibilities, the participation of others was necessary to complete the ceremonial nature of the work. Their presence as co-creators was acknowledged and celebrated by Garneau, and that agency was often received with wonder (as documented by various participant responses in this book). The invitation to be a part of something attractive and unusual, to be a part of a performance rite, was extended and accepted openly and honestly. Learning about a different way to see and make art, or history, gives multiple layers of meaning to the work itself and adds to the chance of its lasting impact.

By directing attention toward concepts/events/places that can be understood easily, Garneau draws people into the art ceremony through an open embrace of the spiritual potential of cultural work. Those of us that love art understand the feelings of pleasure, mystery, or discovery that are accompanied by the art encounter. My heart swells when I find a work of art that I love, and when visiting a museum, I often feel like I am visiting old friends. Many people aren't familiar with that experience, or at least it is not commonly recognized. That swelling of the heart and quickening of the mind's eye are what I mean by 'the spiritual potential of art.' For me, it is proof of something larger than myself, of union. The ritual nature of the UPRISING project seemed to have a great appeal to the public, breaking the cycles of alienation and increasing technological intimacy, which are regularly discussed as part of modern culture (and about which Daniel Tucker writes in his contribution to this book). Garneau's UPRISING created captivating ceremonial art experiences that resonated with volunteer participants and passersby, which is confirmed in the feedback offered by the individuals themselves. Their testimonials are some of the treasures of this book.

The majority of art today, including Garneau's work, transcends any one definition of genre or medium by incorporating varied approaches with the goals of achieving a vision, connection, and growth. In any historical period (especially in the past 150 years), contemporary art production is often about emerging from tradition and crossing boundaries. The boundaries may be subject matter, technique, and/or exhibition spaces, among others. Garneau's work follows this trajectory. It is deeply anchored in and influenced by historical art production, just as it operates outside of some of those expectations.

The roots of Garneau's work can be traced to Neolithic humans' ritual activities, using instruments embellished beyond the role of functionality. These practices were often meant to strengthen the community and mark important occasions. UPRISING echoes this ancient history of aestheticized rituals. The idea of 'artist as shaman' is as old as prehistory and has been revived by many artists over hundreds of years. Artists (and art historians) from around the globe and throughout history have contributed to the formation of that concept. People worldwide share the traits of honoring the earth, ancestors, and a larger spiritual cosmology through creative ceremonies. One could argue that Leonardo da Vinci or Hieronymus Bosch's scientific and philosophical studies of anatomy, astronomy, alchemy, and spiritual iconography qualify them for such a role during the Renaissance. More recently, artists like Vincent van Gogh, Joseph Beuys, or Yoko Ono have taken on the notion of esoteric, sometimes spiritual, cultural production. These artists, too, were drawn to study traditions outside their cultures of origin. Garneau's construction of ceremonial artwork through performance comes from documented historical precedents as well as her own personal journey.

The early performance events of Dada, along with their political motivations and commentary, are clearly part of the historical base from which Garneau draws as an artist. Sociopolitical performance, poetry, theater, and visual art are some of the legacies of Dada, a Western European movement that began in 1916 as a response to World War I. Dada artists focused on chance, the absurdity of the Great War's carnage and rapidly changing modern culture. Garneau's work is actively engaged with issues of social justice and builds upon the foundations of early twentieth-century performance with special attention paid to race, sexuality, and gender. Her personal experiences with the theater in Russia also influence the sociopolitical aspect of her art, as she worked in Russia with colleagues trained amid the backdrop of a rich dramatic and artistic heritage mixed with repression and/or censorship. Garneau learned about the importance of community in the face of such challenges, and how art could function as a tool in a practical sense. Her interest in public engagement beyond the closed spheres of art or theatrical spaces can also be linked to Russian realism, and the happenings of the 1960s–70s, especially Fluxus, and more recently, artists like the Guerrilla Girls and Marina Abramović.

Garneau's work shares much in common with the feminist artists of the 1960s–70s, who emphasized education, history, collaborations, and performance as a primary mode of communication. Her work serves as a continuation of the dialogues around women's art and bodies over the last 50 years. She is able to use her body and the bodies of her collaborators as sites of simultaneous specificity and universality. Just as Hannah Wilke, Ana Mendieta, and Carolee Schneemann before her, Garneau encourages a dynamic reconsideration of gender, performance, and ritual in the context of early twenty-first-century culture.

Garneau differs from many of these earlier artists and movements with regard to her focus on our common humanity and individual power. The inclusive quality of her work, in terms of allowing people to speak for themselves and participate freely, relates directly to her experience as a white student of African-American studies, a queer activist in Chicago, and as a teacher. Consent is a critical aspect of Garneau's work, and she engages strangers and volunteers without intimidation or coercion. Following feminist precedents and centered on our diverse communities, UPRISING offers an animated education about history, social activism, art, and working together, with language and actions that are clear and intelligent.

The word 'revolution' and the concept of revolutionary practices are fundamental to the project. 'Revolution,' as employed by Garneau and as she explains in Revolutionary Practice #6, does not always mean a violent clash; essentially, I see revolution serving as inspiration for Garneau to envision her work as part of a mission to create a more peaceful, equitable society that appreciates diverse beauty. Revolutionary Practices are strategies that can create change in subtle and not-so-subtle ways. Whether a Revolutionary Practice plants the seed of thinking about things differently (we won't fit in the same box; remember to be thankful to those who came before) or the seed of doing things differently (let love help make the art; honor the earth), Garneau's principles offer the possibility for development, for improvement, and for release. The very idea of an art ceremony can seem like a radical one. If that art ceremony is dedicated to the cause of immigration reform or community gardens and requires volunteer participation, then additional dissonance is introduced into the expectations of art's passive consumption. Any reference to the sociopolitical realm can seem offensive or too aggressive to be part of the transcendental atmosphere of art. Never mind the hundreds of years of history that support the radical possibilities of art to transform culture; for many people, being outside of the box is unimaginable and undesirable. Garneau's choice to stress the word 'revolution' reveals the seriousness with which she views not only the thematic issues of UPRISING, but also cultural production itself. In different times and places, making the art can mean risking one's life, and often the value of creation wins the bet.

Even with her concerns and focus on serious sociopolitical issues, Garneau takes great care to ensure that beauty is not lost in the work. When I think about UPRISING, I recall many images: volunteers in white clothing, the vibrant red of beet stains against a white background, a smiling face offering a warm mug of tea to passersby, stones at the lake, embroidered handkerchiefs, white muslin in the wind. Any ritual includes at least an element of formal beauty, and art is often characterized by a visual appeal. The sensual nature of many of the UPRISINGs is apparent through the sharing of tea or beet juice (the mouth, taste, smell, color), whispering, or putting one's hands in the earth. Singing and talking, reading and drinking, UPRISING uses the body to engage mind and heart. The physical connections between strangers as part of the project created moments of exhilaration, of uncertainty, of security. Engaging all the senses, respecting the boundaries and individuality of each participant, UPRISING generates open communion with thoughtful care. Garneau discusses serious problems and issues, she raises critical lenses to culture and its productions, and she does not neglect the power of aesthetic attraction. As discussed in Revolutionary Practice #10, beauty is vital to the success of her art offerings.

Through this book and within it, Garneau addresses the fact that no documentation can reveal the experience of being present with a work of art, whether that work of art is a painting or performance, book or music. The case of an artwork whose form is a time-based event is especially difficult to encapsulate within an image, and therefore the combination of words, memories, and photographs is the best effort to achieve a representation of UPRISING.

This book features the artist's words and the theories and motivations behind the project. It includes responses from individuals who volunteered in UPRISINGs, as well as three essays that provide more structured and thematic reflection from artists and scholars. The compilation of information (about the process, the execution, memories from Garneau and others, along with the visual documentation) provides a comprehensive roadmap for anyone wondering about the composition of a multiyear project such as this one. The writings provide a fuller appreciation of the work itself and its possibilities, a formula for future actions.

Professional artists, art historians, critics, and visual culture experts read and interpret artists' writings for their own understanding and research of a work or period. Artists' writings can be equally enlightening and/or entertaining for the public at large. In fact, it could easily be argued that artists themselves have written some of the most important texts in the history of art. Their interpretations and expectations of their own work can serve as critical signposts along the path to making meaning. For a work like UPRISING, which was site-based and impermanent, a book is exceptionally well suited to capture an overview of both the completed project and its development.

This text serves as a manual for people to create their own UPRISINGs, providing what Garneau refers to as a 'recipe.' The potential for others to make similar art events is a clever way to continue cultural production in a variety of media and situations; it also spreads Garneau's vision of social justice activism. Encouraging others to create ways to honor history, to mark important events, or to celebrate the earth, seasons, people (the list is endless), is part of Garneau's gift. That kind of agency to make art, to initiate a ceremony, is rarely made visible in our society, and recognizing the power and potential of individuals is an explicit feature of Garneau's work.

An artist whose work similarly avoids simple categorization and focuses on the influence and promise of individuals is Félix González-Torres. González-Torres was a Cuban-American artist who worked with readymade materials in unconventional ways, and he is best known for works of stacks of paper or piles of candy from which one may remove pieces. Viewers may become participants by removing (or not removing) a part of the pile through their free choice. It is conceptual art, to be sure, but it generates from and reflects earlier precedents in minimalism, post-minimalism, Dada, and pop art. As with many of his colleagues working in the 1980s–90s, González-Torres infused apparently neutral objects with sociopolitical issues of race, class, gender, and sexuality, emphasizing the work's multiple meanings, always resisting any singular interpretation.

Like González-Torres' creative production, Garneau's work involves chance, the participation of strangers, and thoughtful determination in service of both beauty and critical, contemporary social commentary. Each artist offers an individual the ability to participate without compromising free consent. Each artist offers the opportunity to learn something new, to encounter a moment of reflection, and to connect with people and ideas larger than oneself. Each artist labors with love at the forefront of the agenda. Both González-Torres and Garneau talk about and create art about things that matter to me. Both artists face the challenge of being called 'corny,' 'too political,' or 'difficult to understand as art.'

'The personal is political,' as the saying goes, and cultural production is part of both. UPRISING is personal and political art that practices what it preaches in terms of building a more peaceful, art-filled world. One of González-Torres' works (*'Untitled'*, 1990) is a large, white paper stack with five small words in black on each side of each sheet. The words on one side: 'Nowhere better than this place.' The words on the other side: 'Somewhere better than this place.' In each UPRISING, Garneau exposes this dichotomy by working on the creation of a better place in real time; each UPRISING shows the simultaneous truths of the twin-edged proposition. We work to arrive somewhere better than this place, and through the work find there is nowhere better than this place. Revolutionary Practice #1: Balance Weeks of War with Acts of Love. Turn That into a Working Methodology.

There are no spectators here – only revolutionary, sensual, lovely art.

BALANCE WEEKS OF WAR WITH ACTS OF LOVE. TURN THAT INTO A WORKING METHODOLOGY

REVOLUTIONARY PRACTICE #1

Times when people and planet are in desperate peril call for nothing less than totally audacious propositions. Embrace something you doubt can ever be accomplished in your lifetime, and then commit your time and energy to it. Choose to be 'powerless criminals in a time of criminal power,' like radical peace activist Father Daniel Berrigan (Democracy Now! 2016). Allow that overture to structure your efforts in ways that are symbolically meaningful to you. The United States announced the start of its war against Iraq in March of 2003, and then-President Barack Obama announced its official end in December 2011, but the war continues as of writing this in 2017. We are now in a dangerous normalization of this perpetual state. Cultural critic Henry Giroux explains that 'war has become a mode of sovereignty and rule, eroding the distinction between war and peace. Increasingly fed by a moral and political hysteria, warlike values produce and endorse shared fears as the primary register of social relations' (Giroux 2013).

Count the weeks, days, months, years, or hours we have been at war. Quantify that violence, and match it with generous and compassionate actions that you hope might counteract 'shared fears' as the only way humans have to relate to each other. UPRISINGs happened once a month from 2008 to 2012. We are nowhere near restoring a balance between weeks of war and acts of love. As Chris Hedges stated in an anti-war rally at the White House gates in 2010, 'the more futile, the more useless, the more irrelevant and incomprehensible an act of rebellion is, the vaster and more potent hope becomes. Any act of rebellion, any physical defiance of those who make war, of those who perpetuate corporate greed and are responsible for state crimes, anything that seeks to draw the good to the good, nourishes our souls and holds out the possibility that we can touch and transform the souls of others' (Hedges 2010). The struggle continues.

IN ACTION: UPRISING #1

26 January 2008, 1:00pm | Intersection of Milwaukee, Ashland, and Division in Chicago
Participants: Uncle Bear, Nicole Garneau, Britt Lower, David Ortega, and Bill Van Berschot
Photos: Ruth Robbins | Video: Zac Whittenburg

UPRISING #1 marked 240 weeks of the United States' war against Iraq by offering 240 acts of love to audience and strangers gathered on the Chicago plaza known as the Polish Triangle. I was anxious about who was going to show up in heavy January snow. Uncle

Bear and Ruth had volunteered to help me make the UPRISING, and while we rode our second bus en route to the Polish Triangle, most of the people who had volunteered to perform in UPRISING #1 called to say they were running late or not able to make it. Uncle Bear announced an intention to be miserable for the entire day due to relationship drama. Eventually, we gathered intrepid volunteer performers at La Pasadita restaurant on Ashland for nachos and instructions. I handed out white turtlenecks and jars of fresh beet juice and explained my plan.

I was excited that there were eight audience members who came to watch, because the blizzard had driven away all of the people that normally spend time on the benches of the Polish Triangle. Blowing snow had even discouraged pigeons from hanging around. We emerged from the Division Blue Line subway stairs holding hands in solidarity and walked across the plaza. We stood on the benches surrounding the trees. Performers told stories about a time when they felt like what they were doing was good for humanity: a moment of being filled with love for the world. We poured jars of beet juice on closed mouths and down the front of white shirts. In order to create 240 acts of love, we divided 240 by five performers. Each of us blew 48 kisses to the audience, each other, passing cars, people at the bus stop, and to the world we are trying to cherish.

We made a point of having an intentional target for each of our 240 kisses, so I had the experience of genuinely sending love to people in the performance, in the audience, and on the street. Cars on Milwaukee Avenue slowed and rolled down passenger side windows to see what was going on, and we blew them kisses. A couple of guys walked through the Triangle, suddenly realized they were in the midst of something, and blew a bunch of kisses right back at us, laughing the whole time.

> For the first UPRISING, I remember the amazing sensation of gulping down that glass of beet juice as it splashed down my chest after speaking of the power of love in my work and in my life. Then the fullness in my heart as I blew the kisses out into the world.
> **– Uncle Bear (Participant, UPRISING #1)**

> I got tingles when you were all blowing kisses to the world and the crazy [beet] juice was dripping down to the snow.
> **– Bryn Magnus (Audience, UPRISING #1)**

> It doesn't surprise me that you have walked off the stage and out into the streets. How exciting to perform NOT in a traditional theatre setting. It takes courage to do what you do. I felt empowered.
> **– David Ortega (Participant, UPRISING #1)**

31 January 2008, after the first UPRISING event, I wrote to Nicole Garneau to say, 'I'm way into what you do and how you're doing it, and the fact that you're so dedicated to it happening outside the relatively safe and/but kind of loaded arena of traditional performance venues [...] It does my brain good to be reminded of how simple (and few) the elements of performance are.' I continued to follow the UPRISING project through its four years, attending in person when I could. When I couldn't, photo-postcards sent by mail kept me engaged with and aware of how UPRISING was progressing, evolving and growing. The number of people UPRISING involved as it continued – in terms of participants, audiences and communities – is impressive. I'm heartened and inspired knowing there's a diaspora, so to speak, of UPRISING witnesses all over the Chicago area as well as on both coasts, in Kentucky, Russia and beyond.
– Zac Whittenburg (Videographer, UPRISING #1)

Interjection: Love Letter to Beets

When I was a kid, I thought that beets were sweet and sour slices in a jar that my mother put on her salads, but that no one else in the family even considered eating. It was not until I lived in Russia in the early 1990s that I understood that beets were fist-sized root vegetables that are delicious boiled and shredded for salads, or cooked in a soup called borscht. Somewhere around 2000, I bought a vegetable juicer and discovered the joys of beet juice for nutrition and artmaking.

Beets entered my artwork in 2001, when I filled a glass funnel with beet juice, hung it from the ceiling, and did dive rolls on a crib mattress under the drip. They have made many appearances in my work ever since. I have shredded them into my lap while wearing white pants; fed the audience that freshly shredded beet; scrubbed the streets with whole boiled beets; painted the sidewalk with beet juice graffiti; squeezed beet juice from a sea sponge on my body while singing in white lingerie; prayed over glass bottles of beet juice that hung around my neck, and then convinced strangers to let me put a few drops on their tongues; laid on the sidewalk choking through songs and stories while beet juice was poured down my throat from above; made beet juice handprints with white gloves; scratched fragments of community stories into apple slices and soaked them in beet juice before serving them back to the people; filled up my mouth with beet juice and then dribbled it out over peoples' hearts and cupped hands; and distributed them in raw slices that were held daintily during a performance in an immaculate white apartment.

When I work with beets, they take on many different meanings. Beets and beet juice keep demanding my attention, hoping to appear in performances and visual art works. Audiences have rich interpretations of the crimson splatters they make. Beets and beet juice can be a reference to blood – both the bleeding caused by injury and bleeding not caused by injury. Beets are a source of sugar that comes from the earth. They have a wonderful smell. Many natural health blogs recommend beets for liver cleansing to purge anger from the body. Flower essence practitioners New Millennium Essences (2011) note that beetroot flower is often used in the treatment of post-traumatic stress disorder from war, affecting both combatants and civilians – sometimes even trauma that persists over generations.

For the UPRISINGs, I made the beet juice myself or bought it freshly made right before the performance. It was wholesome and delicious. Beet juice stains are not necessarily permanent. After many UPRISINGs, I gathered a garbage bag full of beet-stained clothing and laundered them myself. My method: a vigorous cold water rinse in the tub, then a regular wash with soap plus a little bit of bleach.

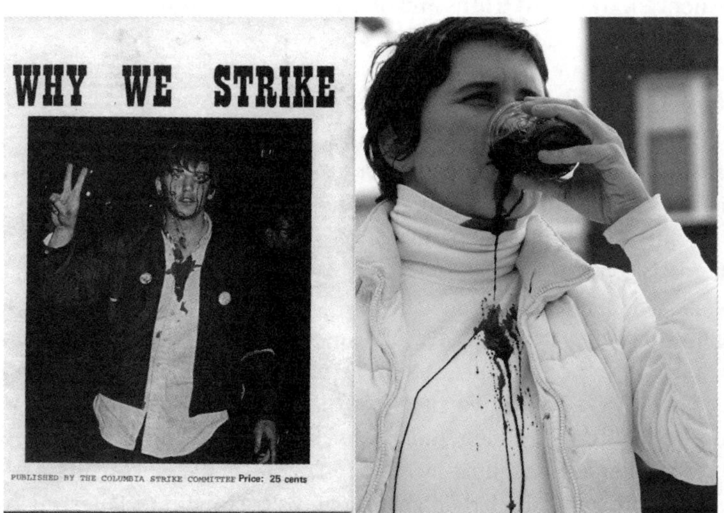

Figure 4: Pamphlet by Students for a Democratic Society (SDS), and Nicole Garneau in UPRISING #1. Photo by Ruth Robbins.

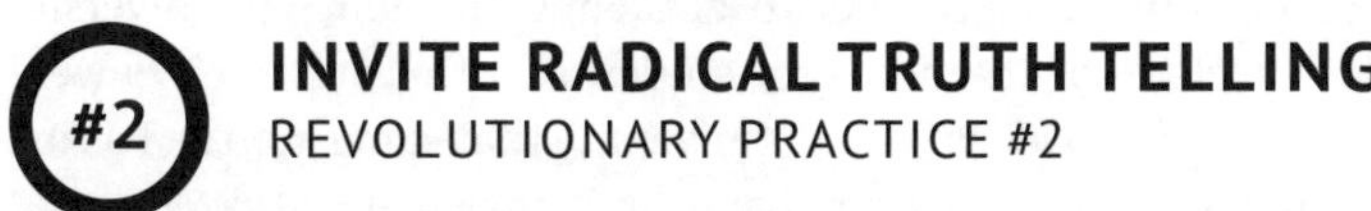

INVITE RADICAL TRUTH TELLING
REVOLUTIONARY PRACTICE #2

#2

Creating and re-creating literal and metaphoric expressions of truth telling draws a direct lineage from the feminist notion that the personal is political. Finding our voices and communicating the truth of our lives is a revolutionary skill worth practicing. We must dig inside ourselves for what we know, and defend our own truths. Your refusal to believe the lies of your oppressors and your actions of resistance are profound gestures of self-love. The act of inviting the truths of others honors their stories, even if we never hear them. In an op-ed inspired by Richard Martinez' words about the murder of his son Christopher, who was killed in a mass shooting at the University of California-Santa Barbara, Adam

Gopnik says, 'Clear speech takes courage. Every time we tell the truth about a subject that attracts a lot of lies, we advance the sanity of the nation' (Gopnik 2014). Novelist Anne Michaels reminds us, 'there are many degrees of solidarity. We must learn the value of each other's words, what they cost' (2009: 211).

I am inspired by a photo of a pamphlet published in 1968 by the Students for a Democratic Society (SDS), entitled *Why We Strike* (Columbia Strike Committee 1968). On the cover is a student holding up a peace sign, bleeding down the front of their shirt. Transforming that image is a way of imagining our mouths as revolutionary tools. How are voices punished and silenced? Tell hard truths and bleed from the mouth.

IN ACTION: UPRISING #2

7 February 2008, 8:30pm | DePaul University Quad, Chicago
Participants: First-year students in Dr Laila Farah's Chicago Women's
Theatre course: Billy, Katie, Lauren, Kaitie, Krystal, Nichole, Theo, Katy, Samantha, Stephanie, Kyle, Jordan, Jenna, Margaret, and Vassaly
Photos: Nicole Garneau

A week before my visit to Dr Laila Farah's Chicago Women's Theatre course, there was a conference organized by the DePaul Academic Freedom Committee. The organization's efforts were inspired by DePaul University's 2007 decision to deny tenure to Dr Norman Finkelstein and Dr Mehrene Larudee, in spite of the fact that both scholars were well respected and recommended for tenure by their colleagues and departments. Finkelstein's work had been very critical of the Israeli government's treatment of Palestinians, and Dr Larudee had supported Finkelstein during his tenure battle (Busch 2008). The conference placed these cases in a larger context of threats to academic freedom on university campuses in the United States. None of the first-year students in Dr Farah's class were aware of this controversy. For UPRISING #2 at DePaul University that same month, I asked students to research student rebellions of 1968 as preparation for my visit. I also requested that someone bring a dance we could all learn.

The students and I met each other for the first time at 6:00pm, and two hours later we were out performing on the frozen quad of DePaul's Lincoln Park campus. In the classroom, we talked about the feminist principle 'the personal is political' and student revolutionary movements of 1968. It was really difficult, in such a short time, to help students have anything approaching a genuine understanding of the student rebellions of 1968. They had trouble imagining the utter seriousness of that moment. It was very hard for them to grasp, given their current context, the idea of a protest or demonstration *meaning* anything or *changing* anything. They got hung up on details about whether students were doing drugs or pissing in the president's office. But I still believed drawing a 40-year line between students of 1968 and 2008 was important.

To activate themselves as creators of the work, I had students write their own radical truths. We designated volunteers for such performance roles as 'telling your truth out loud,' and 'getting beet juice poured over your head.' We dressed in white, dealt with one student's pre-performance emotional breakdown, and walked out to the snowy quad. Performers silently mouthed their stories while they danced an abstracted Macarena, or someone poured beet juice over their heads. It was moving to watch people telling their radical truths without voices, just earnestly mouthing the words. It had the effect of putting them in the space of that truth telling, and letting that read on their faces, but they did not have to share anything they did not want to.

> It sounded kind of stupid when we just talked about it, but when it was actually performed it seemed very moving. With the performance happening at night, and the peace of the winter snow, you could really feel the passion Nicole meant to portray through her piece.
>
> I was so skeptical about the whole idea of performing on the streets when we had to watch the videos of the wild and crazy things Nicole does on the streets of Chicago in order to get her message across. I remember talking to people in the class about how weird it was going to be, and more than that, none of us knew exactly what we were going to be doing, and that fear of the unknown made our anxiety even worse. But once we got around Nicole, and saw how good-natured she was, and how she was so passionate about her message, I could feel the entire class warm up to her. I really felt like we were making some sort of a difference; I didn't know how or exactly why, but it made me feel like I was doing something good for mankind. I now realize Nicole's whole point is to make the world a better place, and help raise awareness about the problems in the world. Some people choose to protest, or riot, but Nicole has found a peaceful, non-violent way to help everyone to realize just how easy it is to help the earth and its people.
> **– DePaul University student (Participant, UPRISING #2)**
>
> Although I was uncomfortable throughout the night, I am really glad I did this. Also, it was really nice telling my radical truth.
> **– DePaul University student Billy Allen (Participant, UPRISING #2)**

I have to say how surprised I was when the beet juice was being poured on me. I felt very liberated and like I was standing up for something important to me – but I didn't know what that was exactly. Maybe it was the fact that I was telling my radical truth when it happened that made me feel so 'free.' I really felt renewed after having the beet juice poured on me. I keep going back to that because it really made me feel something I've never felt before. I really enjoyed this performance – it was so truthful and that's what made it so renewing.

– DePaul University student Katy Barrett (Participant, UPRISING #2)

I believe in stepping out of the box sometimes, and I felt this class was a test to the limits of our imagination. The beet juice over my head was very cold. As a portrayal of blood, it did feel thicker than water. I could feel it soaking in. To be a part of the performance gave me a better understanding of who I am and what I'm capable of doing.

– DePaul University student Vassaly Sivanthaphanith (Participant, UPRISING #2)

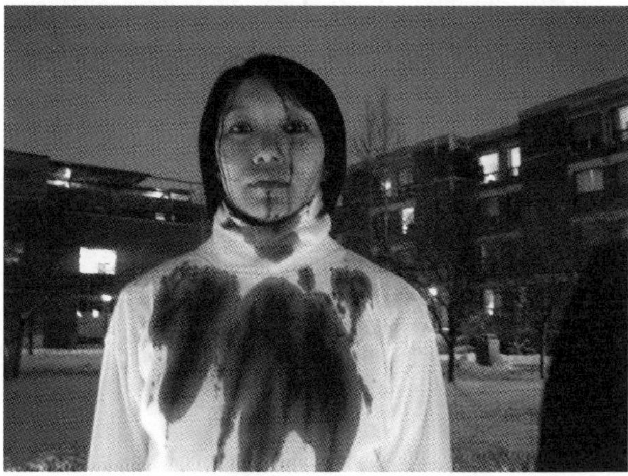

Figure 5: Vassaly Sivanthaphanith in UPRISING #2. Photo by Nicole Garneau.

(#3) CALL FOR VOLUNTEERS. BUILD A TEMPORARY ENSEMBLE
REVOLUTIONARY PRACTICE #3

Make meaningful and heartfelt performative gestures with groups of people. Engaging friends and strangers in world-building activities is a useful tool to deploy in revolutionary service. Experiment in immediacy and reliance on factors beyond your control. Never knowing who will show up makes the work spontaneous and potentially chaotic. Call for volunteers who come together about an hour before the performance starts, do it, document it, and disband. Make the task simple enough for anyone to do, so it never matters if people have performance experience. Create temporary ensembles as a community organizing strategy. Be present and let yourself notice, look, and listen to performances you are experiencing for the first time. Consider alignments between this practice and the definition of the word 'uprising.'

Learn to feel out groups of people in a room. As a starting point, get in among them and be quiet. Observe them and experience their energy in your body. Soften your visual focus, listen, and feel. Notice features about the space that may enable folks to work together, or make that difficult. For example, is it possible for this group of humans to form a circle? How can you arrange the furniture to facilitate the interactions you are hoping for? Who are you in relation to these people? Do they know and trust you, or is what you are about to ask them to do totally outside the bounds of what seems normal to them? Try to find the sweet spot where your invitation balances enough risk with enough pleasurable connection between folks. There is too much emphasis on passive 'consumption' in contemporary culture. Provide models for the participation of artists, non-artists, and activists in purposeful, hope-filled activities. People *want to* and *will* participate in meaningful projects if they are given an opportunity to do so, in a way that is both safe and challenging.

IN ACTION: UPRISING #3

30 March 2008, 1:30pm | Community garden near 6100 S. Blackstone, Chicago
Participants: Nance Klehm, Janet Schmid, Valerie Johnson, Simon, and Nicole Garneau
Photos: Cyrus Rivetna | Video: Steve Cudzilo
Special Assistants: Gina and Jacob Lapalio-Lakin

On the opening day of the community garden at 61st & Blackstone in the Woodlawn neighborhood of Chicago, volunteer performers and I had plenty of time to form a temporary ensemble as we stayed warm inside the Experimental Station across the street. We talked about how and why we were making a performance in the middle of a community garden.

We discussed food and justice. Volunteer performer Nance Klehm is a world-renowned expert on permaculture, land politics, and soil health, and she contributed her wisdom to the conversation. In one of my most beloved revolutionary texts, *Pedagogy of the Oppressed*, Paulo Freire defines liberation as praxis: 'the action and reflection of men and women upon their world in order to transform it' (1970: 79). Pre- and post-performance dialogues were part of the praxis of an UPRISING, as is this book. The people in the group brought individual expertise to the subject matter of the performance, and that felt as much like revolutionary work as bellowing a call-and-response text into a cheerleader megaphone. Here is an excerpt of the words that traveled across the community garden:

> Today, we don't need to create
> An image of the world
> In which we want to live
> Today we can witness
> The image you are already making
> Of the world
> In which we want to live
> We came to see it
> To be inside it.
>
> Today we thank the gardeners
> And the organic farmers
> And all the people
> Who steward the earth
> May your growing season
> Be fruitful
> And may your backs stay strong.

The performers and I emerged from the Experimental Station, crossed the street, and walked down the rows holding hands while the gardeners were getting their plot assignments, paying rent, and sharing food. We dropped off performers in winter-worn beds, and I led everyone in a blessing through the megaphone. Performers got down on their knees and worked their hands in the earth. Then we all held our dirty hands up to the garden and the people. Throughout the process, we talked to gardeners about what they would be planting. We saw kale ready to harvest from cold frames and admired the communal herb plot. We wished them strength and fertility.

I volunteered because I feel aligned with your mission, I have respect for your work, and I am a devotee of all people brave.
– **Nance Klehm (Participant, UPRISING #3)**

CLAIM THE TITLE ACTIVIST
REVOLUTIONARY PRACTICE #4

Transforming our world does not require *everyone* to identify as an activist, but if you do, say it loud and proud! Reject attempts to turn activism into a profession. Cast aside the false dichotomy between art and activism. Employ activist strategies like the people's mic (also known as the human microphone), which was used effectively in the Occupy movement (Moraine 2011). The people's mic is a technology in which people gather around a speaker and repeat their words back to them, amplifying their voice so that it can be heard by large groups of people without the need for amplification equipment, which could require a permit (Lerner 2012). Be a vocal enthusiast of social justice. Embody a form of activism that is not oppositional: it is explicitly about envisioning the world we want, and then practicing to hasten its arrival. Commit to flexible structure, ambitious intentions, and a sense of humor.

IN ACTION: UPRISING #4
19 April 2008, 10:30pm | Version>08 NFO XPO, Viaduct Theatre, 3111 N. Western, Chicago
Participants: Anne Statton, Nicole Garneau, Travis, Andy, Oscar, Nicole, Tim, Ben, Heath, Dana, Gabi, and Blaire
Photos: Rick 'Wiggpaw' Wilson

UPRISING #4 was included in Chicago's Version Fest amongst film screenings, activist art projects, and punk band reunions. It was snowy and miserable that night, and Anne Statton was the only volunteer who came for the purpose of performing, so at the bar in the lobby beforehand, I recruited about twelve strangers and gave them white shirts. In the process of explaining how the performance would involve beet juice, some of the volunteers revealed they were beet farmers! At City Farm Chicago!

In addition to the audience volunteers in white shirts, everyone in the room had both a speaking role and a way to activate our bodies. I used call-and-response to ask everyone to 'check in.' Anne Statton used the cheerleader megaphone to talk us through 25 years of her own revolutionary activism. At one point I interrupted her monologue to ask, 'What about abortion clinic defense?' Anne was funny because she recited her activist history in the clear, authoritative tone of voice that one uses for making a speech at a demonstration.

Meanwhile, I went around the room and tried to get people to hold hands with people next to them. I pulled my white-shirted performers up on stage, took some beet juice in my mouth, and pressed it against their hearts, letting the juice dribble out onto their shirts. I lined up people on the stage arm in arm. The activism monologue and handholding continued until all people in white shirts were lined up on stage.

At the end, I let the audience know that Anne was the only person in this performance that I had known longer than ten minutes beforehand – everyone else had made a leap of faith to stand on the stage before them and be part of the work. I was surprised by the audience reaction to the performance. People came up and hugged me. I saw some people weeping. The whole line of performers stayed present and involved. Someone had Anne and me sign their beet-stained shirt. I liked that everyone in the room had a role. Everyone spoke and engaged their bodies.

UPRISING #4, which featured an explicit narrative of feminist activism, coincidentally served as the opening act of the 30-year reunion concert of an all-male band called The Cunts, considered to be Chicago's first punk band. They were nervous and tipsy and freaked about following what they saw as radical feminist performance art; backstage, they awkwardly begged me to heckle them. To help them feel that punk show vibe, I sat in the audience for their set and used my UPRISING megaphone to scream, 'Show me your cunt!' through their first few songs, which seemed to do the trick.

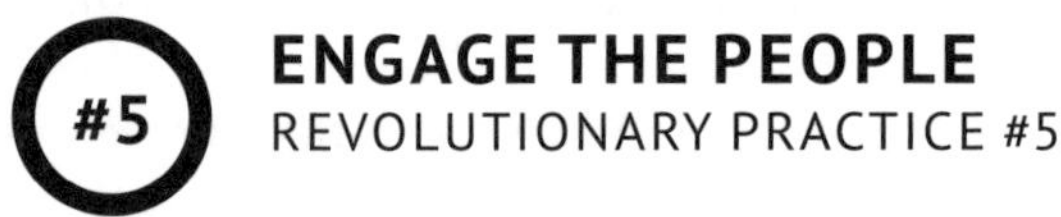

ENGAGE THE PEOPLE
REVOLUTIONARY PRACTICE #5

Step outside the auditorium, where the audience is safely out of reach. Structure improvisations that incorporate participation as a template for people to engage more actively and humanely in society. How can these gestures feel meaningful and accessible to people who do not identify as artists? Can the practice of creating scenarios for expression counteract prevailing beliefs that the voices of the people are meaningless? How can we consciously create an art practice that is about joining together with people to imagine the world in which we want to live, and then enacting that in our bodies? In her dialogue with Franco 'Bifo' Berardi, Ruth Miller imagines this as 'reactivating the sentience of the social body:'

> Building and sustaining solidarity has to be much more than a political project. It is about reactivating the sentience of the social

body much more than it is about political organization. Do you see what I mean? Ultimately, what we have is a problem of therapy, which, in my parlance, does not imply a process of re-connecting, or reducing language, behavior, or feelings to established norms. For me, therapy implies a process of re-activating empathy between living organisms. This empathy is the foundation of the solidarity we need today. (2012: n.pag.)

IN ACTION: UPRISING #5

18 May 2008, 11:00am–2:00pm | Manifest Urban Arts Festival, Harrison Street between Michigan and Wabash Avenues, Chicago
Participants: AJ Sacco, Nicole Garneau, and passersby
Photos: Aurora Tabar

UPRISING #5 was a collaboration with AJ Sacco for Columbia College Chicago's Manifest Urban Arts Festival. AJ Sacco had been a student in my undergrad Making and Unmaking Whiteness class. After the class was finished, we stayed in touch and wanted to work on something together. AJ works as a magician, often in the Chicago burlesque scene. We submitted a proposal to Tic Toc, the time-based offerings of the Manifest Festival. AJ and I were interested in ideas of endless struggle, so we set up a game of tug-of-war. We recruited players for each end of a long rope and asked each person to give us an idea for making the world better. We painted their words on the sidewalk in beet juice. We fired up our teams with megaphones, yelling, 'Pull harder!' I took enormous personal delight in getting Columbia College administrators on the tug-of-war rope. Eventually, some weary participant would ask us how they would know they had won. We just rallied them to keep pulling. We kept it going for three hours, rotating players in and out, and no one ever stopped struggling just because they did not know how to win.

The game structure with beet juice graffiti emerged from dialogue with AJ about what UPRISING was trying to do, and how that complemented or diverged from his ideas about activism and revolution. This is an excerpt from an e-mail AJ sent in the spring of 2008:

Check it – I've been having trouble finding some acts of love that fit into a revolutionary practice. Your philosophy is to create a more just, loving, humane future. Yes that would be brilliant. But I really can't see that happening in America without a violent uprising. America was built on genocide and oppression. American hands are bloody, very bloody.

Flower power doesn't work. John Lennon said it himself. I was at the [anti-war] protest on the 19th [marking 5 years since the United States invaded Iraq], and I was disgusted by the stoned out 'revolutionaries' who were hippie dancing to the beat of the military drums. I was, however, in love with the protesters who refused to move from the path of the police ATVs, eventually provoking the police to retreat. I got butterflies because it almost led to a non-peaceful protest. I was excited. Peace doesn't get recognized. Americans get bored of peace, as much as they want it. No one wakes up or unites without violence.

In my eyes, you're either preaching peace, and looked at as a bit naive, or you preach by any means necessary, and are looked at as a terrorist/communist. So people just stand in the middle ground and complain or remain silent. Because they're safe there. And that's why nothing gets done.

As Rage Against the Machine says, 'Anger is a gift' (2002). I see a rock in a cop's face as beautiful. I see a crowd blocking traffic on Lake Shore Drive as a community united. I see the passion for change to be so great that it causes people to create a rift in civilized life as true love. We've been tricked to think otherwise.

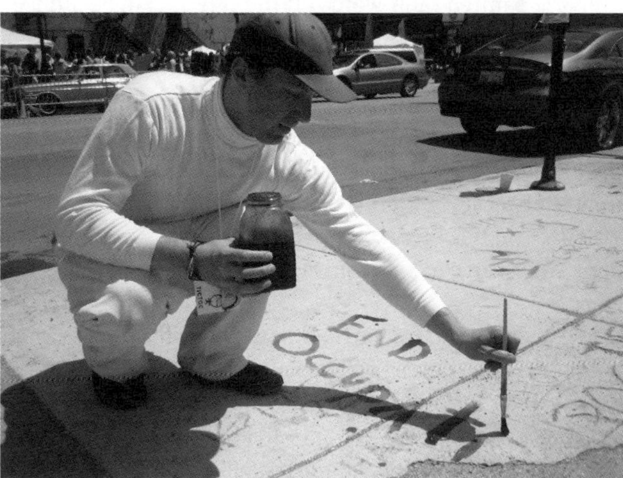

Figure 6: Al Sacco paints beet juice graffiti in UPRISING #5. Photo by Aurora Tabar.

SAY THE WORD REVOLUTION
REVOLUTIONARY PRACTICE #6

#6

Revolution means a lot of different things: violent overthrow of oppressive state regimes, all of the actions and organizing that lead up to that point, the international revolutionary movements of 1968, the Russian Revolution(s), the French Revolution, Gloria Steinem's *Revolution from Within*, the turning of a sacred planet, utopic revolutions of love, the sexual revolution, re-evolution, struggles for justice, anti-racism, feminism, womanism, class struggle, queer liberation, food justice, earth activism, spiritual evolution, and smashing the white supremacist capitalist patriarchy. Beyond those goals and movements, revolution is a concept. We can learn revolutionary histories and strategies.

Revolution is a term that is loaded because it means violent overthrow of the government as well as a Chicago microbrewery and a new development in mouthwash. In 2016, Sarah Palin precisely demonstrated that revolution is not necessarily leftist when she declared, 'we have needed a revolution, and we found our revolutionary. Donald Trump is that revolutionary!' (TRUNEWS 2016). Revolution means so much, and has also been thoroughly exploited by the machine of capitalism, which co-opts everything for its own ends. Revolution has been sloganized and re-branded. It has already been so misused and appropriated that it is once again available for our sincere exploration and interpretation.

There is a perverse privilege in making art that attempts to explore the concept of revolution. Consider Carolyn Kizer's poem 'The Ashes.' This is the first stanza:

> This elderly poet, unpublished for five decades,
> Said that one day in her village a young girl
> Came screaming down the road,
> 'The Red Guards are coming! The Red Guards
> Are Coming!' At once the poet
> Ran into her house and stuffed the manuscript
> Of her poems into the stove. The only copy.
> When the guards arrived they took her into the yard
> For interrogation. As they spoke
> The poet's mother tried to hang herself in the kitchen.
> That's all I know about the Red Guard.
> It is enough. (Kizer 2001: 137)

The elderly poet knows about revolution: it is ushered in by a force so frightening that for the sake of saving the lives of everyone in the house a person would throw 50 years of unpublished poetry on the fire – and then survive to know that loss for the rest of her life, and know something about state power and fear in a way that is not the least bit abstract. How nice to be able to snuggle in bed on an ample rump and think about whether to write more about revolution, or maybe take a walk in the woods.

Russian Gulag prisoners wanted so badly to possess a book of Anna Akhmatova's poems that they copied them from memory onto birch bark – you can see this book in the Akhmatova Museum in St. Petersburg. There are revolutionary acts more courageous than we could ever imagine. At the same time, there are revolutionary heroes who act like assholes. Abbie Hoffman was a visionary, creative leader, but who can stand his homophobic macho swagger?

Try not using the word revolution in a snarky or sarcastic or tongue-in-cheek way. Try things out as revolutionary strategies. Has the last nail been hammered into the coffin of revolution? The urgent struggles of oppressed people everywhere say otherwise. Revolution is for the people, and we always have the option of being noble, courageous, and sincere. In these times, nothing less will do.

IN ACTION: UPRISING #6

28 June 2008, 1:00–4:00pm | Chicago Dyke March in Pilsen:
18th Street from Halsted to Damen
Participants: Liz Digitale Anderson, Hugo Garcia, Nicole Garneau,
Genevieve McClosky, and Jamie Spirakes
Photos: Nicole Garneau | Video: Uncle Bear

The three-day workshop 'Learn and Make UPRISING #6' was presented as part of Links Hall's professional development offerings for artists, in partnership with Insight Arts. In this workshop, participants studied theory and history related to the UPRISING project, shared personal connections to social change, moved our bodies, and created an outdoor performance exploring revolution to be enacted on Sunday afternoon during the Dyke March.

Workshop participants imagined how to articulate solidarity using bodies and markers. Hugo and Liz created a dance of solidarity gestures and taught it to the rest of us. Genevieve showed us how to draw her solidarity symbol. Where folks gathered in Pilsen for the Chicago Dyke March on Sunday, we moved in and out of a chalk circle to make our dance. Meanwhile, each performer talked to marchers about revolution, freedom, and liberation – all the while drawing our solidarity tattoo on the inside of as many wrists as we could. The Dyke March was raucous and gorgeous; inside it, UPRISING #6 performers in white asked strangers to engage critically using their own voices. The action was both intimate and public: holding a hand, drawing on a forearm, and simply asking folks, 'What about this event is revolutionary?' We were not telling them anything or projecting our ideas. We were genuinely curious. We were listening.

> Curiosity was far greater than our fear
> It felt so simple, so prodigious at the same time
> Incredible things are happening in the world
> Magical things are happening in the world. (Iron & Wine 2009)

LIBERATE OUR SEXUAL ENCOUNTERS
REVOLUTIONARY PRACTICE #7

The revolution should be sexy in all the ways that are possible, not just in the bedroom. Be in your body and remember that everyone else has a body. The work we do to liberate our own sexuality and that of our lovers is essential world-building work. Give thanks for all of our feelings of pleasure. Healing is an active project that does not always have an end point. Too many revolutionaries have been sexually traumatized. In the world we are trying to build, sex will be enthusiastically consensual and self-determined, but until we get there, create tasks or gestures that allow us to practice consent in low-stakes ways. Acknowledge the people, pictures, and books that have revolutionized your own gender and/or sexuality. Feel your own edges and articulate them.

IN ACTION: UPRISING #7
24 July 2008, 11:30pm | Bijou Theater and Sex Club, Chicago
Participants: Erica Mott, Jane Fresne, Sheelah Murthy, Madsen Minax,
K. Bradford, Samantha Miller, Coman Poon, Nicole Garneau
Assistants: Savannah, Sky, Nino Dorenzo
Photos: Tara Malik | Video: Tamale Sepp

Think Pink Radio was a queer people of color collaboration between DJs Erik Roldan and Ruth Batacan. When they decided to bring their regular radio broadcasts to a close, they held their 'Transition Party' at the Bijou Theater, the oldest gay porn theater in the United States, which featured two floors of play areas for casual sex and cruising. But by 2008, the Bijou was not as popular as it once had been, and the folks at the Bijou decided to make a little extra money by renting out the place to young queers who wanted to throw parties. There were DJs, performances, and a keg out back. (Rest in Power, Bijou Theater! It closed in 2016.)

In the summer of 2008, my dear friends (and notorious sex-positivity advocates) Red Tremmel and Jessica Halem were moving out of Chicago, so I dedicated a pervy UPRISING to them. Eight performers stood before the audience, reading simultaneously from books that had revolutionized our understandings of sex, feminism, and gender. As we stood in white reading our books to the audience, queer feminist porn projected onto our bodies and the screen behind us.

The performance was designed to encourage young, queer partygoers to explore the whole space of the Bijou, which was understandably intimidating to folks who had never been in a gay male sex club before. We split up and invited audience members upstairs to cubicles in the sex club to give them private, flashlight readings from books that had changed our lives. Then we negotiated kisses. In these brief moments of intimacy, we made it known that explicit communication about sexual boundaries and desires is what we want from our revolution.

UPRISING #7 and the party at the Bijou was such a powerful experience for me that two years later, it became the launching point for a collaboration between DJ Erik Roldan and myself. We had so much fun working on that party in 2008 that we created our own sexy, weird, queer performance and dance party we called Northern Lights, which we threw monthly from October 2010 to October 2013 at Parlour on Clark.

The integrity and dedication of UPRISING volunteer performers cannot be understated. I discovered along the way that other artists were also hungry to take part in work that felt meaningful to them, often in ways that were highly personal:

Hello Nicole,

I am interested in volunteering for Uprising #7: Sex & Revolution. I currently have my BA in dance from Columbia College Chicago. My senior choreographic project was on issues within the transgender community and exploring alternative forms of masculinity and femininity. I chose this topic because I have been in the queer community for years. I was not aware of the issues within the transgender community until I met my now boyfriend, who is transgender. His radical views on gender expression have been life changing in terms of my own views.

I ran into Peter Carpenter (former professor of mine) at the last Poonie's Cabaret and he mentioned that I should know who you are. I have read the material on your website and watched some of your work on YouTube. I am inspired by the political viewpoints of your pieces and how you bring awareness to issues you find important through the performance art genre.

Please let me know if you are interested in having me volunteer for
Uprising #7.

Samantha

Performed by a group of folks who are accomplished artists in their own right, UPRISING #7 provided by far the most detailed portrait of participant experience. We had shared a performance moment together on the stage, but then we all split up for a couple of hours to deliver individual readings to folks we invited upstairs to the sex club. I was curious about their experiences of the UPRISING since I did not witness most of them. Each volunteer performer found a different way to articulate their relationships to the people with whom they were interacting; they called them clients, guests, and audience. My impression, and feedback from the party organizers, was that we did indeed tune the party by helping people to explore a space they might not have otherwise. I had some fascinating conversations and felt genuine moments of intimacy with strangers.

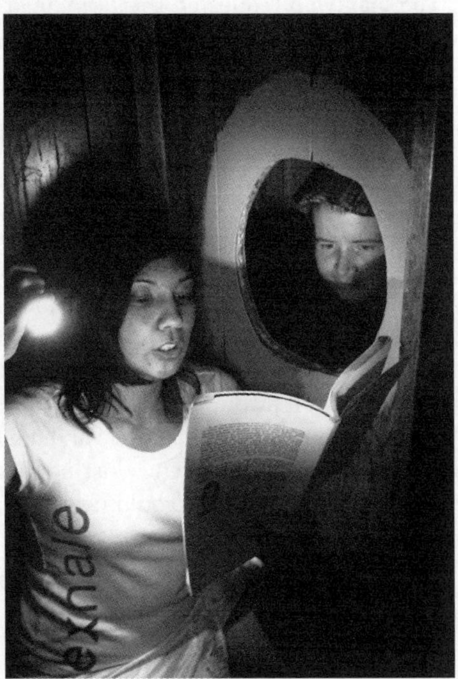

Figure 7: Sheelah Murthy reads to Red Tremmel through a glory hole in UPRISING #7. Photo by Tara Malik.

Reflections on UPRISING #7

Sheelah Murthy, Samantha Miller, Coman Poon, Jane Fresne

SHEELAH MURTHY

I read a poem called 'My Shadow' from *A Child's Garden of Verses* to my first 'client' on a leather hammock-style sex sling. We both sat in the sling and read it to each other. In that dimly lit space it felt more effective when he read it. He chuckled at all the masturbation innuendos. Another memorable performance: read a steamy passage from another book about the powerful calming effects of cunnilingus and nipple pinching on women in labor from a book I own called *Birthing at Home*. This felt very transgressive for me; reading such a biologically female book in a space designed for sex among male-bodied people. I read to two men. The man who requested the *Birthing at Home* text watched through the glory hole (and is someone I personally know and feel safe with), but then there was another man who wanted to join. I thought he followed us because he was interested in my friend. I felt the unknown man was getting into it. I ended the session with the ritualistic kiss. My friend and I did the amicable peck, and the other man and I tongued. He felt dry and wanting, but gentle. I felt like the compassionate nurse. We smiled. He said thank you. I left him alone. I did not think he wanted to be led back down the stairs.

Then I read a passage from a book called *Transformative Emotional Bodywork* to a trans* guy through a glory hole. The intimacy of this performance led to conversation. We discovered we were both moving for teaching gigs in progressive schools, and had a nice conversation about the blur between sexual healing and massage therapy. It felt serendipitous. We were both embarking on pivotal life-changing journeys. I told him that I was supposed to ask him for a kiss to end the performance and did he think his partner would mind? What proceeded was quite the erotic French kissing session. He was a lovely kisser. As we were kissing through the glory hole, I could hear other couples inside the darkened secret corridors having sex.

SAMANTHA MILLER

Most of the audience members, in my opinion, were receptive to the UPRISING. I only had one individual decline. In most instances, they almost seemed delighted to be chosen. I could hear the whispers when my guest(s) realized that I was taking them upstairs. Not only did they receive permission to see the space, but also the light from the flashlights allowed them to experience what the typical patrons don't see. I could tell that they were REALLY listening to me. I experienced some self-doubt, and wished I had picked a longer passage with more information. The guests were very open to the kisses. In my crowd of friends, we always kiss on the lips. I know this is odd but I've gotten used to it. Most guests freely allowed me to kiss them on the cheek. Only men allowed me to kiss them on the lips.

I had one extremely intense moment with a guest. I had given him and his friend a reading. He came back later to find me and tell me a story. He said that he had taken too many drugs once and went into a psychotic episode. The police were called and were concerned that he would harm himself and others. In the police station, they put him in a small, enclosed space, similar to the closet that I read to him in. He said that eventually the calmness overwhelmed him. He said that he is thankful that the police did that, and now goes to enclosed spaces to calm himself down. He said that by taking him into that intimate space, I brought him back to that time in the police station. He smiled, touched my arm, and walked away. I was stunned. Wow. It was such a personal thing to share with me. I think I probably experienced something similar to what the guests were experiencing. I felt privileged.

In terms of my own feelings, I enjoyed myself. After about an hour of talking to people, I started to feel exhausted emotionally. I think this was caused from having to stay so open to the experience and to try not to judge or make assumptions. It was such an odd experience. I didn't even know places like the Bijou existed. Sky and I have quite a few friends who have HIV/AIDS. It was hard for me to push my concerns for the patrons out of my head. I was just shocked! However, I am also respectful of the range of freedom that we all deserve to have to pick who and what we are sexually. Ultimately, they have the right to make their own choices and it is not my place to worry for them. I'm glad that places like the Bijou offer such freedom if so desired.

COMAN POON

As a seasoned performer, I especially appreciated the freedom of personalizing with both text and site-specificity while knowing that we were a diverse but cohesive whole: I enjoyed the act of reclaiming and recharging the usually exclusive, male, anonymous sex space of the Bijou with acts of intimate disclosure, and intellectual and performative provocation. My primary text was *Refusing to be a Man* by John Stoltenberg (a close ally of Andrea Dworkin).

Coman Poon: Highlighted Performances

Single Male

Someone recommended that I approach a man who was standing alone by the wall in the theater. Despite the fact that I was most interested in performing with those who would not normally have access to the Bijou (women and trans* folk), I approached P and invited him to join me upstairs. P presented as a semi-awkward Caucasian young man in his mid-to late twenties, sporting glasses, seemingly without social connection, and perhaps newly 'out of the closet.' After brief introductions, I escorted him into a booth near the top of the spiral staircase, told him what I would be doing next, and asked him to sit down with his face beside the large glory hole (like a confession booth).

I read him an excerpt from *Refusing to be a Man,* which analyzed the relationship between pornography and homophobia (Stoltenberg 1984). I nonthreateningly asked him to name or point to three places where he would like to be kissed; in response, he named 'my head,' 'my heart,' and, after momentarily pausing, sweetly pointed at his lips. In response, I went around, entered his booth, and closed the door behind me; with nonverbal permission, I kissed him on the forehead, over his heart, and paused before we kissed tenderly on the lips.

This was a beautiful and pure moment where performance boundaries blurred. An authentic and charged person-to-person connection transpired between two strangers. I consciously allowed it to go there and in retrospect, it made for a very unique performative moment, one where real sexual desire was expressed and exchanged in a specific moment without necessarily being formed just as an act of performance. This stretched boundaries on many levels; personally, artistically, and ethically (I am in a monogamous relationship). After lingering in the liminal moment of connection and desire, P asked me, 'So what is this?' I responded by verbally explaining that it was part of a group performance around exploring sexuality in public spaces and that it was in honor of two sexual and gender mavericks in the Chicago community who are leaving the city and are being feted tonight. He understood, and after a long embrace, we exited the booth and I escorted him back down the stairs to the first floor.

Young Dyke Couple

After the first performance ended, I immediately spotted two young women (whom I assumed to be a couple) sitting down; I introduced myself and found out that one or both of them had just come back from receiving a performance. I invited them to hold hands and follow me for a second performance and led them to a booth with chicken wire on one wall, with an entrance located in the middle of the dark back alleyway behind the sex booths with glory holes. From an adjacent room (separated by the chicken wire) I read the two women (still holding hands) a text from *Refusing to be a Man* on the re-conceptualization of the fetus as a penis, critiquing male (sexual) self-interest in light of reproductive rights (Stoltenberg 1984). Then I asked them to turn to each other and point to a place on the other where they personally would like to be kissed; both were initially shy but both pointed to their lips and (upon encouragement from me) kissed each other lovingly. Thereafter, I escorted both back down to the base of the spiral staircase. Both held hands for the duration of the performance and thanked me at the end.

Two Gay Male Friends

I roamed out into the backyard/garden space where I bumped into M and B, two gay men who I know only through a Sunday night queer meditation group at the Shambhala Center in East Rogers Park, and who I have never socialized with outside of Buddhist contexts. We were all friendly acquaintances, both are highly intelligent and I invited both to join me in the dark BDSM room. Someone (likely a man who was cruising at the Bijou) remained in the dark corner of the room. My intention was to read them a story. After letting them struggle (valiantly and ever-so-body-respectfully) to both get on the sling in a back-to-back way, I got inspired to intervene. I commanded them to start again and to arrange themselves so that M was lying on the sling, legs hanging off the one end, and B was straddling and sitting directly on top of M's crotch; they happily agreed.

I read them a section from *Refusing to be a Man* on hetero fear of disempowerment in the act of being penetrated, and its transgressive embrace in gay male porn scenarios of taking sexual humiliation as a erotically charged act (Stoltenberg 1984); both seem to enjoy this immensely and engaged with the irony of being in the pose and context. To create contrast, I asked them to kiss each other in the tenderest way in an erogenous zone, and to direct each other to where they would like to be kissed; M directed B to kiss him on the neck behind his right ear and B directed M to kiss him on his pierced left nipple. I escorted them both back to the garden.

Jessica Halem and Red Tremmel

I looked all over for Jessica and Red and finally located them in the upstairs space, at the tail end of receiving a performance from K. Bradford. I waited for Red to gather and after assenting to his request to not have the camera follow us, I led them to Blow Job Alley (one of few places left in the play area where I had scouted out remnants of sexual activity still happening). We entered one of the semi-enclosed corners and I stepped up onto a platform seat, standing above Red and Jessica. Save for the single light source from the two LEDs on my bike light/headlamp, it was pitch dark inside; we heard some noises in the nearby dark corners and were aware that there was a man voyeurizing the three of us (in performance). I read from *Refusing to be a Man* choice excerpts of graphic porn dialogue between a male and female (Stoltenberg 1984); but in honor of both Red and Jessica, I randomly and intentionally mixed up all the pronouns to undermine the dominant/submissive intent of the original pornographic dirty talk. When I finished, without instruction, I squealed in pleasure to find that Red and Jessica were already making out under the halo of light that seeped over the contours of the book.

JANE FRESNE

UPRISING #7 was really fun for me. It was interesting for me as I waited to begin and then realized that I could go into the porn theater and enjoy the evening before we began the performance. Looking back, I smile at myself wondering how much of life I missed by being inside a box of behavior... thinking that's the way things should be instead of just jumping in. I loved that I saw a 'real' lesbian sex movie. I've only seen the kinds made for men before – not for women – that was super fun. Of course we like to get pounded now, don't we? The little spaces were great. I loved taking people into them and being intimate by reading and kissing. People weren't quite sure what to expect. I really liked wearing a different identity that night.

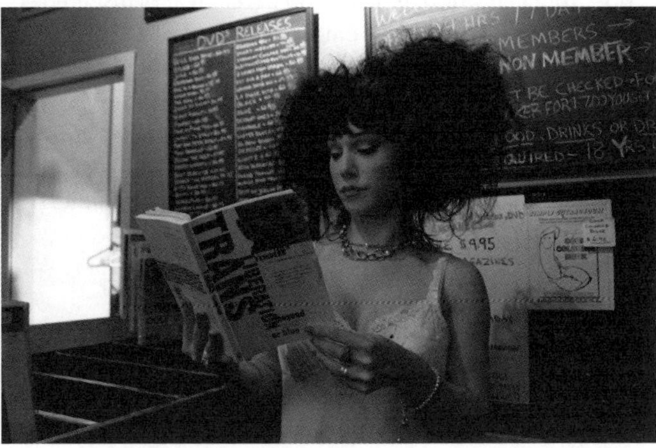

Figure 8: A book that revolutionized Sky's understanding of sex/gender in UPRISING #7. Photo by Tara Malik.

OCCUPY PUBLIC SPACES WITHOUT PERMISSION
REVOLUTIONARY PRACTICE #8

It is a specific political stance to refuse to ask permission to do things in public. Reclaim our common spaces! Make art in the streets! Do not wait for a commission or an institution to legitimize working outside. Do not hurt anyone, and try to avoid making people feel harassed. Highlight and critique how privatized and policed public spaces are. Practice this skill: put your body in public spaces, and do things outside of generally accepted social norms.

Working outside or in public charges the energy of the performers and audience. Inside a theater or a performance space, everyone is so comfortable with their respective roles that it is hard to surprise anybody. If people have paid $15 at the door, there is not much you can do to shake them up. Suzi Gablik highlights some reasons why it is very challenging to make politically engaged work inside the safe confines of a performance space:

> In the normal physical environment of the theater or concert hall, the purchase of an admission ticket indicates to the audience that it does not have to earn its way in; the audience is not required to work, learn, act or participate in any way. All that is required of customers is that they be able to afford the price of admission. Performances are usually given in the evening, at a comfortable temperature, preferably on a full stomach, and with a time limit of 3–4 hours, so as not to interfere with work schedules. (Gablik 1992: 86)

Be conscious of the ways that working in public is easier or more difficult based on the kind of body one has, or is perceived to have. Understand that performers on the street may be subject to different kinds of scrutiny based on who they are or how they look. Talk to pedestrians, security guards, and cops in the simplest and most humane way possible. Build the common spaces and respectful public interactions we need now.

IN ACTION: UPRISING #8
24 August 2008, 1:00pm | Grant Park, Chicago
Participants: Peter Carpenter, Leah Mayers, Emily Smith, Clara Kim, Uncle Bear, Julie Ann Downey, Ian Hatcher, Karen Christopher, Suzy Grant, and Nicole Garneau
Photos: Tara Malik | Video: Unattended

In my artist/activist circles, there was a lot of talk about 2008 as the 40-year anniversary of the worldwide revolutionary movements of 1968. Chicago was marking 40 years since student demonstrations at the Democratic National Convention (DNC) sparked a police riot that earned the city an international reputation for police brutality. I was personally interested in the 40-year interval because I was soon turning 40 and some part of me was trying to reckon with the world into which my parents had brought me. When I asked my mother what 1968 was like for her, she recalled how after she and my father were married in 1965, they tried earnestly to get pregnant to keep my father from being drafted into the Vietnam War. A pregnancy did not manifest in time to excuse my father from military service, but they were lucky that my father was sent to Korea instead of Vietnam. She remembers drinking a lot in 1968, smoking cigarettes, sleeping in her childhood bed, and praying not to be widowed.

August 2008 marked 40 years since the 1968 Chicago DNC, and UPRISING volunteers and I gathered at the General Logan statue in Grant Park to reimagine the image made famous during mass anti-war demonstrations in the park across the street from the hotel where the DNC was held. We fanned out to talk to folks in the park that day about their visions for a better world. We wrote or drew those ideas on a plain white flag and promised to wave it. The people in Grant Park had great visions that made beautiful flags. We also wrote our own intentions on flags. Then we met at the top of the hill and waved our flags like crazy, sending our hopes out on the wind.

Working in public is not without risks. We had a video camera set up to record the UPRISING and I foolishly left it on a stone pillar quite a distance from us, pointed at us to get the long shot. When we finished I went down the hill to retrieve it but it was gone. It was a really nice camera that belonged to my employer. Suddenly the photographer, Tara Malik, took off, running after some people we saw walking away from the spot. She caught up to them and managed to negotiate a return of the camera without humiliating them or threatening violence. That in itself was miraculous. But when I returned to the rest of the group and told them the story, one of the performers said that one of the folks involved in the theft had participated in the UPRISING and that she had been waving his flag during the performance. His vision for liberation was 'Love Respect Dignity!' There are no guarantees of rainbows and flowers, but maybe something about the piece made him give the camera back, and besides – who am I to say that petty thieves do not have valid ideas for a better world?

Ian Hatcher wrote about his experiences in the park that day:

> When we dispersed to talk to strangers I made an arbitrary rule for myself: if I didn't feel like I should approach someone because they seemed somehow intimidating or unlikely to be receptive, I had to approach them. This led to me first talking with a Spanish-speaking couple that was with their son who was perhaps 6 or

7. The son spoke English so he translated for us. The three of them seemed slightly baffled but amused and warm. After a bit the son stopped translating and the couple said, 'Next time.' Off I went.

I tried approaching a few other people but they didn't last more than a sentence or two. I emerged on Adams and found myself in a large crowd of marathon runners (I think?) who were definitely not interested in talking to me. I started thinking about groups, about how the likelihood of adults being receptive to talking about what would make the world a better place in a genuine manner seemed, in general, inversely proportional to how many of their friends and acquaintances were surrounding them.

Next I started looking for people with kids, but there weren't many kids running the marathon, so I went back into the park. I walked to the shady area overlooking the disused train lines. An older African-American man was sitting there reading a book. I walked up to him and began speaking. He looked up, and stared in silence as I introduced the project and myself. Then he slowly, barely perceptibly, shook his head, and his eyes returned to his book.

I was getting a little worried because I still needed my second flag drawn/written upon and was running out of time. I walked back through the grass and came upon a girl sitting beside her bike. She was shy at first but after I convinced her I wasn't trying to sell something or induct her into a cult, she took the flag and marker and sketched her bicycle.

Then I returned to the statue and joined the others in flying our flags. Karen Christopher was standing beside me holding her flags upward and outward, not flying them, or rather, allowing the wind to fly them. That looked beautiful to me, so I did the same. After a while I tried flying them more actively, but wasn't sure what to do (my last flag-waving experience was probably Boy Scouts, age 13) so the cloth was in a constant state of near-entanglement. The entire time we were holding and flying the flags I felt very peaceful, as well as grounded in the solidity of the stone beneath my feet and the ring of people. It was quiet up there and the wind was the loudest sound around.

Then we ran down the hill, and I remember noticing the sound of the wind and the silence otherwise, aside from the rustling of my own movement.

The last woman I spoke to, upon returning to the hill, was a woman who had been at the DNC in 1968! She approached me and asked about the performance, and I told her what we were doing and invited her to contribute to the flags. She decided to draw a peace sign on the first one. But then she couldn't quite remember it. Then she laughed quietly to herself, incredulously, and said aloud, 'I can't believe it... I can't even remember what the peace symbol looks like.'

That, and a sense of calmness and buoyancy that lasted through the rest of the day, was my experience with the flags.
– Ian (Participant, UPRISING #8)

Sometimes, volunteer performers wrote reflections years after the fact. I received this message from Suzy Grant in January 2012:

Dear Nicole,

I can physically remember the UPRISING event I participated in a few years back, the anniversary of the 1968 Democratic National Convention in Grant Park – when your camera was stolen and then returned and we all felt that moment of true community.

I remember how the air felt that day as we waved our fabric, and the way the sun was shining through the trees as I walked around talking to people and having them write on my flag. I connected and talked to people regardless of how they looked, and that genuine kindness and sharing filled the park that day. That was energy we all sent out and which, in turn, got your camera returned without police involvement but just by you talking human to human with another person. I knew who you were before then but I don't think I had actually met you before that day. The openness and kindness you carry is wonderful and inspiring. Knowing you and people like you make me reconsider why I'm reacting to situations in a certain way or when I'm feeling negative and angry or judgmental. Letting those kinds of weights fall away and enacting change through community and compassion is something I'm really thinking about and working on within myself.

– Suzy Grant (Participant, UPRISING #8)

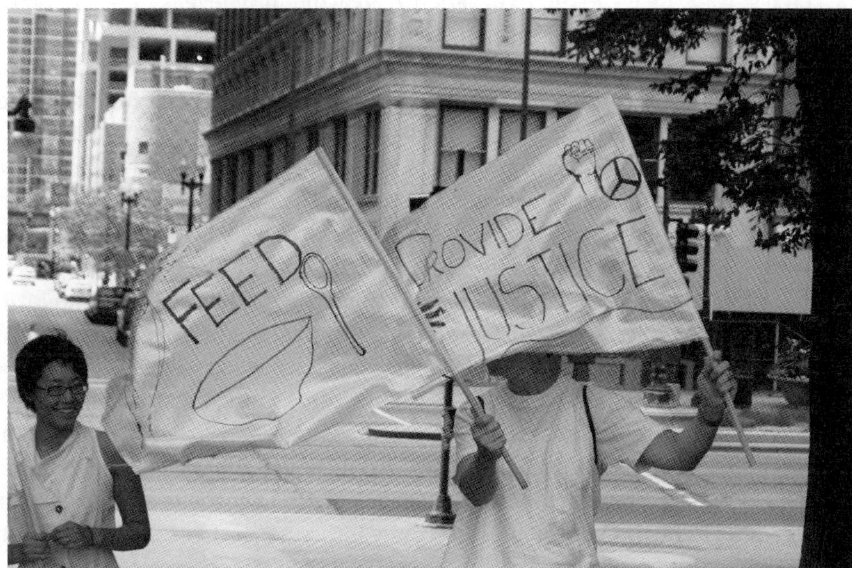

Figure 9: Clara Kim and Ian Hatcher in UPRISING #8. Photo by Tara Malik.

Interjection: Remember That Cops Are Human Beings

One of the starkest ways I have found to experience my white privilege is to reflect on my interactions with the police. Even if those interactions involve the police stopping and/or questioning me in relation to my public artmaking, I have never thought one of them was going to kill me for doing something unusual on the street. The Movement for Black Lives and many other activists have done incredible work to highlight the vastly different ways in which white people are assumed to be automatically law-abiding and nonthreatening, and people of color are assumed to be automatically criminal and dangerous. Those assumptions often mean the difference between life and death when it comes to encounters with the police.

Working out of doors, making art in public settings, I have had a good amount of interaction with the Chicago police. The simplest things might seem shocking or provoking on the street: cups of water on the pavement, blowing kisses at strangers, waving flags, drawing chalk paint flowers, or asking someone to sing a song. I have collected some entertaining stories about police interactions over the years, but in contrast to an unrelenting media barrage of images of police violence against people of color, they hardly seem funny anymore. How dare I laugh in the face of the very real terror that my friends of color experience on a daily basis in relation to their own lives and the lives of their children?

To make UPRISINGs in public, I developed some principles for what happens when the police stop by to find out what is going on. Nowadays, most of our public spaces are 'policed' in a way that does not become obvious until one starts doing something slightly unusual. Then security guards come out of the woodwork. Spaces that we may think of as public are increasingly controlled by private security.

My interactions with the police are privileged because I am white, middle-aged, English-speaking, female, and a US citizen. Cops approach me with a mixture of suspicion and curiosity, but I have never thought that someone was going to pull out a gun and shoot me. What they do not know from looking at me is that my maternal grandfather was Sergeant Orville C Kent, who dedicated 33 years to police work in several South Side Chicago neighborhoods before retiring at age 63. My mother strongly identifies as being from a police family. Growing up, I heard many stories about him being a good and gentle cop, refusing to take bribes, and priding himself on defusing hot situations rather than pulling his gun.

The Movement for Black Lives (2016) articulates a position toward the police state and the prison–industrial complex that I find useful: they demand divestment from policing and incarceration, and reallocation of funds into 'long-term community-based safety strategies such as education, local restorative justice services, and employment programs.' As Mychal Denzel Smith writes in *The Nation*:

> The police are not performing the function we say they are, and there are real ways to achieve a world with less violence that don't include the police. We simply haven't tried. Until we invest in full employment, universal healthcare that includes mental health services, free education at every level, comprehensive sex education that teaches about consent and bodily autonomy, the decriminalization of drugs and erasure of the stigma around drug use, affordable and adequate housing, eliminating homophobia and transphobia – things that actually reduce the amount of violence we witness – I don't want to hear about how necessary the police are. They are only necessary because we are all too willing to hide behind our cowardice and not actually put forth the effort to create a better world. (2015: n.pag.)

I support the position that working toward full social and political equality will eliminate the need for a police force, at the same time as I regard individual police as mostly blue-collar workers in an oppressive and brutal industry. I believe that the revolution will liberate those workers who are engaged in activities that uphold state apparatuses of oppression. In the world we are trying to build, cops, prison guards, soldiers, and many others will be able to heal from the damage done to their humanity.

For an UPRISING in public with other people, I was explicit about my hoped-for interactions with cops, security guards, and other authorities. I told my volunteers that if they were approached by a cop or a security guard, to try and send them to me. I suggested they say something like: 'See that big white lady over there? She is in charge.' Second, I explained that cops and security guards are human beings working within an extremely dehumanizing system. Private security guards could be harder to deal with because they report to property owners, and have less training and less actual authority than police. They also have less job security, so if something happened on their watch (beet juice graffiti, filling cups of water from a fountain) they had good reason to fear that the repercussions would land squarely on them. I encouraged UPRISING volunteers to give individual guards and cops the benefit of the doubt and try to engage with them in a genuine conversation about the art and why it was happening. When stopped by the police, I could usually explain the performance to them in simple terms. Sometimes they seemed to really enjoy being 'included' in the ideas behind the UPRISING. Sometimes they just acted like jerks.

When there has been some kind of police or security intervention in a performance, it is easy to retroactively decide that that particular performance had a more radical edge than others. I never set out to do things that will purposely attract police attention, and it is not my intention to be arrested doing performance art. I understand those things are out of my control, and my safety or danger has a lot to do with how I look as a racialized person. But if the point of the UPRISINGs is to practice building the world we want to live in, that ethic has to apply to my interactions with police and security.

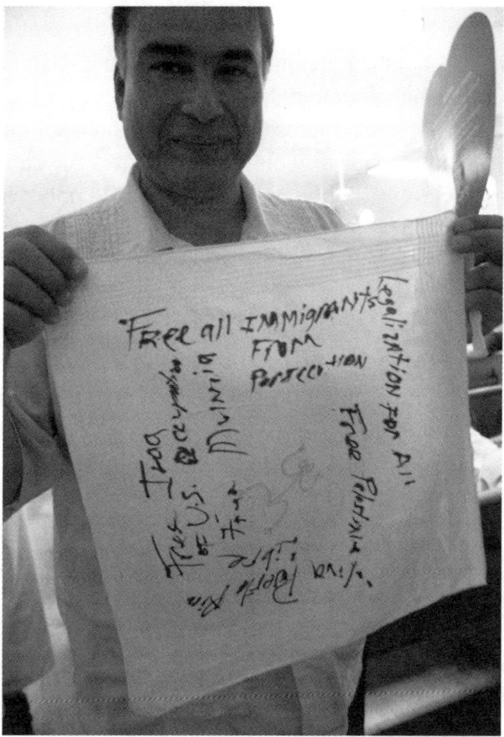

Figure 10: Visions of liberation on a handkerchief in UPRISING #9. Photo by Tara Malik.

#9 SUPPORT RADICALS OF COLOR
REVOLUTIONARY PRACTICE #9

Revolutionary performance art does not escape entrenched race and class segregation. It affects our neighborhoods, schools, and every aspect of our social lives. Many of us are dedicated to racial justice and have individually meaningful relationships across racial lines, but we find very few truly integrated social spaces – especially in my hometown of Chicago. In 2016, Ta-Nehisi Coates called Chicago 'the capital of black America,' saying, 'you guys have so much, so much culture, so much history [...] which doesn't mean everything good about being black. If you want to experience pure racism, you come here too' (Miller 2017: n.pag.). Of course this is mirrored in art communities as well. A lot of the self-identified radical art crowd is terribly earnest and very white. We have meetings in which we agonize about the 'effectiveness' of our political art.

But the fact remains that the structures of white supremacist capitalist patriarchy are killing our planet and ourselves. These systems must be dismantled. What do we need to do to manifest the moment(s) of transformation? How can our work respond to and participate in this particular political moment? How can we be of vital service to social and political movements? One way is to explicitly support the work of progressive people of color whose work is leading the way in struggles for social and racial justice. For some of us white folks, this means stepping out of our normal social circles and working with communities of color in supportive ways, guided by them and responding to their needs and requests. This requires vigilance: maintaining a rigorous intersectional analysis and checking our actions. Daring to maintain a critique of our work and ourselves sheds a light on the systemic oppression that keeps us separated from others, and therefore from our own humanity. We do this by putting our often simultaneously oppressed and over-privileged bodies and selves in spaces where we are strangers, listeners, humble students, encouragers, and not the stars of the show.

 IN ACTION: UPRISING #9

21 September 2008, 2:00pm | 40-Year Struggle: Young Lords Celebration, Chicago
Participants: Emily Smith, Angel Nava, Ahalya Satkunaratnam, and Nicole Garneau
Photos: Tara Malik

The Chicago Young Lords were the children of the first Puerto Rican immigrants, and they built a grassroots movement for human rights and self-determination within the barrios of the United States. So when I heard that they were planning the '40-Year

Struggle: Young Lords Celebration,' I contacted the founder José (Cha-Cha) Jimenez and offered an UPRISING for his event. He and I had talked about the content and the participatory nature of the work, and he was supportive even though we did not know each other personally.

I learned that one of the ways the US companies historically exploited the labor of Puerto Ricans was through embroidery. Puerto Rican women and children were employed embroidering handkerchiefs, often in their own homes, and they were paid by the piece. Then the handkerchiefs were shipped back to the United States to be sold. To reference this history, UPRISING volunteers distributed 40 handkerchiefs I had embroidered with an image of El Coquí, cultural symbol of Puerto Rico. We asked participants at the event to decorate the handkerchiefs with their visions for liberation. People in attendance did beautiful work on their handkerchiefs. Children took the task especially seriously. Our plan was to decorate the handkerchiefs before and during the event. At an appropriate moment in the program, José would introduce us, and I would briefly explain the UPRISING project, thank folks for participating, and then invite everyone to wave their flags in the air as a way of celebrating and releasing their visions of liberation.

I do not think José really knew how many people would show up to this event, or how long it would go on, or that prominent activists would continue streaming in for hours, requesting time on the microphone. So the program, understandably, kept changing all afternoon. I never thought our UPRISING should take precedence over a speech by former Black Panther Kathleen Cleaver or Fred Hampton, Jr. The celebration went on for hours, long past its scheduled end time. Finally, it was time for José to close the event. I connected with him one more time to assure him that our action would take no more than five minutes and would be a really beautiful closing. He said that sounded good, and he said he would go up and do final thank-yous and then introduce the UPRISING. He did all of his final words of gratitude, and then thanked everyone for coming and welcomed folks to a potluck meal downstairs but did not mention the UPRISING. After nearly five hours of speeches, folks understandably leapt to their feet to go to the buffet, and then José looked at me and remembered that he had not introduced the UPRISING. It was a simple mistake. There was so much going on, and José was holding it all, and he just forgot. He felt badly, I felt badly, but there was nothing to be done. The event was over.

UPRISING #9 was the first one that felt like a colossal failure to me, and as soon as I had thanked the volunteers and said goodbye, I walked to my bus stop on North Avenue, started crying, and never stopped for the next two hours. The build-up of hours of anxiety and adrenaline were mixed with my awareness of being an outsider in that community and my fear that I had disappointed volunteer performers who had given an entire day to this action. I came to understand that the gift we all received from UPRISING #9 was an adventure in revolutionary social relations. It painfully demonstrated that stepping into a space where I had no social capital, I had to release my expectations and encounter the UPRISING exactly how it happened: 40 intimate interactions, 40 beautiful handkerchiefs, and one of the most fascinating afternoons of radical teachings from people of color that I had ever been privileged to share.

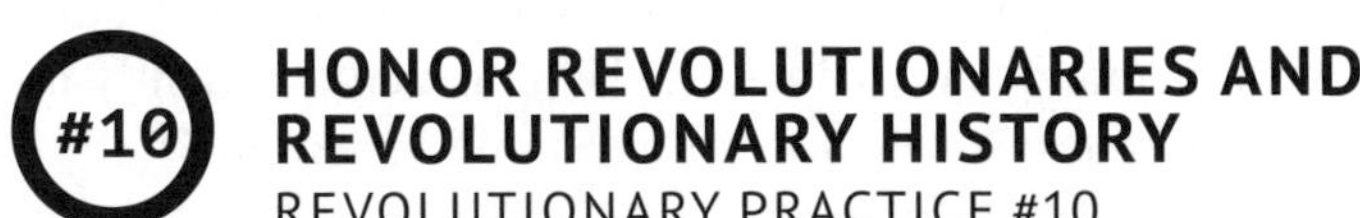

HONOR REVOLUTIONARIES AND REVOLUTIONARY HISTORY
REVOLUTIONARY PRACTICE #10

Most people educated in the United States possess an appalling lack of knowledge about world history. Why not use art as a tool to further our own education about revolutionary events and practices? Design projects that require research, information sharing, and conversations. Revolution is a dialogical process. Learn the courageous stories of historical freedom fighters. When violence and oppression seem overwhelming, hold those examples in your heart and on your tongue. Draw on them for strength and inspiration. Say their names, and give their legacies life.

One way to actively honor folks is to build a public altar or shrine. If this prospect triggers your anxiety about doing things correctly and respectfully, take this valuable piece of advice from artist and ceremonialist Ruth Robbins: *make it beautiful*. Release analysis about the politics of revolution and who is a revolutionary person. The way we honor our beloved dead is by making their altars gorgeous.

IN ACTION: UPRISING #10
18 October 2008, 9:00pm | Sappho's Salon at Women and Children First Bookstore, Chicago
Participants: Jane Haldiman, Linda Horwitz, Maggie Barrack, Nicole Garneau, and 30 audience members/altar builders
Photos: Tara Malik and Ruth Robbins | Video: Uncle Bear

UPRISING #10 honored revolutionary women who have left this world, as part of a performance evening called Sappho's Salon at Women and Children First Bookstore. One of the few longstanding independent feminist bookstores in the United States, Women and Children First and its staff play a vital role in holding and promoting the ideas, writers, and texts that a revolutionary movement needs. UPRISING volunteers and audience members were invited to write the names of revolutionary women on long strips of white fabric, and then these flags were added to an altar that had been installed in a doorway alcove on Clark

Street, right outside the store. For the purposes of the altar, 'revolutionary' was broadly defined, and we did not attempt to be all-inclusive.

While I tied flags to the altar, Linda Horwitz and Maggie Barrack read aloud the names and contributions of some of the revolutionary women who were on the altar. Jane Haldiman contributed a poetry reading to the occasion. The building of a shrine to revolutionary women was itself a ceremony, but we also performed a shrine-activation ritual to turn it on: the assembled crowd was invited to take a moment to silently fill their hearts with gratitude for all of our revolutionary heroines, and on a count of three we blew those prayers of thanksgiving into the altar. Everyone present was deputized 'altar maintenance crew' for the next month. We left little flyers explaining the altar and inviting passersby to feel free to add a name of a revolutionary woman or other offering to the altar.

The next month, the Chicago Tribune ran an article with the headline, 'Three weeks later, literary shrine still just fine.' Reporter Patrick Reardon called it 'a minor urban miracle' and quoted Linda Bubon, owner of Women and Children First Bookstore, as saying: 'I thought the artist was naïve in thinking this would not be vandalized. I'm so glad I was wrong' (Reardon 2008). By the time I deconstructed the altar several weeks later, community members had lovingly added flowers, stones, photos, and an additional 150 names of departed women they considered revolutionary.

Feminist Art Activism and UPRISING

Anne Cushwa

The 1960s saw the growth of the feminist, civil rights, and anti-war movements throughout the United States. These movements have continued to grow and shape the cultural landscape of the United States over the past 50 years. Feminist art collectives are some of the products of this time of change. Collaboration, education, and activism were and are some of the principal goals and methods of these artists. From California and artists like Judy Chicago and Betye Saar to New York and artists like Faith Ringgold and Nancy Spero, feminist projects included artworks, public programs, and opening woman-centered galleries and businesses. Chicago fostered its own feminist art scenes, as well as being a hotbed of civil rights and anti-war demonstrations and organizations.

Beginning in 1973, two Chicago groups, Artemisia and ARC Galleries, provided models of women trying to effect change in their communities through collaboration and shared power. Artemisia and ARC Galleries were women-only collectives founded within weeks of one another. Membership through the payment of annual dues guaranteed an artist one show each year, a way of circumventing traditional institutional venues and their patriarchic concentration. The members worked together on exhibitions, seminars, education, and programming. Chicago's large metro area, public transportation system, and lower rents (than the major cities on the coasts) give the city more accessible, practical avenues for smaller groups to create a foothold within communities. The work of Joanna Gardner-Huggett of DePaul University speaks specifically and eloquently about the histories and impacts of these women's groups, and her scholarship helped me see the depth of the roots of Garneau's work through the lens of Chicago (Gardener-Huggett 2007, 2012). An example of the close connections among feminist groups in Chicago, Garneau showed work in a group exhibition at Artemisia in 2001, before the gallery closed in 2003. She also performed at a benefit for the ARC Gallery in 2002. Her experiences with each organization show the endurance of their mission and the fruitful interactions with a diverse assortment of artists, which are made possible through these feminist collectives.

One of the biggest critiques of women's movements both historically and in the present is the predominance of white women in such groups and the lack of representation of women of color. That was certainly a critique of both Artemisia and ARC over the years. More recently, one of the stories that emerged from the January 2017 Women's Marches in the United States was the conflict in leadership and organization between white women and women of color. The notion of 'checking one's privilege' is still a thorny problem for feminism. Interest in addressing this problem encouraged associations to emerge that were explicitly about inclusion and representing more accurately the diversity of Chicago's women. Garneau cites several of these smaller groups (WAC Chicago, Big Smith, Queer White Allies Against Racism, etc.) and their open struggles with race as central to her development as a practicing performance artist with a primary interest in social justice. Her background in teaching also informs her work and shows her commitment to tackling divisive issues like race and privilege.

The influence of the city of Chicago, its sociopolitical history, and its networks of feminist and social justice activism could be explored in much greater depth as contributing factors in Garneau's work. For the scope of this writing, it seems enough to note the vectors of germination and cross-fertilization that helped bring UPRISING into existence – the city of Chicago and its history, feminism, social justice, LGBTQ rights, the theater and arts communities, and multilayered spirituality.

Garneau's art, as I mention in my appreciation of her work, defies neat categorization. Framing the work broadly as 'activist art' may encourage more readers to participate, especially if they are already identifying as activists, artists, or both. On the other hand, framing the work as 'activist' will exclude those for whom art is something separate from political action, everyday life, and the social arena. Some folks disregard the terms 'activist' or 'spiritual' out of hand, especially as they relate to art.

Complicated by the very nature of art and history, the definitions of terms, and the perspectives of those writing the histories, any discussion of the history of activist art is fraught with limitations. Can one argue that all overtly political art is activist in nature? Some believe that all art is political on some level, even if it is not conscious. Others believe that politics are involved with everything already, so art does not need to be openly political to serve a political function.

There are many different types of 'activist' art. Many artists make objects that are explicitly or implicitly political, with messages that are conveyed through text, image, or the material object itself. Other artists use their bodies to create performances, happenings, and other live events with a focus on political turmoil, social injustice, or other major themes.

Activist art became more popular and common as the civil rights, feminist, and anti-war movements developed in the later twentieth century. Following precedents from Dada,

Futurism, and other avant-garde waves of the early twentieth century, politically charged objects and performances were produced in order to shock, to compel thought and/or actions, and to reveal more about individuals and their cultural positions.

Understanding Garneau's earlier work in theater and how it transformed into the hybrid performance art of UPRISING is deeply related to her commitment to activism, which dates back to her youth. Having a political awareness of questions related to gender, identity, and race at a young age encouraged Garneau to become a member of activist groups associated with feminism, queer rights, and issues related to people of color. Her involvement in groups like WAC, which combined political activism with protest actions filled with musicians, artists, and thinkers, helped link art and activism openly for Garneau, even as it would take a few years to seep into her professional practice.

Feminism and activism are linked directly in the well-known work of the Guerrilla Girls. The Guerrilla Girls are a collective that began working in the 1980s. In their interventions using billboards or posters, and at protests, performances, and speaking engagements, these anonymous women call attention to politics within the arts and art institutions in addition to politics in society at large. Often, the Guerrilla Girls will use statistics about representation of women or artists of color in art institutions, or about economic injustices for women in the arts. Their work provides excellent context for understanding some of the activist precedents that inform Garneau's work.

Language is a key component of their work, and speaking engagements in educational venues have been part of their approach to stimulating change. One such example is the Guerrilla Girls' 'Guide to Behaving Badly, which you have to do most of the time in the world as we know it' (2011), presented at the College Art Association annual conference as part of a panel about feminism. This work features a list of suggestions for how to be an active feminist, many of which resonate with Garneau's UPRISING project and revolutionary strategies. Among the Guerrilla Girls' imperatives are 'Be Crazy,' 'Be Anonymous,' and 'Be an Outsider. And Act like an Outsider Even on the Inside.' Garneau's work on the streets and in public spaces, her work inside of others' events, and her lack of reliance on major institutional interventions all speak to the spirit of the Guerrilla Girls' directives on making a noticeable impact. Another prompt from the 'Guide to Behaving Badly' is 'Just Do One Thing. Then Do Another' (Guerrilla Girls 2011). This instruction corresponds with Garneau's approach to creating the five-year UPRISING project, and echoes her Revolutionary Practice #37 (Make the Road by Walking) and #56 (Attempt Impossible Tasks).

The Guerrilla Girls practice strategies that combine the creation of an object (whether a poster or billboard) with the creation of performative speaking engagements/protests, while Garneau's work is often only tangible after an UPRISING through photographic evidence. For Garneau, the influence of the Guerrilla Girls came from familiarity with their works individually, but also through the anonymous collective's effect on the protest actions of WAC. WAC took strategic and practical notes from the activism of the Guerrilla Girls in the 1980s, and as WAC branches opened around the country, different locations led to variances in the type of cultural interventions WAC led around the country. Garneau observed WAC's impact in a 2011 discussion with Daniel Tucker: 'WAC Chicago met weekly at Randolph Street Gallery. And I think it's important that it met at Randolph Street Gallery because there were a lot of women artists that were involved in WAC, so there were a relationship between Randolph Street Gallery, which was a kind of alternative or progressive art space, and the Women's Action Coalition so I think that thing of space is really important' (https://never-the-same.org/interviews/nicole-garneau/). The collaboration between artists and activists – and artists who are activists – proved to be an important step in building the foundation of Garneau's aesthetic practices and sensibilities.

Another powerful artist who sometimes makes objects, is a performer, and speaks about social justice is Guillermo Gómez-Peña. Gómez-Peña is a conceptual and performance artist who has been actively producing work since the 1980s as an individual artist and in collaboration with the group, La Pocha Nostra. La Pocha Nostra conducts workshops and trainings internationally for artists and others. Garneau has trained with La Pocha Nostra and Gómez-Peña in their workshop format, and their attention to themes of gender and sexuality is an aspect of Garneau's study of their work. Gómez-Peña's work has connections to Garneau's practice through a shared interest in history, beauty, spirituality, and subject matter that is often difficult. In their book, *Themes of Contemporary Art: Visual Art after 1980*, authors Jean Robertson and Craig McDaniel discuss the work of Guillermo Gómez-Peña:

> In his installations and performances, the artist asserts a proud hybrid identity even as he portrays the uprootings and disjunctures that are products of colonialism. Gómez-Peña's confrontational art reflects a root optimism – a faith that clashes of cultures and ideologies can fuel a creative synthesis that is ultimately beneficial to many. (2005: 119–20)

Garneau works with ceremonial performance and seeks to unite people through a fusion of art, research, awareness and openness.

If an UPRISING involved objects, they were generally readymade, everyday kinds of materials that served as metaphors and could be reused. The muslin rope of names created at UPRISING #31 is a good example of a metaphorical object Garneau used to embody a social justice principle. The ecru strips of fabric were covered with names in black marker and bound together to create a rope of humanity, showing our unity as one human family, showing our greater strength when we are working together.

Often, Garneau offers experiences rather than objects in the service of social justice. UPRISING #21 created the opportunity for many different kinds of people to share an intimate moment of connection. As discussed in Daniel Tucker's essay, the crowd of people was gathered in an event to support prison policy reform. Incarceration in the United States is a booming business, and one that impacts people of color disproportionately and severely. Lawyers, family members of prisoners, philanthropists of social causes, artists, and others were assembled at this function, and Garneau asked the group to stand physically behind one another, with a hand on the shoulder of the person in front, and whisper words of care and support. Rather than drawing attention to the prisons themselves, Garneau focused her attention on the people who had chosen to be there through their own experiences. She wanted to show that people really can 'have each other's back.' She emphasized the creation of community that this event engendered and provided a simple, sincere gesture to offer a reminder of the strength we must rally in dealing with real problems.

In her influential book, *One Place after Another: Site-Specific Art and Locational Identity* (2004), Miwon Kwon offered analyses of public art and included examples of art works and the words of various art critics to illustrate her positions. Kwon spent a good deal of time discussing 'art-in-the-public-interest,' or 'new genre public art,' the category in which Garneau's work might be placed. Kwon described this type of cultural production as being 'distinguished for foregrounding social issues and political activism, and/or for engaging "community" collaborations' (2004: 60). Kwon presented an examination into how power roles can be emphasized, undermined, or reinforced through these community art projects; how certain collaborations contribute to unsettling expectations or bolstering the status quo; and how the push and pull of institutions, artists, and residents can prove to be a balancing act of the problematic and positive, sometimes without a fulfilling result for anyone. Garneau's ability to work with minimal institutional frameworks and responsively according to inspiration from site, community, or history allowed her to avoid some of the common snafus in new genre public art.

The kinds of intimacy and the sensual immediacy of Garneau's work seem ever more significant as people have grown accustomed to having digital or virtual contact without touching or speaking, eliminating the need for physical interaction on even the most basic levels. Spikes in hate crimes also speak to the growing alienation of humans from one another. Replacing screens or fists with outstretched hands offering encouragement and empathy seems like a good start, as there are many who feel downtrodden and unsupported. The temporary stepping outside of one's comfort zone in the space of an UPRISING may not effect lasting change in a participant's life, but it may serve as a powerful moment, recognizable for its difference from a habitual routine, operating on a slightly different level of sensation. That heightened sensory response is indicative of an art experience. As Kwon summarized:

> Thus, it is not a matter of choosing sides – between models of nomadism and sedentariness, between space and place, between digital interface and the handshake. Rather, we need to be able to think the range of the seeming contradictions and our contradictory desires for them together; to understand, in other words, seeming oppositions as sustaining relations. (2004: 166)

Kwon's idea of 'sustaining relations' is precisely what I believe UPRISING sought and what it achieved. Through UPRISING, Garneau encourages us look around with critical appreciation and look forward with optimism and belief in our possibilities as humans.

Is Garneau's work successful? If so, how? In gauging participants' responses, it seems the work is indeed successful, as it moves folks from one state of being/feeling/seeing into another new state of being/feeling/seeing. Even if no one felt connected to the Arab Spring (UPRISING #38), there was a connection manifested in that place with everyone together aware of their contact with other humans, strangers in a communal, public space. As the artist Suzanne Lacy described new genre public art: 'what exists in the space between the words public and art is an unknown relationship between artist and audience, a relationship that may *itself* be the artwork' (cited in Kwon 2004: 105, original emphasis).

If one's measurement of success has to do with whether each participant chose to pursue activism or philanthropy, or change any habits, or if success is measured through monetary gains or typical career advancement ideas, then no, it is not successful. If one's measurement of success means having an object or many objects to sell, show, or give away, then it is only partially successful. (This book is perhaps the largest artifact, and even that is mediated by time and money.)

When I think about whether the work is successful, I think about the fact that the issues Garneau raised in UPRISING are all still relevant and important. I also think about the fact that Garneau is using all of the techniques and strategies of both outsider and insider art of the past 30 years, taking into account their shortcomings and critiques. Her themes, her methods, and her understanding of the power of presence are all positioned within and comfortable in contemporary art, art practice, and art education. For example, Robertson and McDaniel identify six themes into which contemporary art can be divided, eliminating a focus on traditional mediums like painting, sculpture, etc. (Robertson and McDaniel 2005). These themes are Time, Place, Identity, the Body, Language, and

Spirituality. UPRISING could be discussed in each one of these categories and combines them all.

The goal of this book initially was to document and reflect upon a project that felt significant during and after its existence. It was also meant to be a book that could be read by anyone, not only art professionals or activists or specialists (or friends of Garneau).

The book has a new relevance after events of the past few years, including and especially the 2016 US presidential elections. Protest, activist, and explicitly feminist movements have strengthened. Art's possibility to provide social critique, to hold a mirror up to culture and document its beauties and injustices, is ever more urgent. The 2017 Whitney Biennial opened recently in Manhattan, and many of the works have overtly political, feminist, and spiritual subjects. Over the past few years, I have been struck by how relevant Garneau's themes continue to be. Her recipe for UPRISING could be a powerful model for meaningful protest, action, and art all over the world.

ENVISION THE WORLD IN WHICH WE WANT TO LIVE
REVOLUTIONARY PRACTICE #11

The late poet and musician Sekou Sundiata's final project was *The 51st (dream) State*. At the 2006 Imagining America Conference, Sundiata called on artists to 'uncover a transcendent vision of society that lifts our visions to the highest possibilities of human conduct. What might such a vision be? What would it take to imagine, to create, and to ritualize such a vision? How can artists and activists and scholars and others take up this challenge?' (2006: n.pag.)

Many of us are so alienated by our current economic, political, and social structures that we cannot even imagine what a loving, compassionate, creative, and revolutionary global culture would feel like. We are paralyzed by the incessant, soul-sucking negativity of our politicians and our media. The book *The Reenchantment of Art* advocates for 'a socially or morally sensitive art' that takes up the challenge 'of trying to construct a new vision and put it into practice. It is not part of our legacy to view ourselves as powerful agents of change; however, we are being confronted with the necessity of transforming our old modes of understanding if we are to survive the predicaments that are our collective fate right now. To create today is to create with responsibility' (Gablik 1992: 8).

Stay grounded in the belief that we are fully capable of building a better, more humane, more just, more loving, more earth-reverent world. We can feed, clothe, and shelter ourselves without destroying the planet and each other. Work to expand your capacity for love, joy, creativity, cooperation, spiritual connection, and culture-making. Imagine it, again and again, over shared meals, construction projects, and arms linked together. Try and create moments in the present that contain intimate glimmers of the possibility of moving forward together.

IN ACTION: UPRISING #11

11 November 2008, 5:00pm | Nelson Algren Fountain, Division/Milwaukee/ Ashland Streets, Chicago
Participants: Mark D'Neal, Cheryl Doyle, Anita Evans, and participants of Free Street Theater, ages 16–22
Photos: Nicole Garneau | Video: Anita Evans

Chicago's Free Street Theatre Youth Conservancy focuses on social justice, using art to build community through ensemble-based practice. As their guest artist, I asked them to imagine the world after some problem is solved, and then write about how it looks, feels, smells, what colors it is, and how people interact within it. From their writing we developed the following performance: half the group swept mud and fallen leaves from the inscription on the Nelson

Algren Fountain, and the other half crouched down close to the sweepers so that they could give a detailed description of their gratitude for the sweeper's humanity and for this humble service to the space. We took our inspiration from Algren's words, inscribed at the fountain's base: 'For the masses that do the city's labor also keep the city's heart' (1998).

Before I arrived at Free Street, Anita Evans faxed me some of their sensual descriptions of the world we desire:

> If we could eliminate the awful mannerisms that exist within people today the world would be light and bring about a lot of graciousness and gratitude. People would thank each other for their lives and their health. Big toothy smiles, gleaming warm eyes, healthy minds with beating healthy hearts. Laughter and handshakes!
>
> Just walking the streets in hot pink heels, chanting 'we got each other if no one else does.'
>
> Your warmth my warmth mingling to create the sound of success. My skin is no cause for cringing but an embrace of individuality and a lasting faith that for decades had been silenced through annoying men talking through me but I'm OK now.
>
> What happens when I can't picture the picture...? I can lie and say the grass is greener the sky is bluer there is no more trash in our streets everything everyone is nice and perfect but it's not. I can't picture anything because these problems won't go away they're implanted into our minds well into my mind anyway and they will never leave not now anyway so I can't picture it until I see it.
>
> It smells like water. You know. The way it smells after it rains. Just lovely.

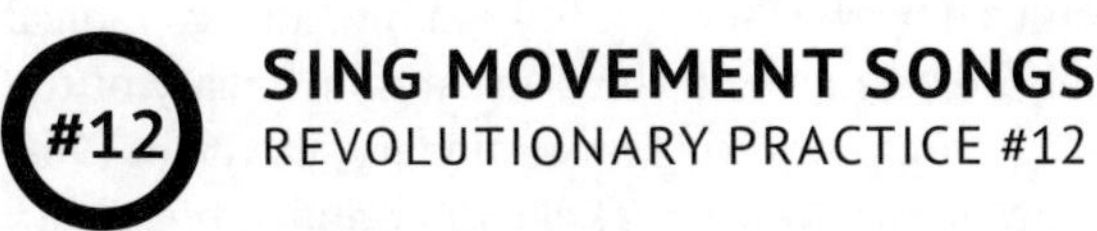

SING MOVEMENT SONGS
REVOLUTIONARY PRACTICE #12

All revolutionary movements have songs. There is a rich tradition of social justice music in the United States. Pete Seeger said, 'there's a lot of good music in this world, and if used right it may help save the planet' (in Pareles 2014). But nowadays, many of us are mortified by the idea of singing in public. Somehow we have internalized the notion that the only people who are allowed to sing are the 'real singers.' This is tragic. How can we be so ashamed to raise our voices? I believe we will never be able to make a revolution if we do not sing. Mario Benedetti, the literary voice of the progressive left in Latin America, died in 2009 in his home country of Uruguay and left us this revolutionary poem, 'Por qué cantamos?' ('Why do we sing?'):

> We sing because it rains on the furrow
> and we are militants of Life
> and because we cannot and do not want to
> let songs become ashes.
> We sing because a cry is not enough
> and neither are tears or anger.
> We sing because we believe in people
> and because we will overcome defeat. (1983: n.pag.)

If you are lucky enough to be in a place where a song leader is working to inspire a group to make music together, breathe and give the song everything you have in you. You will not regret it. Alternatively, you may find a room filled with people who strongly identify as left activists, but asking them to sing even a little bit might seem like a totally radical act in the face of their reluctance. Witness the beauty of voices singing from a place of sincerity, not performance. Push through resistance, share a moment of relief when it is over, and see how much that feels like world-building.

IN ACTION: UPRISING #12

6 December 2008, 3:00pm | Jane Addams Hull House Dining Room, Chicago
Participants: AJ Sacco, Rose Camastro-Pritchett, Bonnie Garneau, Nicole Garneau, Cate Plys, Carly Garzotto, Chelsea Culp, Sonya Dekhtyar
Photos: Tara Malik

In the first year of UPRISING, I was energized by the fact that folks in my Chicago radical artist community were initiating critical projects around the 40-year anniversary of the Democratic National Convention in Chicago, and worldwide revolutionary activity of 1968, particularly Daniel Tucker and AREA (Chicago Art, Research, Education, and Activism). In December 2008, they published their '68/08' issue of *AREA* magazine, which included an article I wrote about UPRISING. In the Introduction, Rebecca Zorach writes:

When people who weren't there, and some who were, think of Chicago in 1968, they generally think of one thing: dramatic televised scenes of protest and police riot outside the Democratic National Convention. But Chicago in 1968 was much more (and perhaps in some ways less) than what could be seen on TV. For many, it meant facing discrimination, coming together in struggle, as in the important but nearly-forgotten first Rainbow Coalition that brought together the Black Panthers, the (white) Young Patriots, and the (Puerto Rican) Young Lords. It also meant working creatively to imagine alternatives. Younger activists now are in a position to sift through the legacy: what can we discard, what can we retain? What are the moments of relevance for us today; what are its moments of stunning irrelevance? What is the unfinished business of '68? (2008: n.pag.)

To celebrate the '68/08' issue release, folks gathered at the Jane Addams Hull House Museum for a range of fabulous presentations and speakers. As a closing, we worked on the revolutionary tool of singing. UPRISING #12 got an intergenerational group of about 80 people on their feet, in a circle, holding hands, singing, and listening to each other's voices. We mapped our circle by asking folks who were alive in 1968 to stand in the south end of the circle, and everyone else in the north. Each person was invited to conduct an experiment in courage by stepping forward and singing a little bit of any song they knew by heart. Sometimes others joined in. Folks who had been on the streets in 1968 reminded the crowd of old protest songs; children and young ones sang everything from Public Enemy to camping songs.

Nicole,

Thanks so much for your contribution to [*AREA*'s '68/08' issue] and the [launch] event. I had no idea what you were going to do but I think it was a great way to wrap up the event and gave people a real altered sense of how they related to the event. They cannot deny now that they were participants. And the nature of that participation is complicated and unique and something they were likely not expecting. It was a really great performance!
– Daniel Tucker (Participant, UPRISING #12)

MAKE SPACE FOR CHILDREN
REVOLUTIONARY PRACTICE #13

In his *Truthout* op-ed 'The violence of organized forgetting,' cultural critic Henry Giroux calls out the ways in which children and young people are systematically excluded from the making of the world. He writes,

> What is particularly new is the way in which young people have been increasingly denied a significant place in an already weakened social contract and the degree to which they are absent from how many countries now define the future. Youth are no longer the place where society reveals its dreams. Instead, youth are becoming the site of society's nightmares. Within neoliberal narratives, youth are mostly defined as a consumer market, a drain on the economy, or stand for trouble. (Giroux 2013: n.pag.)

The world we are building must include space for children and the adults who care for them. How can we design actions in which children can truly participate, not just appear as cute appendages? How do their voices and desires impact the work? Whenever possible, involve youth in the work. Create collaborations with them. Encourage their agency. Allow them to discern what they care about and want to express. Be inspired and changed by their ideas. Help them acquire the habit of thinking of public spaces as *their* spaces.

IN ACTION: UPRISING #13
3 January 2009, 10:00am | Live webcast performance: 24hours24artists.com
Produced by Jump-Start Theater Company, San Antonio, TX
Participants: Nicole Garneau and her niblings Renée and Natalie Garneau
Photos: Ruth Robbins

On the first Saturday of every year, Jump-Start Performance Co. in San Antonio, Texas, celebrates with a performance party. For their 24th anniversary, they went global with *24 Hours 24 Artists*, a marathon webcast featuring performers from all over the world. Representing Chicago, UPRISING #13 featured live artmaking by my niblings Renée and Natalie Garneau (aged 8 and 6), who faced the camera while painting on sheets of clear Plexiglas, an image from the vault of childhood memories of the TV show *The Electric Company*. I stayed off-screen, providing audio for the performance by reading favorite selections from *New Genre Public Art*: 'within a listener-centered paradigm, the old specializations of artist and audience, creative and uncreative, professional and unprofessional – distinctions between who is and who is not an artist – begin to blur' (Conwill Màjozo 1996: 88).

Ruth, Renée, Natalie, and I made the performance in the basement of my parents' house in the Chicago suburbs, while the rest of the family was upstairs watching it streaming live on the computer.

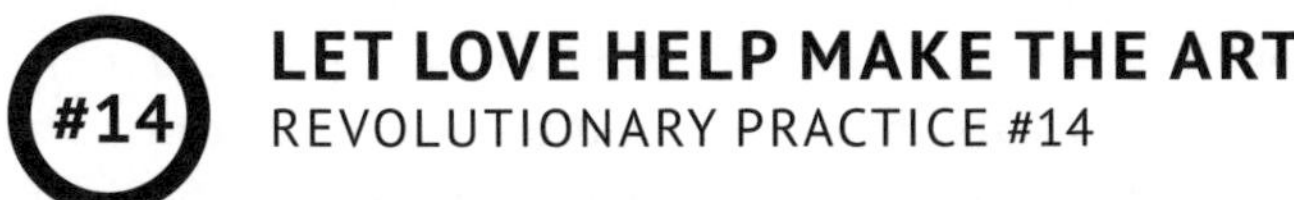

LET LOVE HELP MAKE THE ART
REVOLUTIONARY PRACTICE #14

If you need a way to feel hope for humanity, invent a way to allow folks to work together on something positive, and then repeat it over and over, until it really sinks in.

In 2008, Derrik Jensen was named one of Utne Reader's '50 visionaries who are changing your world,' after the publication of *Endgame Volume 1: The Problem of Civilization*. Permaculture expert/activist Nance Klehm felt so strongly about the work that she handed me a badly xeroxed copy of Jensen's twenty Premises. He makes an activist call to love:

> **Premise Fourteen:** From birth on – and probably from conception, but I'm not sure how I'd make the case – we are individually and collectively enculturated to hate life, hate the natural world, hate the wild, hate wild animals, hate women, hate children, hate our bodies, hate and fear our emotions, hate ourselves. If we did not hate the world, we could not allow it to be destroyed before our eyes. If we did not hate ourselves, we could not allow our homes – and our bodies – to be poisoned.
>
> **Premise Fifteen:** Love does not imply pacifism. (Jensen 2006: n.pag.)

'*Love does not imply pacifism.*' We can clearly see that when people are legitimately suffering, whipping up xenophobic fear is an effective political strategy for electing a sociopathic fascist. As Charles Eisenstein (2016) writes, 'hate and blame are convenient ways of making meaning out of a bewildering situation.' But if our goal is a more just, humane, and compassionate global culture, then we must infuse our actions with love and beauty that is irresistibly infectious. Turn the care and support you receive from others into fuel for your creation. Plug into whatever source of divine love you can access, and then burn brightly. Feed your work with self-respect and self-love.

Advocate for social and racial justice in a manner that increases *our own capacity* for love. Remember Che Guevara's famous declaration: 'At the risk of seeming ridiculous, let me say that the true revolutionary is guided by a great feeling of love. It is impossible to think of a genuine revolutionary lacking this quality' (March 2005: 74). In the face of the daily, lived reality of oppression, truly loving each other and ourselves takes real courage. Movements for social and racial justice have love at their core: we defend the lives we know are precious, even when we see those lives devalued all around us. Stay grounded in the belief that we all deserve better. Acknowledge the deep wounds that are inflicted on us by violence and injustice. Build the revolutionary discipline of offering artworks that are gifts of love to the world. We can all share a revolution that is filled with feelings of great love (March 2005).

IN ACTION: UPRISING #14

14 February 2009, 2:00pm | Berkeley, CA
Participants: Julie Caffey, Morrison Lyman, Jen Zoom, Lisa Ruth Elliot, Gabriel McCabe McNidder, and Nicole Garneau
Photos: Ruth Robbins | Video: Wafaa Yasin

UPRISING #14 referenced the 40-year anniversary of the self-immolation of Jan Palach and Jan Zajíc, two Czech students who burned themselves to death in January and February 1969 in Prague to protest the Soviet invasion of Czechoslovakia. I was curious about whether any of us had ever had the feeling that there was something we would die for.

UPRISING #14 was featured at She Works Flexible, Lynne McCabe's critical artistic exploration which in 2009 was centered in Berkeley, California (now it is a gallery and art space in Houston, Texas). She Works Flexible housed a variety of artistic endeavors from child rearing to occasional performances to project research and development – all in a domestic sphere. For the performance, we crawled on hands and knees up Martin Luther King Blvd to Lynne McCabe's front yard while the audience watched from the porch. One by one, we told stories about what we might be willing to die for. After each person's story, I kissed them over their hearts, staining their white shirts with beet juice from my mouth, and then dribbled beet juice into their cupped hands. Performers held the beet juice in their hands as long as they could. The last person to be stained with beet juice was Lynne's 5-year-old child. The mood at the end of the performance was somber, and we welcomed the warmth of the fireplace inside.

STOP CARING ABOUT WHETHER OR NOT IT IS CORNY

REVOLUTIONARY PRACTICE #15

In *The Reenchantment of Art*, artist Amy Olds asserts that contemporary artists have internalized a culture steeped in cynicism, snark, and bombastic rhetoric:

> When we see cynicism even in our art, it reinforces our belief in a negative, cynical reality. We've come to appreciate and expect cynicism in art as an intellectual game about the definition of reality. Artists as well as art critics teach us that cynicism is interesting because it relates to life. Hope and optimism are generally hated, made fun of, considered hokey, childish, and sometimes fanatic, simply because they are not concepts that people of intellectual stature believe in. But the truth is that people actually do want to believe in a positive worldview [...] We've seen that art has the power to form negative visions of the world through magnifying the undercurrents of cynicism, so it must be possible to create a positive vision of the world through focusing the aspirations of hope. (Gablik 1992: 28)

Under these conditions, a project that is explicitly about hope and positive visions might sound ridiculously naïve and even corny. Even if we are motivated by genuine outrage at the injustice and violence we see and experience in the world, some of us battle with the idea that our work should be harder-edged and more obviously legible as protest. We must decide that our political, social, and ecological situation is too urgent to worry about our insecurities and fears. We must tell others and ourselves: 'It does not matter if it is corny. We're at war. People are dying.' Discover the people who are ready to be galvanized to activate a better world. Be inspired by their bravery and the ways in which they take world-building ideas and make them fiercely their own.

IN ACTION: UPRISING #15

22 March 2009, 1:00pm | State of the Nation Festival, New Orleans, LA
Participants: Maunglwin, Rocio, Chao, Isa, Marcus, Landry, Heidi, Ashley Sparks, Claudia Garofalo, Berk, Kathie DeNobriga, Artemis, Joanna Russo, Lizzy, Nicole Garneau, and Stanford Talisman choir
Photos: Carlton Turner | Video: Nick Slie and Bruce France

UPRISING #15 was a culminating performance of the 5th State of the Nation, a festival bringing together artists from across the United States who are committed to addressing social, political, and economic issues facing the Gulf South and the country at large. Performance material for UPRISING #15 was generously developed by participants in a workshop I taught earlier in the week called 'Tipping Point of Courage: Outdoor, Public Performance.'

The site of the UPRISING was the front steps of the Colton School in New Orleans, a building that was a school until the day before Hurricane Katrina, but was then mostly empty and being used as artists' studios. The chalk we used in the performance was gathered from classrooms where the homework assignments written on the chalkboard were dated 26 August 2005.

The performance itself incorporated 40 volunteers who practiced two essential skills needed for tipping over into a more just and humane world: Letting Go, and Making More. Performers circled an audience seated on the school's front steps, leaving the building and entering in an inside/outside circle. As performers emerged from the building, they named something they would be Letting Go, and as they entered the building, they named what they wanted to Make More. Audience members seated on the front steps of the school formed a human amplification system: they passed each word on to someone sitting next to them until the whole space was filled with the repeated intentions of the performers. Stanford University's eighteen-member Talisman Choir just happened to be touring and performing in New Orleans that week, and on the morning of UPRISING #15, they led the gathered crowd of performers and audience in a celebratory rendition of the song 'Glory, Glory, Hallelujah (Lay my Burden Down).'

> The most moving part of an UPRISING for me was that it put the notion of revolution in a person-to-person experience. Sometimes, we mistake the revolutionary act for something grandiose, forgetting that the simple act of listening to someone, sharing a dream or singing out loud for a brief minute can be so transformative. I remember walking in and out of those doors at the Colton school in New Orleans, following people with a camera and thinking that this was one of the most simple, yet profound things I did the entire State of the Nation Festival that year. It works because we are invited into an intentional act that each participant gets to interpret. Intention with a splash of autonomy is a potent cocktail.
> **– Nick Slie (Festival Producer/Videographer, UPRISING #15)**

> I remember holding hands with a stranger, walking in a circle.
> **– Ashley Sparks (Participant, UPRISING #15)**

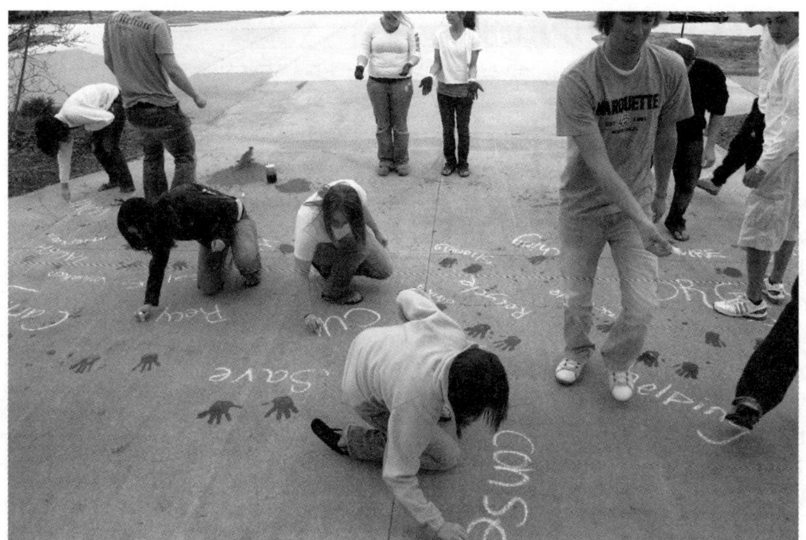
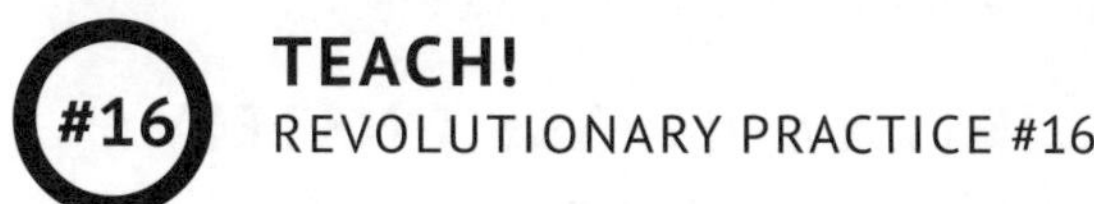

Figure 11: University of Wisconsin-Oshkosh students write one thing they are already doing to make the world a better place in UPRISING #16. Photo by Nicole Garneau.

#16 TEACH!
REVOLUTIONARY PRACTICE #16

In participatory art projects, the artist Ruth Robbins had a useful shorthand for a practice of sharing information with people so that they would know what is going on and want to be part of it: she reminded herself and others to 'help them care.' In making activist street performance we necessarily and frequently return to the question, 'How much explanation do the people need in order to care?' The point of revolutionary teaching should be to ignite a heart-centered connection to material that might otherwise feel abstract. Working with revolutionary histories makes that education explicit and action-based. Performances, ceremonies, songs, and tasks are pedagogical tools. Volunteers, audience members, and participants are genuinely curious: they want to understand what is going on. In turn they teach us by sharing their visions of humanity and liberation. We are all trying to make sense of ourselves as agents of change in a bewildering world. We are all invited to learn and grow. Jump into the continuous cycle of teaching, learning, and practicing the skills we need to make a revolution.

IN ACTION: UPRISING #16

28 April 2009, 7:00pm | University of Wisconsin-Oshkosh
Participants: 42 students in James Chaudoir's Music and War Course
Photos: Julia Barnard and Nicole Garneau | Video: Karl Buelow

I met James Chaudoir while we were both artists-in-residence at Ragdale in December 2008. I was editing UPRISING video documentation, and he was composing music. After we each shared what we had been working on, he invited me to make an UPRISING with the students in his Music and War course at University of Wisconsin-Oshkosh. The class was studying music of the 1960s, so I brought in 'Eve of Destruction,' made popular in a recording by Barry McGuire but written by P. F. Sloan (1965). I asked students to write short paragraphs about what they are currently doing to make the world a better place and then boil this down to one word. For our outdoor performance, volunteer performers poured beet juice into the gloved hands of a classmate. The soaked gloves were used to make handprints on the pavement, next to which students wrote their one-word contributions in chalk. Meanwhile, other students accompanied the action singing the chorus to the song: 'but you tell me, over and over and over again my friend, ah you don't believe we're on the eve of destruction' (Sloan and McGuire 1965).

ASK QUESTIONS. LISTEN COMPASSIONATELY
REVOLUTIONARY PRACTICE #17

Engaging in compassionate and curious conversations with strangers is a revolutionary skill, as is respecting the boundaries of people who do not want to engage. It is really important, especially at events where there is a lot of information being distributed, to have moments (however contrived or engineered they might seem) when the people have the opportunity to use *their* voices and speak from their own expertise. How can everyone in the space be invited to share something simply from their hearts?

IN ACTION: UPRISING #17

9 May 2009, 7:00pm | Open Source Gallery, Brooklyn, NY
Participants: karen g. williams, Nicole Garneau, and attendees of Gallery Opening
Photos & Video: Rebecca Gee

UPRISING #17 explored the revolutionary practice of local community building. 'Are we not famous men?' was the question Gary Baldwin asked in the photographic portraits of people in his South Slope neighborhood: ordinary people who are, of course, extraordinary. Gary and his partner Monika Wührer invited UPRISING to their Saturday potluck dinner in the gallery, with food provided by the artist and the individuals in the photos. karen g. williams and I probed the event by asking guests to tell us stories about their community. We then carved phrases from these stories onto slices of apple, dipped them in beet juice, and served them back to the people.

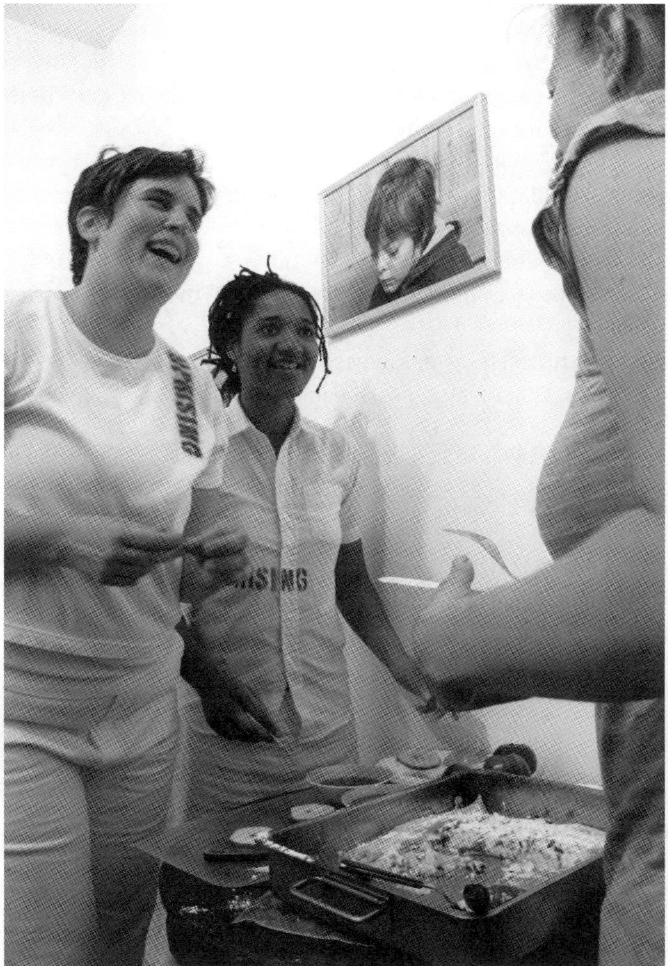

Figure 12: Nicole Garneau and karen g. williams in UPRISING #17. Photo by Rebecca Gee.

Interjection: All the Questions

During an UPRISING we often asked the people questions, really listened to their answers, and turned their responses into the content of the work:

> Tell a story about a time when you felt the high of doing something that made the world better. (#1)
>
> What is your radical truth? (#2)
>
> What cause are you fighting for today to make the world a better place? (#5)
>
> What makes this event revolutionary? (#6)
>
> What is a book that revolutionized your ideas of sex and/or gender? (#7, #34)
>
> May I kiss you? (#7)
>
> What is your vision for a better world? (#8)
>
> What is your vision of liberation? (#9)
>
> Who are your departed revolutionary heroines? (#10)
>
> What do you want to whisper in the ear of your friend to encourage them while they sweep the street? (#11)
>
> What is a little bit of a song you know and could sing right now? (#12)
>
> What would you be willing to die for? (#14)
>
> What are you giving up to make the world a better place? What are you adding to make the world better? (#15)
>
> What is one thing you are already doing to make the world a better place? (#16)
>
> What is your favorite thing about this community? (#17)
>
> What do you need in order to continue making art? (#18)
>
> Check your labels: Where were your clothes made? (#18, #39, #52, #54, #56, #57)

What is one memory you have from childhood that took place in a public park? (#19)

What is your unique gift to the world? (#20, #43, #45)

What words of encouragement can you give to the person in front of you to support them in the struggle? (#22, #29, #33)

Understanding that the Winter Solstice is the longest night of the year, what part of your own shadow side do you wish to bring to light? (#24)

Would you sing me your favorite Russian song? (#25)

What is your favorite passage in *The Communist Manifesto*? Would you read it aloud into this megaphone? (#26)

What is the radical truth you have never shared with anyone? (#27)

What are the contributions you made to this event? (#28)

What are your visions for Health and Healing Justice? (#30)

What is your first name? (#31)

What is one important thing an adult did/said that had a positive impact on your childhood? (#32)

What are you leaving behind in 2010? (#36)

How do you want to thank local abortion providers? (#37)

What does the Arab Spring mean to you? (#38)

Who are your revolutionary heroes? (#44)

Would you like a cup of hot tea? (#49)

Was there ever a moment when you truly thought the world might change for the better? (#50)

What prayers/wishes are you sending with this feather on the wind? (#51)

What do Alexandra Kollontai's theories about love and relationships mean to you? (#53)

Tell me a story about economic crisis. (#55)

Would you like to sit in silence for an hour in this chapel? (#58)

Instead of torture and murder, what would you like to see taught at the School of the Americas? (#59)

Where are you right now in your life with social/racial justice? How can we as a community support you? (#60)

RESPECT THE EARTH AND THE BEETS THAT GROW IN HER
REVOLUTIONARY PRACTICE #18

World-building must include planet tending. A revolutionary art practice honors the earth, the air, the fire, and the water(s). In the book *Eco Amazons: 20 Women Who Are Transforming the World*, the artist Agnes Denes explains:

> Making art for me is synonymous with assuming responsibility for my species and the planet we live on. Art is the essence and a reflection of life. It sees the past and the present and shapes the future. My role as an artist is to create art that questions the status quo, helps the environment, and offers coming generations a meaningful legacy. (Keehn 2011: 58)

Whenever possible, choose artmaking materials that do not damage precious natural resources. The use of beets and beet juice is only one example of a gorgeous, affordable, sensual, evocative, renewable art material. Beets come from the earth, they are incredibly nutritious, and they do not poison the soil, water, or air. Rain will eventually rinse them off of sidewalks and streets. Choose revolutionary supplies from places of intellectual curiosity, spiritual connection, symbolism, and deep intuition. When you drench volunteer performers in vegetable juice, make sure you give them laundry advice.

IN ACTION: UPRISING #18
25 June 2009, 7:00pm | 9th and Michigan Avenues, Chicago
Participants: Students in Jeff Abell's Art as Practice course at Columbia College Chicago, Linda Torres, Jeff Abell, and Nicole Garneau
Photos: Ruth Robbins | Video: Steve Mancione

Jeff Abell invited me to be a guest in his Art as Practice course, so naturally I took the opportunity to put folks to work making an UPRISING. Since a great deal of revolutionary activity has stemmed from the garment industry worldwide, the first thing we did was to check all of our labels and make a list of the countries where our clothes were made. Then we did some personal exploration: we wrote about what we all need in order to continue to make art, and we recorded these ideas on white handkerchiefs. At the corner of 9th and Michigan, I lay down on the ground and Linda stood over me, pouring multiple servings of beet juice in my mouth while reciting the list of places where our shirts, pants, and shoes were fabricated. Jeff Abell used the handkerchiefs to swab my face after every splattered dose.

I had invited Nicole to visit my class on professional artistic practices, to talk about her work. Since by that time she was embroiled in the UPRISING series, she decided the best way to share what her process was about would be to actually make a work together. We set out for the corner of Michigan and 9th St. (about a block from my classroom), to enact the performance.

It was a tricky situation: balancing roles as instructor and performance participant. I was trying to monitor what was happening with my students, and also trying to give myself as completely as possible to facilitate my guest speaker (a former student). I know there were other people on Michigan Avenue that evening, some of whom seemed taken aback by what was happening. (We were standing right outside of a bank as I recall, and I was grateful that it was after the branch had closed for the day; surely the bank would have found some way to interpret what was happening on the street as a critique of their practices.) The beet juice, with its echoes of blood, splattering on Nicole's face, drew a surprisingly emotional response from me. I was dressed all in white, and by the end of the evening was splattered with beet juice; I looked like someone who had been a close witness to a violent crime, and sort of felt that way, too.
– Jeff Abell (Participant, UPRISING #18)

I remember we all helped each other look at our clothing tags to find out where they were from. I remember making a list and then writing on the white handkerchief where my pants were created, most likely in a sweatshop. We tied them together and headed for our location on foot!

I remember being an intimate part of that performance. When you asked for a volunteer I jumped at the chance and was invited to pour the beet juice into your mouth. You were lying on the ground and you were chanting something. I stood over you and as you chanted I gently poured the deep red juice onto your face and mouth. I remember pouring as slowly as I possibly could… mainly because I was pouring from above you. I remember feeling exhilarated. I remember feeling empowered by the idea that brought you to perform about the deeper issues revolving the garment industry.

I felt proud to be a part of something bigger than myself, an idea
that meant something, I was proud to be an activist in that moment.
Thank you for letting me explore that part of myself within your
performance and through your ideas.
– Linda Torres (Participant, UPRISING #18)

PRODUCE BEAUTIFUL IMAGES
REVOLUTIONARY PRACTICE #19

If you are lucky enough to be in a relationship with someone who is an excellent
photographer and you can convince them that they should document Revolutionary
Practices beautifully and for free, then good for you. Otherwise, find photographers who
are also change-makers. The most challenging documentation task is trying to capture
moments of interaction between a performer and a participant. It is the heart of the work,
and it is also the least represented.

In spite of the proliferation of easy video technology and our inundation with video
documentation of all kinds, I maintain that if we are trying to achieve truly honest
and genuine connections between folks, we cannot shove a camera in their faces to
capture it. The documentation of anything live is challenging, but when the art is
the precise moments that cannot be witnessed in a photograph, then other strategies
for recording become even more critical. Figure out how to ask participants for their
feedback and learn about their experiences as a critical research strategy. Understand
something about the impact of this work on the people who are making it. Share the
stories and feelings they express in words, and allow these words to create pictures in
the imagination.

IN ACTION: UPRISING #19
10 July 2009, 1:00pm | Washington Park Lagoon, Chicago
Participants: Rebecca Zorach and eight University of Chicago students
Photos: Ruth Robbins | Video: Nicole Garneau

UPRISING #19 merged the goals of Rebecca Zorach's Art in Unexpected Places course at
University of Chicago with the UPRISING project. In preparation for my visit to their class,
Rebecca forwarded to me student proposals for public art works, and the UPRISING was
an attempt to mash-up a collaboration. In class, I asked them about their relationships
to nearby Washington Park, which was the proposed site for Chicago's unsuccessful bid

to host the 2016 Olympics. Hosting the Olympics in Washington Park was a popular idea with many Chicagoans, but was also criticized as an attempt to expel the African American population of park users (Joravsky 2007).

The most surprising part of this UPRISING was learning that in spite of the fact that the 372-acre Washington Park was only a ten-minute walk from their current classroom, none of these University of Chicago students had ever been there. They explained that the University actively discouraged them from going to the park. They reported various other race and class-based barriers that prevented them from thinking of the park as a safe or welcoming place for them. As we walked the path of the butterfly sanctuary on this sunny afternoon, they joked about getting mugged. These preconceived notions made Washington Park an even more politically meaningful location for the UPRISING.

We developed a multilayered game structure and performed an ongoing feminist gender analysis of our process and its results. We marked flat, round cookies with childhood memories of parks, worked our bodies in a game of chase, and finished with students and professor floating their memory-cookies out across the surface of the Washington Park lagoon. In the same way that we honor our ancestors by building altars to them that are lovely to behold, I believe we honor the earth by creating beauty with our gestures. I wanted to see all of those white-shirted performers lying on the pier in the midday sun. I loved the round cookies and their plain surfaces now embossed with words evoking childhood memories. I enjoyed the grace that was required to gently nudge those offerings out away from fingertips dipped in the water.

CREATE OUR OWN MEANINGFUL CEREMONIES (AND THEN GET CALLED OUT FOR CULTURAL APPROPRIATION)
REVOLUTIONARY PRACTICE #20

For the most part, audiences passively watch performances. Ceremonies are things we all make together and they *enact* something on us and on the world. One thing we can do is allow seasonal changes and moments in time to serve as metaphors and occasions for reflection. Doing that does not require us to sign up for any religion or dogma. Let us invite that thing we call Divinity, that goes by many other names, into the spaces of struggle, and create our own rituals to knit together our communities and support our social movements.

Many revolutionaries talk about the importance of sacred space. As art critic, curator, and historian Nicolas Bourriaud asserts in *Relational Aesthetics*, 'Sacredness is making a comeback, here, there, and everywhere' (2002: 60). There are activists, labor organizers, radical researchers, genderqueers, prison abolitionists, relatives of incarcerated people, environmentalists, political witches, and healers who explore the role of spirituality in left politics. We are asking: within progressive movements, dare we try to build a shared vocabulary of words, gestures, and ceremonies that radically acknowledges our shared humanity and our relationship to the earth and the Divine? Could we do this together in openness and patience, even as we acknowledge that religious violence and oppression have destroyed loving communities and colonized our ancestral spiritual practices? Could we come together, acknowledging many diverse teachers and traditions? How much do we all have to know about the origins of our ceremonial practices in order to benefit from the experience? Can we understand that the urgency of rekindling our sacred relationships to the earth and each other means that we need to work swiftly and efficiently in order to create new, loving, compassionate templates in our communities?

People often respond to ceremonies with an enthusiasm akin to accepting a drink of water while they are dying of thirst. Some folks are so starved for sacred places that feel safe and accepting that they often cry and pour out their hearts when the space is opened to them. Participants express gratitude for *letting them take part*.

But there are also those whose defenses and barriers go up at the first mention of anything that could be interpreted as spiritual. This resistance is often a symptom of the spiritual traumas so many people in our community suffer. Many of us were raised in religious traditions that are deeply patriarchal, woman-hating, racist, homophobic, and body/sex phobic. These forms of oppression damage our relationships with the Divine. Many of us grew up being taught that God/Creator/Divinity is not accessible to us because of who we are, or whom we love, or how our bodies are. We have come to suspect that we are not included in the beloved community of blessed beings. We have been shamed. We have also been implicated. Many of us were raised in religions that were actively involved in the violent destruction of indigenous spiritual practices around the world. The founders of many faiths seized goddess wisdom and earth-honoring traditions. At best, they appropriated them into patriarchal religious traditions, and at worst, they tortured and murdered the wisdom-keepers, healers, *curanderos*, medicine people, and witches. That blood and suffering stain the pages of the hymnals we hold in our hands.

It is no wonder that people are suspicious and wary of ceremonies and contemporary spiritual practices. It is no wonder we dismiss them as New Age nonsense. Invite people to participate in a way that allows them to exercise their own agency. Never shame anyone for opting out. Create rituals that cannot be done wrong. Create spaces in which nothing happens without consent. Make a ceremony of collecting three bags of trash from the site where the UPRISING will take place the next day. Enact rituals of gratitude, memorials to dead revolutionaries, personal release, marking of moon cycles and changes of season, and public pledges of commitment to social justice.

Stay present and open to critical analysis when you receive a call from the anti-racist white person who has been appointed to talk to you about cultural appropriation in your ceremonial work. Listen to stories of folks who were turned off or offended. Hold those experiences as valid and real. Be ready to talk about your training and the lineages of your ceremonial work. Be guided by useful texts like the *Healing & Health Justice Collective Organizing Principles* from the 2010 US Social Forum in Detroit:

> We are learning and creating this political framework, about a legacy of healing and liberation, that is meeting a particular moment in history inside our movements. This framework seeks to regenerate traditions that have been lost; to mindfully hold contradictions in our practices; and to be conscious of the conditions in which we are living and working as healers in our communities. (Page 2010: n.pag.)

Healers are wounded and imperfect people who can cause harm to others, even when their intentions are good. Resist the urge to think that being a healer makes you or anyone else immune to the political implications and context of your work. Appreciate communities where all of us are invited to hear critique without running away or being banished, where we can learn and grow together with love.

IN ACTION: UPRISING #20

15 August 2009, 9:00pm | Alternate ROOTS meeting, Arden, NC
Participants: Tracy Broyles, Kathy Randels, Sage Crump, Moose Jackson, Marcia Jones, Kathie deNobriga, Eleanor Brownfield, Dan Brawley, Carlton Turner, Nicole Garneau, and 100 artist/activists of Alternate ROOTS
Photos: Kiah Green

As a Chicagoan, I did not understand why so many of my southern friends were encouraging me to come to the annual meeting of Alternate ROOTS, a multidisciplinary organization of artists dedicated to social and racial justice, most of whom center their work in the United States South. I went in 2009, and was blown away by the sheer power, dedication, and diversity of the cultural workers who gathered at that retreat center outside of Asheville to learn from each other and lift each other up. This community of people is working on some of the most urgent political projects in the United States, and doing it with song and style.

Even though it was my first ROOTS Week, I was assigned the task of creating the final evening of performance and closing ceremony. That ceremony became UPRISING #20. The theme of 2009's meeting was Rebirth of a Nation, and that was what the UPRISING attempted to portray through a large lakeside ceremony in which we declared our individual contributions to a world being reborn.

My call for volunteers was specifically a call for those who self-identified as 'ceremonialists,' whatever that meant for them. The people who came forward to help hold space for community transformation at ROOTS were Tracy Broyles, Kathy Randels, Sage Crump, Moose Jackson, Marcia Jones, Kathie deNobriga, and Eleanor Brownfield. After the final night of performances and presentations at ROOTS Week, we asked folks to bring two stones, and Dan Brawley led them on stilts them to a lakeside outdoor chapel, where Ana was already tending the fire. We called in ancestors and formed inner and outer circles with one of the stones. We invited people as they wished to step into the inner circle and name their gifts to the world. Our final gesture was launching our second stones into the lake. The Rising Appalachia ensemble emerged as a flaming bird from the water, fireworks appeared in the sky, and we sang and danced around the fire for hours.

> I remember a fire and silence that lasted a long time.
> **– Ashley Sparks (Participant, UPRISING #20)**

DO NOT ADD MORE EVENTS TO THE CALENDAR
REVOLUTIONARY PRACTICE #21

Consider whether what your community needs is a new 'event' for which performers *and* audience will have to be recruited. Is there a way to bring the work to places where people are already gathering? This is an explicit strategy for staying connected with social movements, and it is a way to introduce other kinds of creative elements into programs and demonstrations. At events where individuals have been listening politely to designated expert speakers for a while, actions that require personal interaction can release the pressure valve in a gentle and intentional way. Keep track of activities around your community and either call ahead, or show up unannounced. Consider issues of privilege when deciding where you and your body might be automatically welcomed, and into which spaces you should do serious preparation, build social capital, and check in deeply with the gatekeepers before entering. Examine the power dynamics implicit in just showing up. Design actions that support what the event is trying to accomplish.

IN ACTION: UPRISING #21

15 September 2009, 9:00pm | Tamms Year Ten/Party on the Right Side of History, Chicago
Participants: 100+ loved ones of prisoners, and prison reform activists
Photos: Wayne Cable | Video: Gretchen Haase

In January 2013, Illinois' Tamms Supermax prison finally closed its doors after fifteen years of operation (Reynolds 2013). The Tamms Year Ten (TY10) campaign was dedicated to closing the prison, where every prisoner was held in permanent solitary confinement indefinitely. Four years before Tamms Supermax closed, TY10 founder Laurie Jo Reynolds called me because she heard that an UPRISING could mean 100 strangers in a room doing something beautiful together. The event was a fundraiser and award ceremony for ongoing work to reform and/or close the prison. Politicians, lawyers, and activists received plaques and accolades for their contributions to the campaign. Laurie also made a point to acknowledge that every person in attendance was 'Not a Bystander.' She hoped that the UPRISING could feel like an award or a gift to the ex-prisoners, families, artists, and other concerned citizens who had joined the movement to end long-term isolation at Tamms.

After all of the certificates and speeches, I requested that everyone in the room form single file lines and place their hands gently on the shoulders of the person in front of them. Then I asked each person to lean forward and quietly speak some words of encouragement. We thanked each other for our work for justice. We remembered that behind us is a long lineage of struggle. We took a moment to feel that someone has our back, and we were fortified by their whispers of support. The program for the event featured artwork and writing by Tamms prisoners:

> My name is Richard. I'm from Kansas City, Missouri. I am somebody. I'm somebody with feelings and emotions like you. I'm no harden criminal as most news flashes, newspapers, film portray most-all prisoners. I've much love and joy within my heart and soul [...] Yall are our voices out there. We can only tell yall. I have learned to trust yall now. I see yall are for real. Thank you. (Reynolds 2009: n.pag.)

VIOLATE NORMS OF TIME AND SPACE. PARTICIPATE VIRTUALLY
REVOLUTIONARY PRACTICE #22

Contributions of precious life energy do not always require physical presence. Show up hours before the activists to a site where a demonstration is scheduled for later that day in conjunction with a global day of environmental action. Conduct your own ceremonial preparation of the ground. Note the security vans across the street pulling into formation; know that you are being watched. Since police and security guards are already on high alert, do not invite other bodies. Put out a call for virtual participation, and collect documentation of actions conducted in solidarity.

IN ACTION: UPRISING #22

24 October 2009, 11:00am | Dvorak Park, across from Fisk Energy Processing Plant, Chicago

Participants: Nicole Garneau with virtual collaboration from: Anita, Anne, Anne Elizabeth Moore, Julie Ann, Beth, Kevin Valentine, Nora Dunlop, Jeff, Peg, Ruth Robbins, Sarah Jackson, Therese, and Zac Whittenburg

Photos & Video: Nicole Garneau

UPRISING #22 was performed on the international day of climate action before world leaders gathered in Copenhagen for climate talks. The focus was on the number 350 – as in parts per million, the level scientists have identified as the safe upper limit for CO_2 in our atmosphere according to the environmental advocacy group 350.org (2009). At 1:00pm in Chicago there was a rally in Dvorak Park, across from the Fisk coal plant in Pilsen. I was not there. Instead, that morning I went down to the site and did my best to lay a beautiful ground for the demonstration to come. I purposely did not invite anyone to join me in the park because I knew security forces were amassing for the rally later that day. I wrote an invitation for folks to participate by sitting at an altar or nice sunny window to visualize peaceful and just solutions to the climate crisis. I suggested shaking a feather, folding paper into a fan, flying a flag, writing a poem, drawing a picture, taking deep breaths, or anything else that seemed appropriate and supportive. Across the street from the coal plant, I cleaned the space and used rainbow chalk to answer a call by 350.org to create visual representations of the number 350. Thirteen virtual collaborators e-mailed me reports of how they prayed, breathed deeply, envisioned clean air, ate raspberries, talked to children about the effects of climate change on animals, listened to wind chimes, and conducted their own actions of solidarity.

> During your preparation period [for UPRISING #22 at the Fisk Coal Processing Plant], I spoke with my 5-year-old friend Gabriel about the carbon situation. He is quite the naturalist and understood the implications immediately: 'Uh oh, that would be bad for the tapir.' Gabriel would like to add the tapir is a South American animal in the rhino family. All four species of tapir are endangered.
> **– Ruth Robbins (Virtual Participant, UPRISING #22)**

GIVE THANKS
REVOLUTIONARY PRACTICE #23

When you are exhausted, give thanks. When you are out of ideas, give thanks. When it is time to take stock of what has happened in the last two years, give thanks. Make the thanksgiving as active, sincere, and pretty as you can. Sit with the discomfort of gestures that feel miniscule in comparison to the gratitude they are meant to symbolize and the enormity of the challenges of sustained arts activism. Enjoy it when two of your collaborators appear without invitation to the time and space for giving thanks. Give them thanks.

IN ACTION: UPRISING #23
22 November 2009, 2:00pm | Loyola Park (Morse Ave. and Lake Michigan), Chicago
Participant: Nicole Garneau
Photos & Video: Uncle Bear and Nicole Garneau

UPRISING #23 was the result of a rush of gratitude for how many people had participated in UPRISINGs since the beginning. As of November 2009, I calculated that 264 people had been involved as volunteer performers and/or subscribers to EVIDENCE. In honor of these wonderful, generous, often brave souls, I gathered stones from Chicago's lakeshore and wrote on them the names of all of the UPRISING participants. I arranged them to spell the words THANK YOU on the wintry beach. As if by magic, UPRISING stalwarts Uncle Bear and Maggie Ananda showed up to witness the giving of thanks and take photos.

(#24) BRING THE SHADOW TO LIGHT
REVOLUTIONARY PRACTICE #24

Oppression is stored in places we lock up for fear of unleashing it on the world and ourselves. What are the things we have tried to hide for too long? Where is that pit of shame? What is the unspeakable thing, the words we fear releasing? How can we transform them by bringing them to light? Embrace the teachings of Joan Halifax, who writes in *The Fruitful Darkness* that

> Whatever I have learned about the nature of the self, both the local and the extended self, has been by going inward and down into the fruitful darkness, the darkness of culture, the darkness of psyche, the darkness of nature. The most important secrets seem always to hide in the shadows. (1993: 17)

Do it in a circle, on the longest night of the year, in the deep Northern winter, surrounded by warriors, lovers, friends, and angels of solidarity who are strangers with open hands. In the dawn of the first day on the road to returning light, three of those beloved siblings will be your agents of release, and your offerings will sparkle on the surface of a lake so big it is a sea. Bring the shadow to light.

IN ACTION: UPRISING #24
22 December 2009, 7:00am | Lake Michigan – Pratt Beach pier, Chicago
Participants: Nicole Garneau, Anne Statton, Cate Plys, and attendees of a Winter Solstice ceremony the night before
Photos: Ruth Robbins

Sunrise on 22 December 2009 was the end of the longest night of the year. The longest night of the year seemed like a good opportunity to press on the notion that an exploration of the dark sides of our social change movements and ourselves is essential if we want to avoid recreating oppressive regimes. UPRISING #24 began the night before, when guests at a Winter Solstice celebration were asked to write about their shadow sides: about something dark that they wish to bring to light. The next morning at daybreak, Ruth Robbins took photos while Anne Statton, Cate Plys, and I read these anonymous texts aloud over the frigid lake and offered bread to the circling birds.

SING ON REVOLUTION SQUARE
REVOLUTIONARY PRACTICE #25

In Moscow, surrounded by images of heroic revolutionaries, it is hard not to be seduced by the romantic propaganda elevating proletariat farmers and laborers: women with broad shoulders and head scarves and eyes always lifted beyond the horizon, as if seeing the shining future beyond the battle. If nothing else, there is something poetic about standing in a place called Площадь Революций (Revolution Square) and trying to get busy Russian commuters to sing songs. There is a power to being in a place where one of the most impactful revolutions in human history occurred, even if one of the current-day manifestations of that revolution is tourists from all over the world posing for photos with life-size SpongeBob Squarepants just a stone's throw from the tomb of Lenin.

IN ACTION: UPRISING #25

14 January 2010, 3:00pm and 30 January 2010, 10:00pm | Revolution Square, Moscow, Russia and Chicago
Participants: Nicole Garneau, with seven strangers on Revolution Square
Photos: Nicole Garneau

UPRISING #25 happened on Russia's 'Old New Year's' holiday (14 January, which is when the new year fell on the lunar/Julian calendar, used until 1918). It was also a new moon day. Since singing is a traditional part of a new year's celebration, I stood near Revolution Square and asked passersby to sing their favorite Russian songs. One person gave a hearty endorsement to 'Katyusha,' a Soviet war song about a young woman pining for her beloved who is away fighting for the motherland. Back in Chicago, on the 30 January full moon, I sang that song out to the night:

> *Пусть он вспомнит девушку простую*
> *Пусть услышит, как она поет*
> *Пусть он землю бережет родную*
> *А любовь Катюша сбережет.* (Isakovsky 1938)

> Let him remember an ordinary girl,
> And hear how she sings,
> Let him preserve the Motherland,
> Same as Katyusha preserves their love. (Koplevsky 2006: n.pag.)

SWEETEN THE DEAL WITH COOKIES
REVOLUTIONARY PRACTICE #26

Yes, it is good to crash other folks' programs instead of adding more stuff to the calendar, but if you are nervous about busting uninvited into someone's event and recruiting people to do a participatory performance, consider ways to sweeten the deal. Think of it as a form of sacred reciprocity: you are asking strangers and friends to lend their voices to your action, so why should they not get a treat? Spend some energy ahead of time considering how to thank the participants, and then bake that gratitude right in.

IN ACTION: UPRISING #26

27 February 2010, 2:00pm | FAIR: local maker and publisher fair, Gallery 400, Chicago
Participants: Nicole Garneau, Salem Collo-Julin, Bonnie Fortune, Matthias Regan, Elvia Rodriguez Ochoa, and other FAIR attendees
Photos: Nicole Garneau

To celebrate the 162nd birthday of Karl Marx and Friedrich Engels' revolutionary text *The Communist Manifesto*, which advocates the abolition of all private property and promotes a system in which workers own all the means of production, land, factories, and machinery, UPRISING #26 crashed the local maker and publisher fair at Gallery 400 with a lunchbox full of homemade cookies, a cheerleader megaphone, and a 20-year-old undergraduate copy of the text. Six participants happily accepted chocolate chip cookies as a reward for reading this important theory out loud into a megaphone. Periodically throughout the day the conversations in the room would be interrupted to introduce the next reader, and then someone would take the megaphone and read aloud a favorite section from the Manifesto. It was good to hear the theory out in the air.

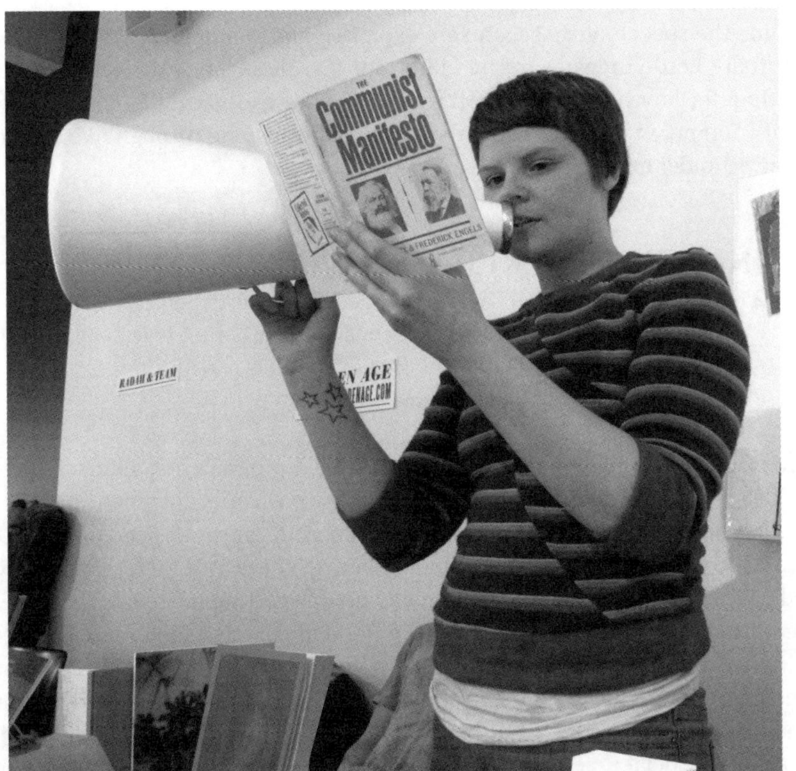

Figure 13: Reading aloud from *The Communist Manifesto* for UPRISING #26. Photo by Nicole Garneau.

SPEAK BRAVELY IN SPITE OF OBSTACLES
REVOLUTIONARY PRACTICE #27

Our bodies, how much money we have, our citizenship status, where we were born, what kind of regime we live under, and the ways in which all of those things are perceived (along with a million other conditions) determine any person's ability to speak freely without fear of violent repercussions. Yet brave people speak out constantly, in spite of terrible obstacles and repression. Writing in 'Performance practice as a site of resistance,' feminist/womanist scholar bell hooks reminds us that 'from times of slavery to the present day, the act of claiming voice, of asserting both one's right to speak as well as saying what one wants to say, has been a challenge to those forms of domestic colonization that seek to overdetermine the speech of those who are exploited and/or oppressed' (1995: 212). The great poet Audre Lorde urges us not to 'allow our fear of anger to deflect us nor seduce us into settling for anything less than the hard work of excavating honesty' (1984). We witness that triumphant moment when the words come gasping through. We can practice communicating under extreme duress.

IN ACTION: UPRISING #27

25 March 2010, 2:30pm | California College of the Arts, San Francisco, CA
Participants: Nancy, Anna Martine, Joanna, Weston, Katie, Steve, Dante, Amanda, Alex, Ana, Maiya, Taylor, Mateo, Yanika, Crispin, Julie, and Aaron
Photos: Ruth Robbins | Video: Malak Helmy

When Ruth Robbins enrolled in the Social Practice MFA program at California College of the Arts (CCA), I was already in the practice of sending postcards documenting UPRISING to 'fancy art people' who I hoped would have interest in my work. One of the people I sent postcards to was Ted Purves, who founded the Social Practice MFA program. (Rest in Power, Ted!) Without knowing who I was or why he was getting postcards from me every month, he started hanging them up in his office. Ted Purves was a fan of postcard art. One day Ruth was in his office and she asked him how he had all of these postcards. He said he did not know; they were just arriving in the mail for him. Ruth laughed and pointed out that she had photo credits on a lot of the postcards. CCA invited me to do a lecture and studio visits for the Social Practice Graduate Program. Obviously that meant creating a San Francisco UPRISING!

For UPRISING #27 at the CCA, I asked a group of about 25 student performers to remember a time they told a bold or radical truth about themselves. My prompt was to write about a memory of feeling silenced, of someone telling them to be quiet, of having the wrong opinion, of trying to tell their truth but having it shut down. I asked: 'How old were you? What were the circumstances? What did it feel like? Why did it matter? Were you ever able to resolve it?' Then I invited students to tell this story to the person sitting next to them and then draw a picture or write words from their memories on a white handkerchief.

Then four brave volunteers lay down on the sidewalk and spent 30 minutes trying to sing while beet juice was poured from above into their open mouths. Periodically another performer would stop the pouring and tenderly wipe the faces of the singers with the decorated handkerchiefs. They continued singing and choking, holding hands through it all, until the beet juice was gone and our moments of truth-telling were soaked red.

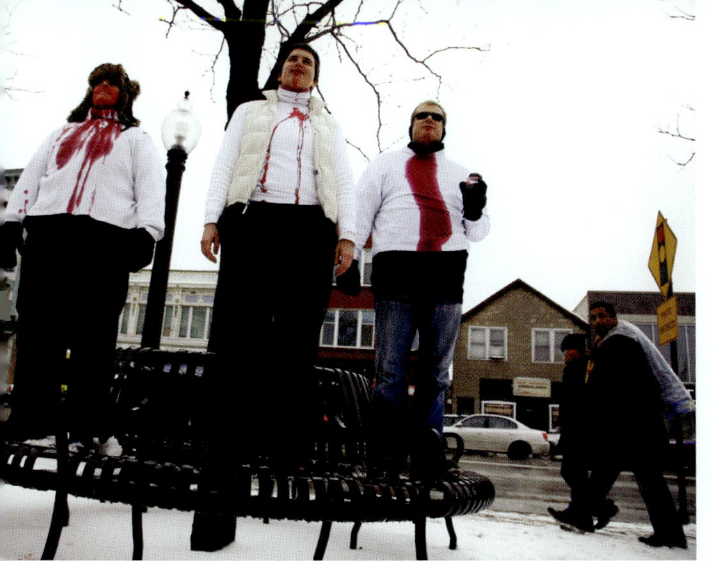

Figure 1a: Uncle Bear, Nicole Garneau, and Bill Van Berschot in UPRISING #1. Photo by Ruth Robbins.

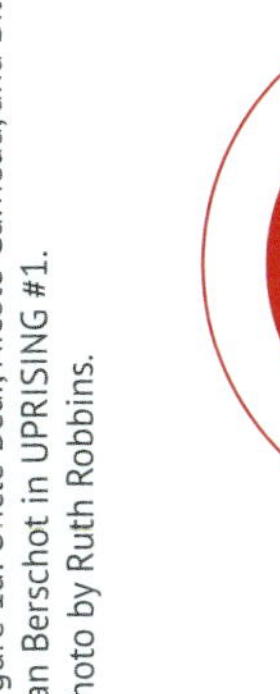

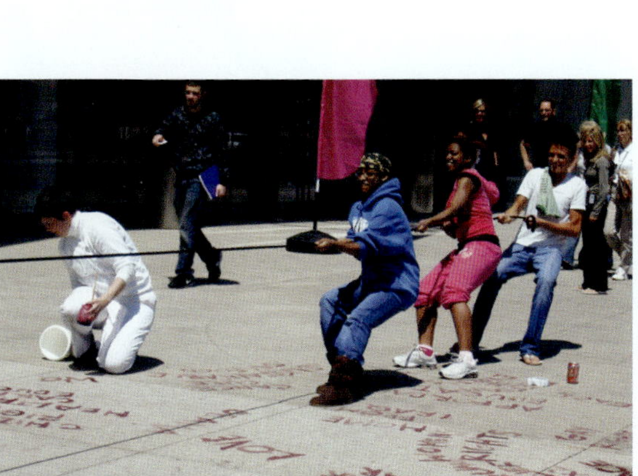

Figure 2a: Nicole Garneau paints beet juice graffiti during tug-of-war game for UPRISING #5. Photo by Aurora Tabar.

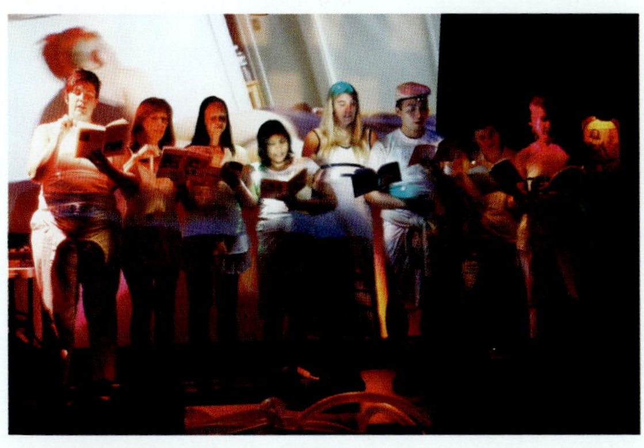

Figure 3a: Nicole Garneau, Jane Fresne, Samantha Miller, Sheelah Murthy, Erica Mott, Coman Poon, Madsen Minax, K. Breadford read texts that revolutionized their ideas of sex/gender in UPRISING #7. Photo by Tara Malik.

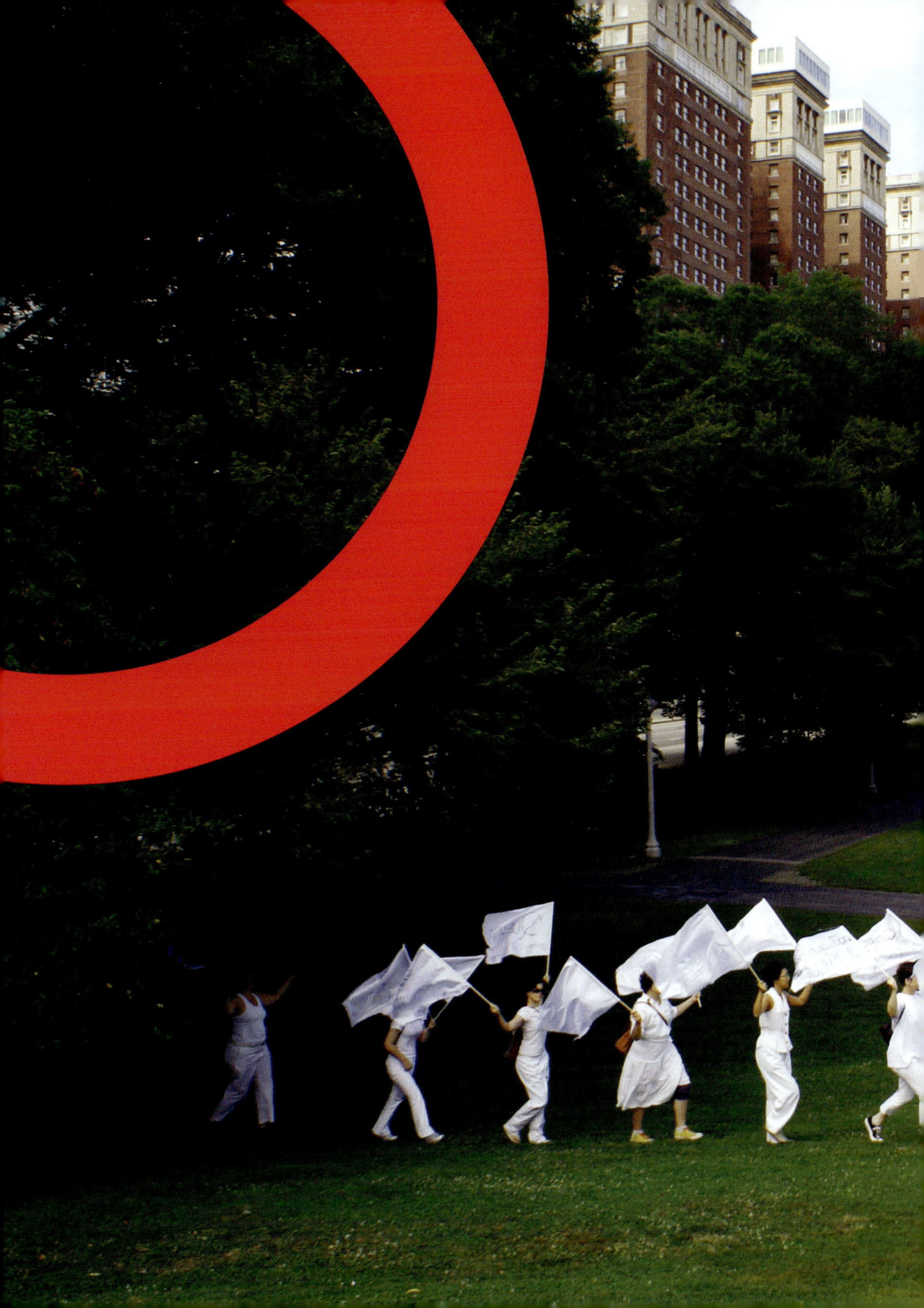

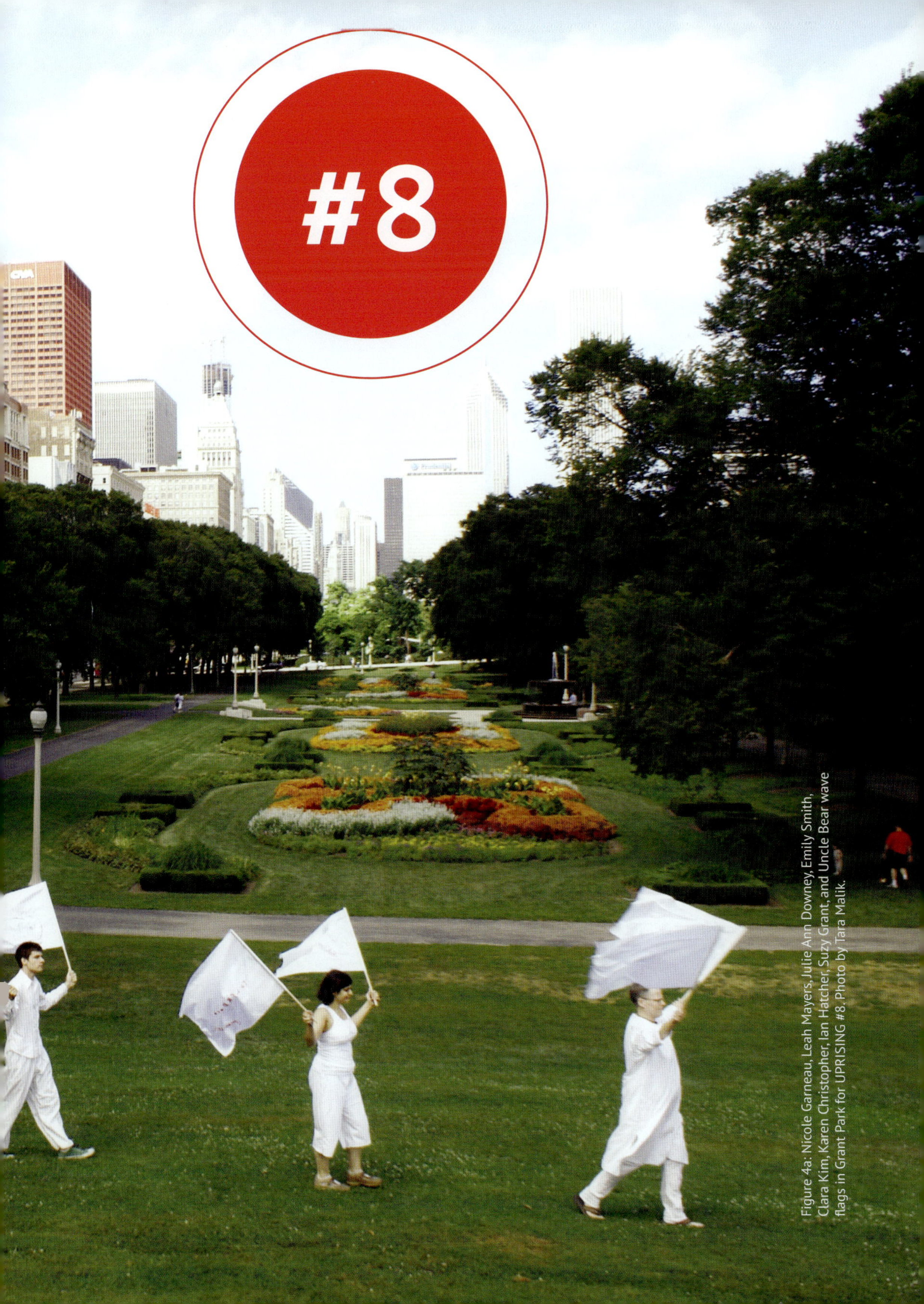

Figure 4a: Nicole Garneau, Leah Mayers, Julie Ann Downey, Emily Smith, Clara Kim, Karen Christopher, Ian Hatcher, Suzy Grant, and Uncle Bear wave flags in Grant Park for UPRISING #8. Photo by Tara Malik.

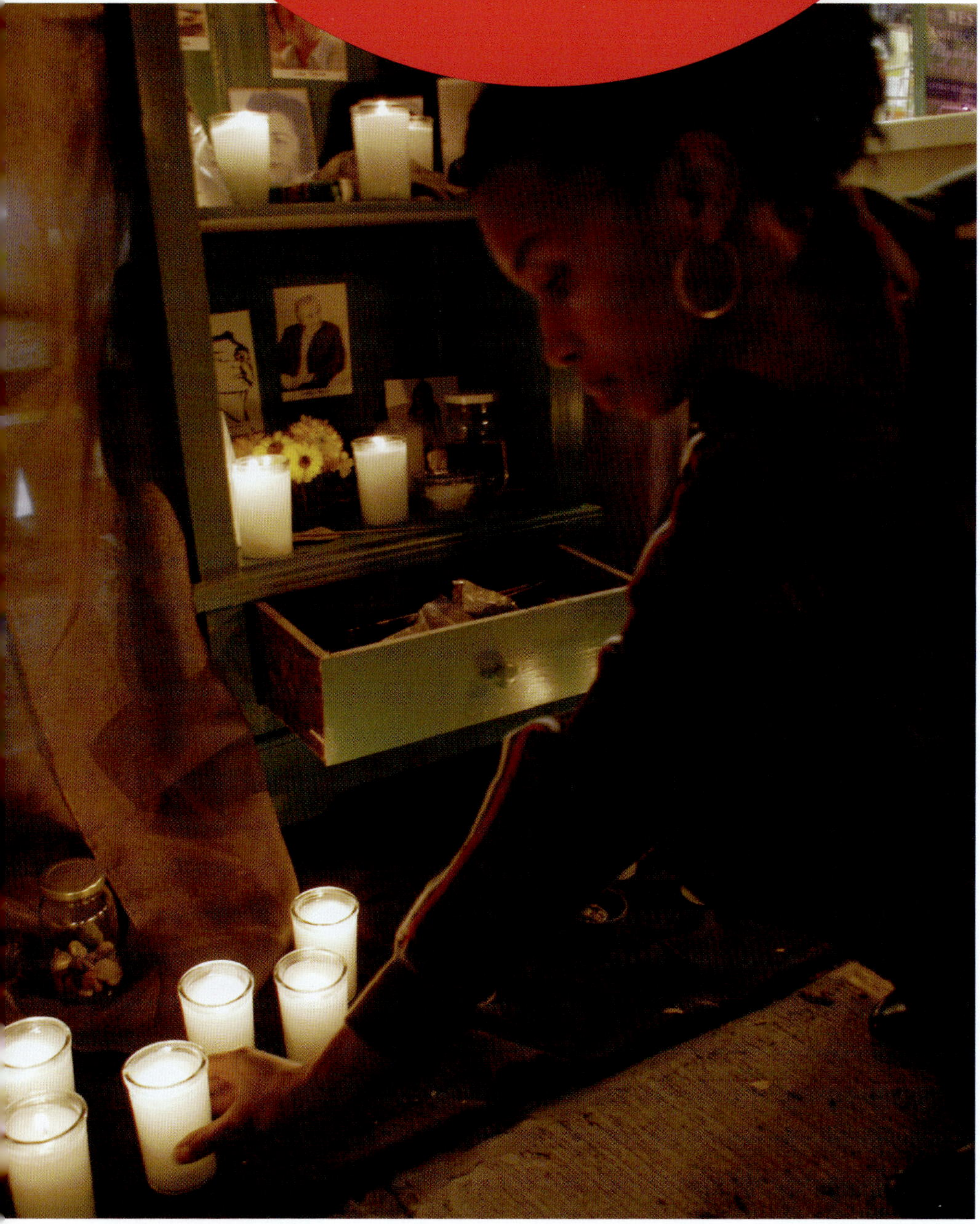

Figure 5a: Red Summer makes an offering at the altar to revolutionary women for UPRISING #10. Photo by Tara Malik.

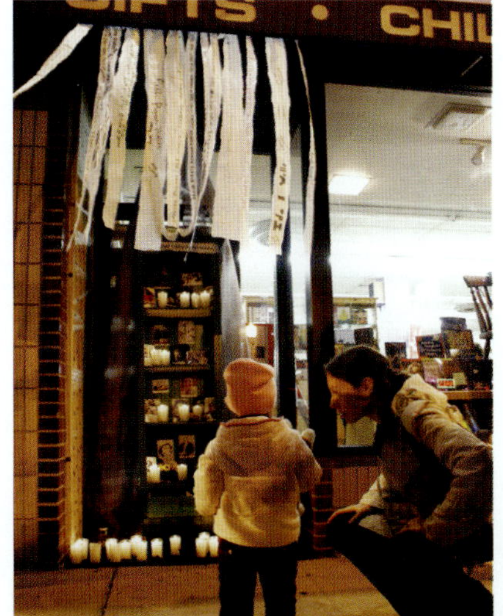

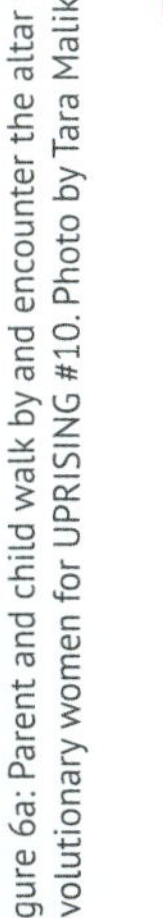

Figure 6a: Parent and child walk by and encounter the altar to revolutionary women for UPRISING #10. Photo by Tara Malik.

#10

#11

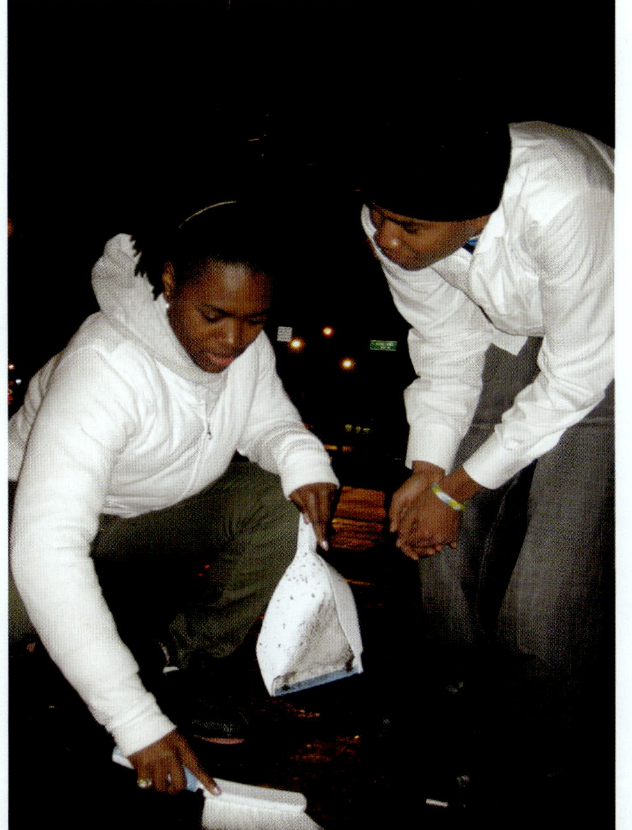

Figure 7a: Two members of Free Street Theatre sweep up around the Nelson Algren fountain and offer words of gratitude during UPRISING #11. Photo by Nicole Garneau.

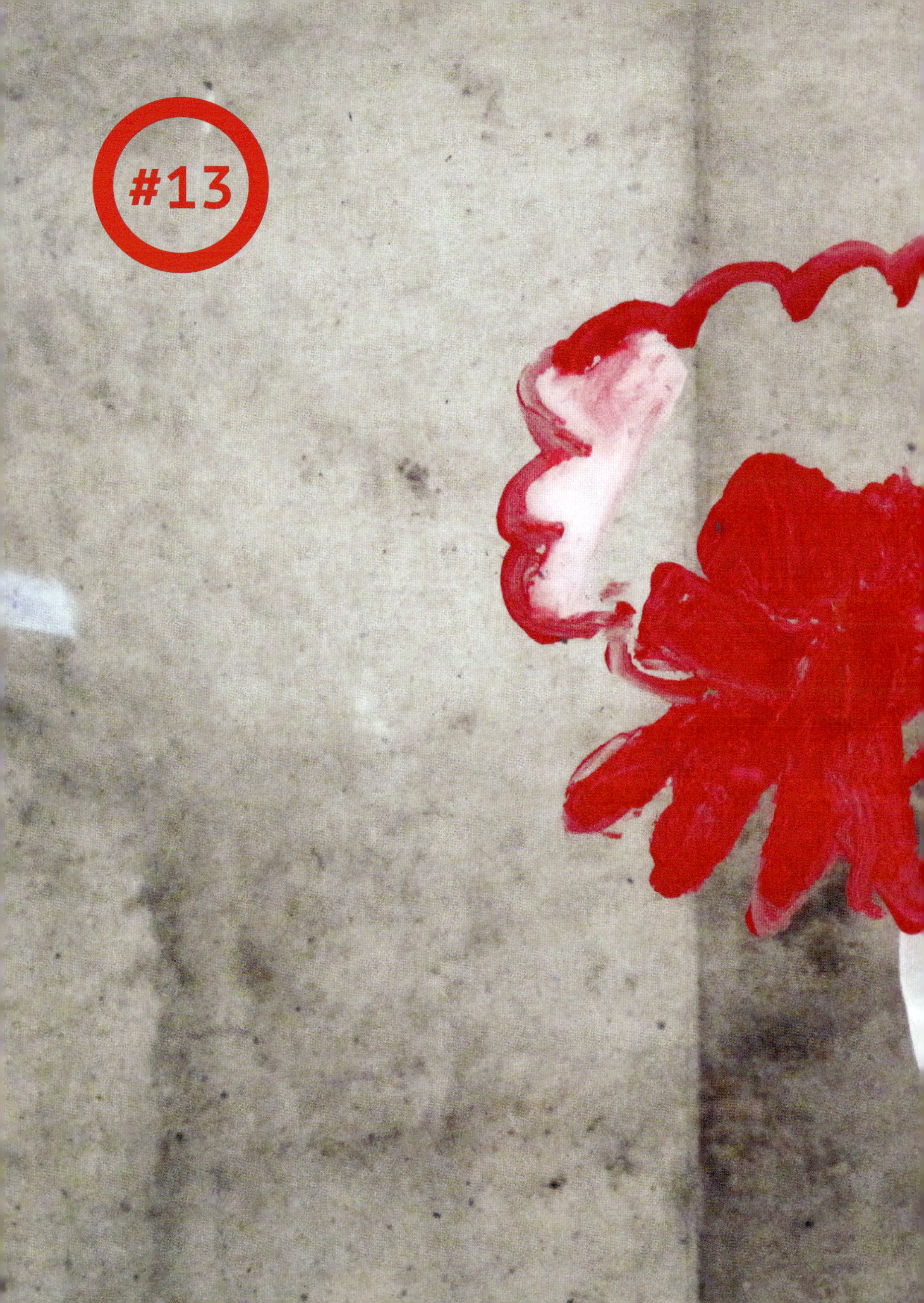

#13

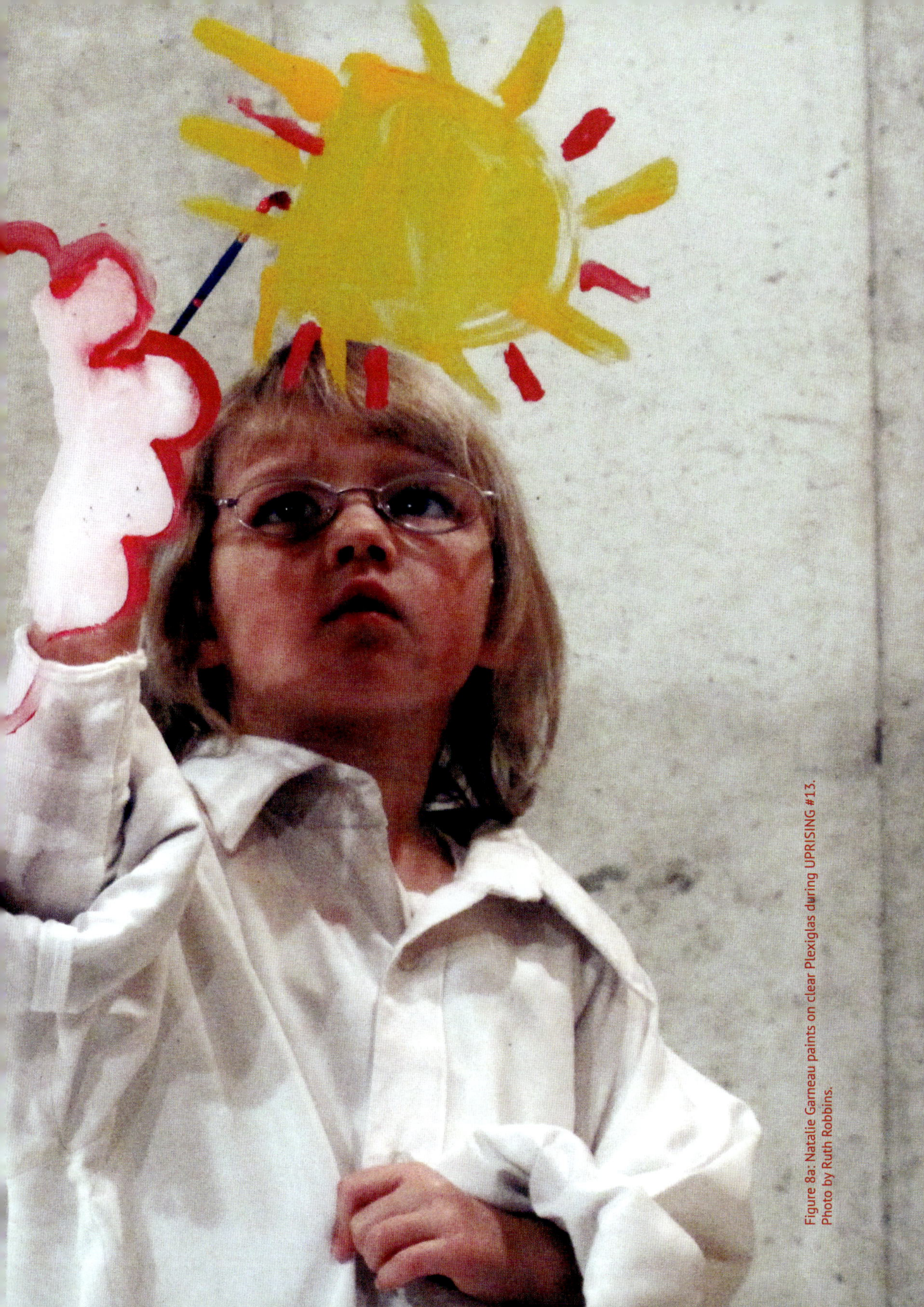

Figure 8a: Natalie Garneau paints on clear Plexiglas during UPRISING #13. Photo by Ruth Robbins.

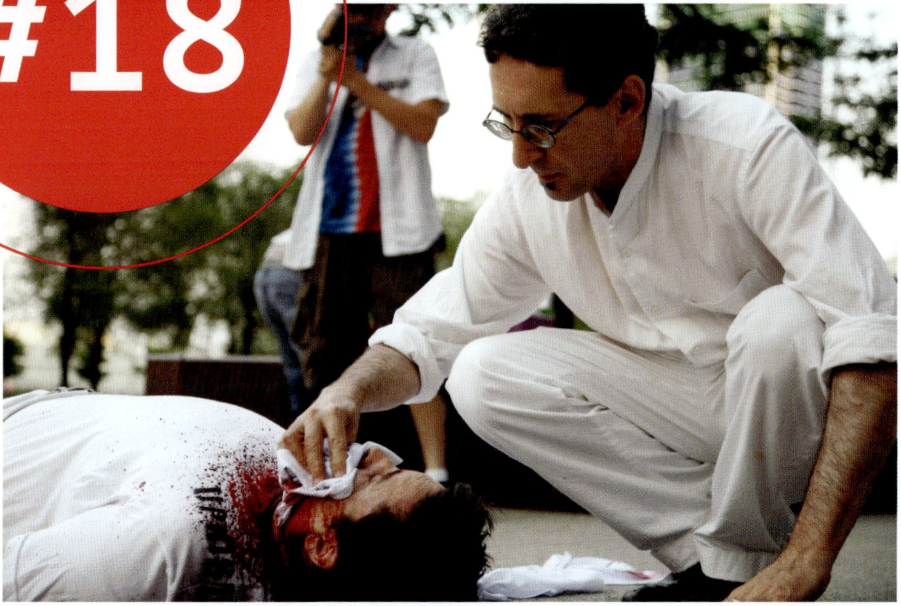

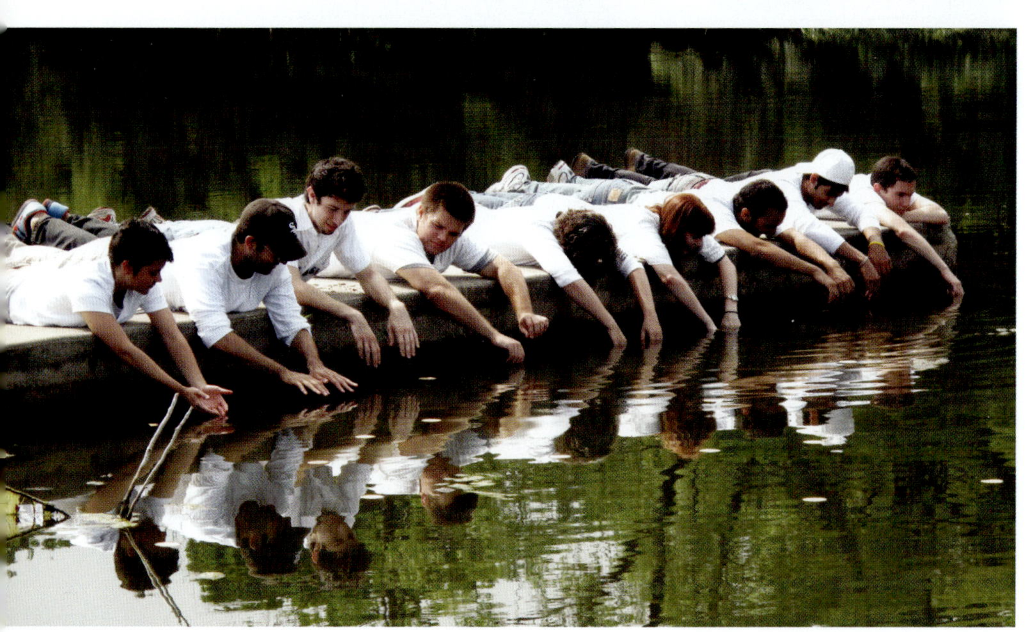

Figure 9a: Jeff Abell dabs Nicole Garneau's beet juice splattered face in UPRISING #18. Photo by Ruth Robbins.

Figure 10a: Rebecca Zorach and University of Chicago students offer cookies to the Washington Park lagoon for UPRISING #19. Photo by Ruth Robbins.

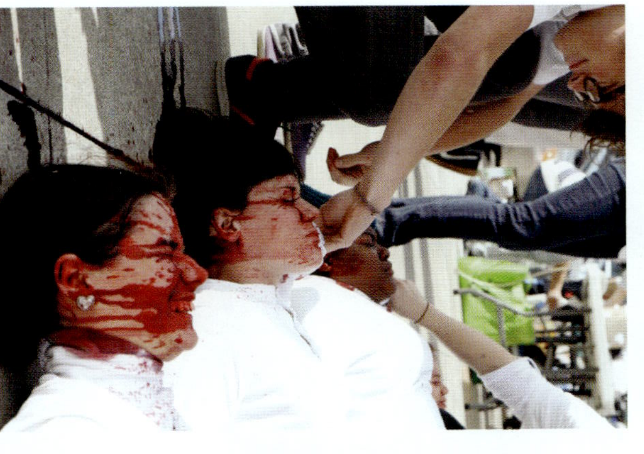

Figure 12a: Students at the California College of the Arts perform in UPRISING #27. Photo by Ruth Robbins.

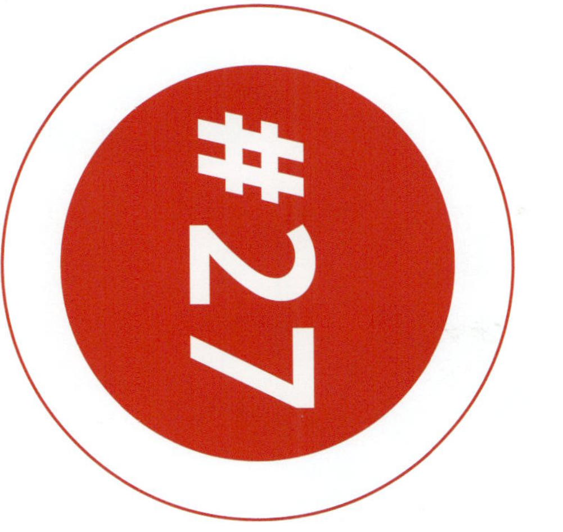

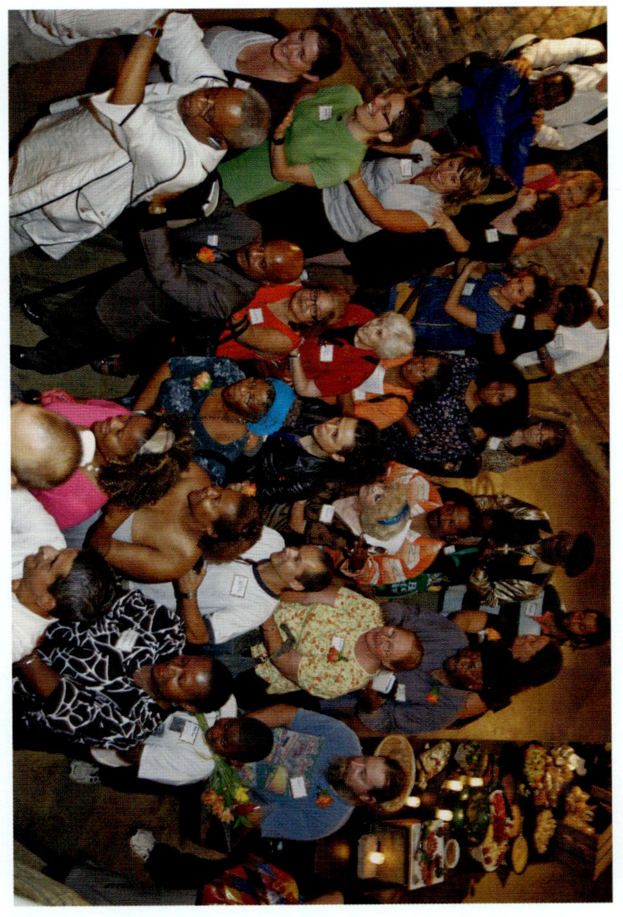

Figure 11a: Prison abolitionists, politicans, and families of prisoners offer each other words of support during UPRISING #20. Photo by Wayne Cable.

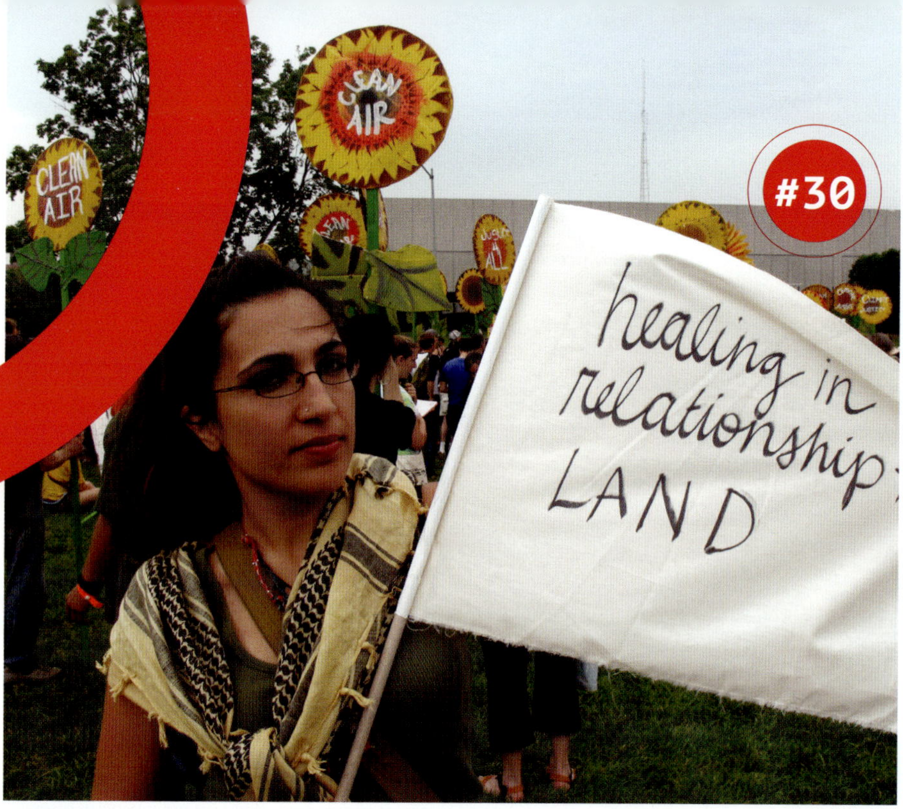

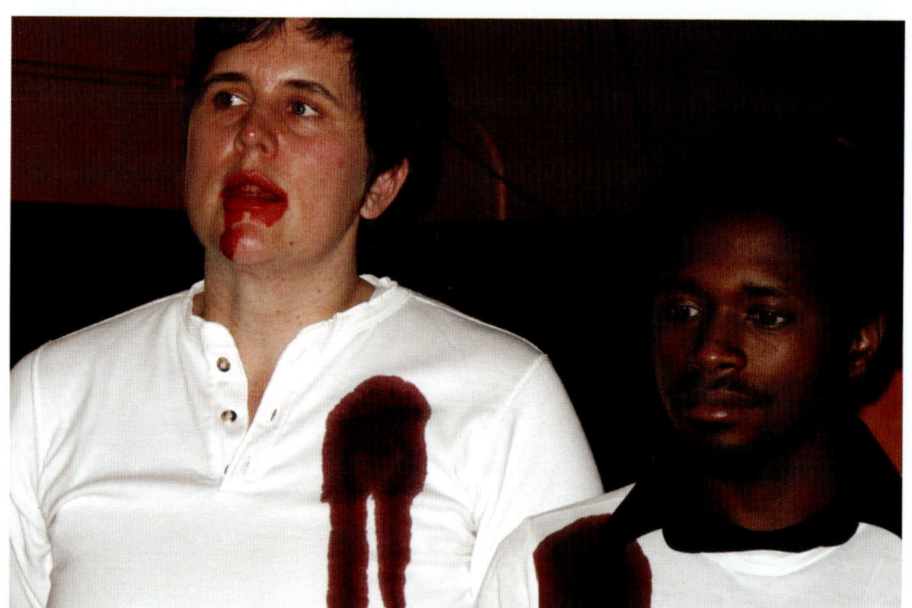

Figure 13a: Nisa Joorabchi carries a flag during the March for Clean Air, Good Jobs, and Justice and UPRISING #30. Photo by Nicole Garneau.

Figure 14a: Nicole Garneau and Domenichi Morris perform in UPRISING #38. Photo by Amara Martin.

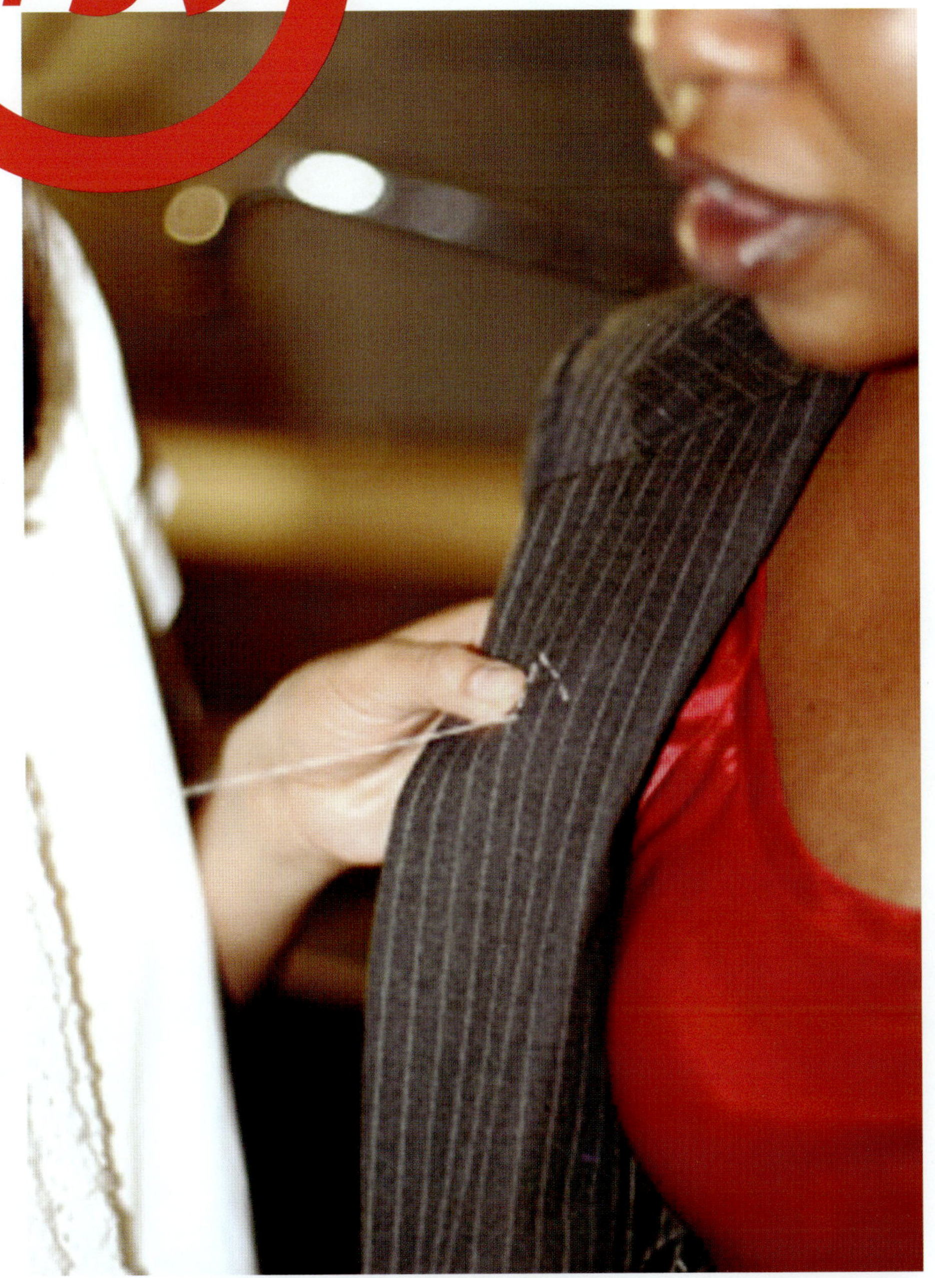

Figure 15a: Silvita Diaz Brown sews a white triangle onto Felicia Holman's jacket in UPRISING #39. Photo by Maria Hadden.

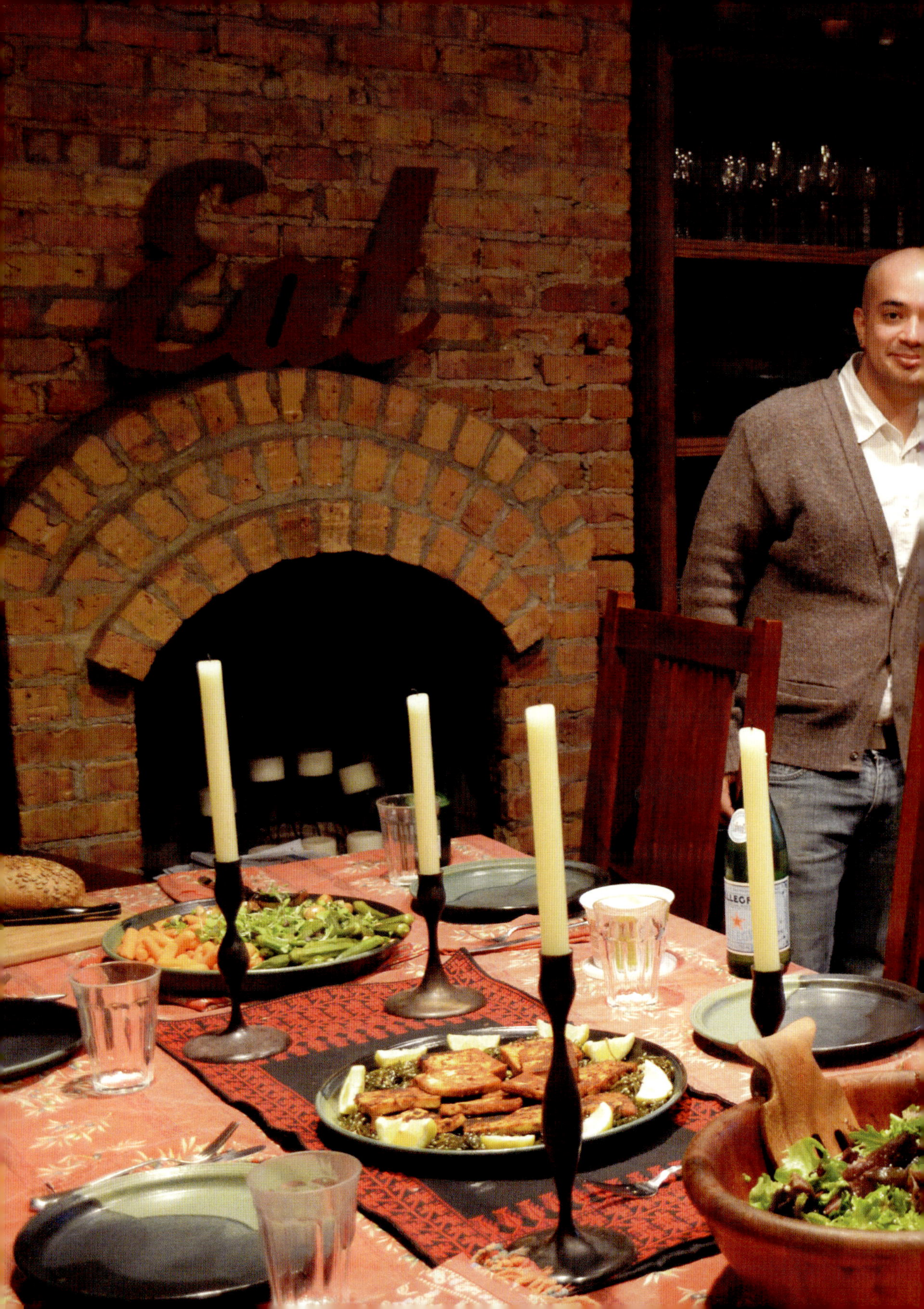

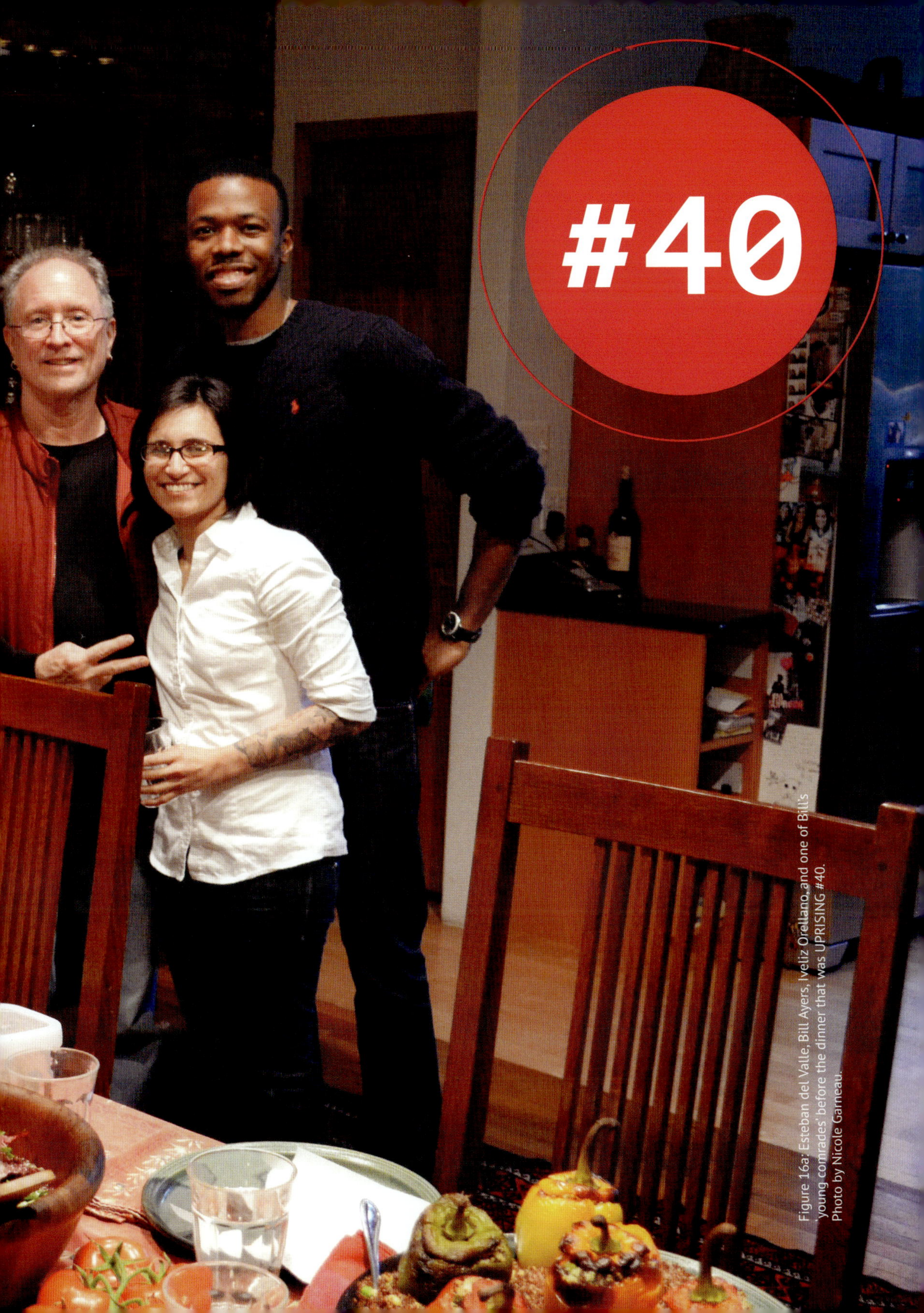

Figure 16a: Esteban del Valle, Bill Ayers, Iveliz Orellano, and one of Bill's 'young comrades' before the dinner that was UPRISING #40. Photo by Nicole Garneau.

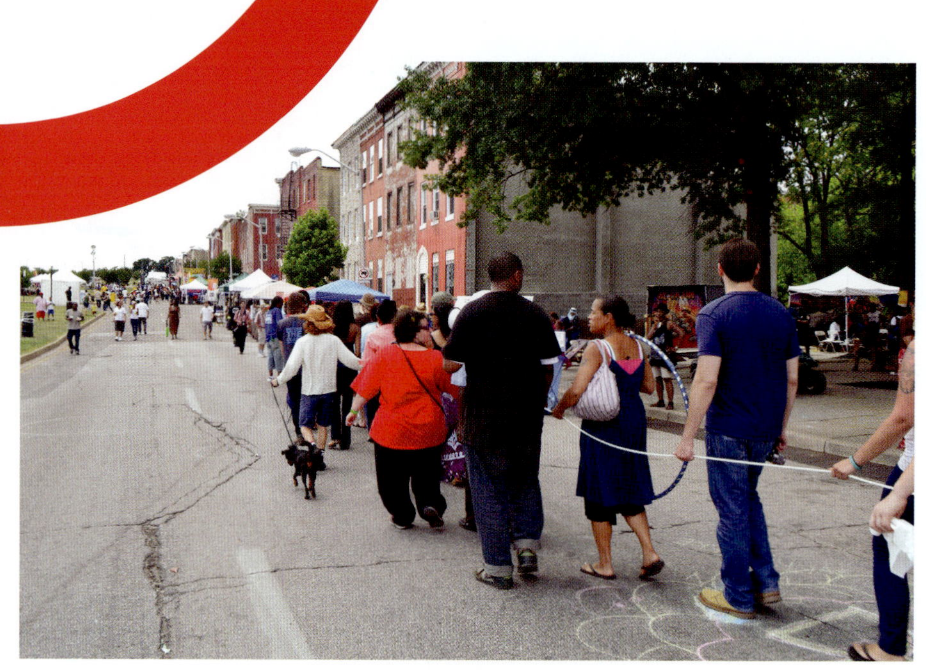

Figure 17a: West Baltimore residents and ROOTS Fest 2011 attendees parade with rope along the Highway to Nowhere for UPRISING #42. Photo by Nicole Garneau.

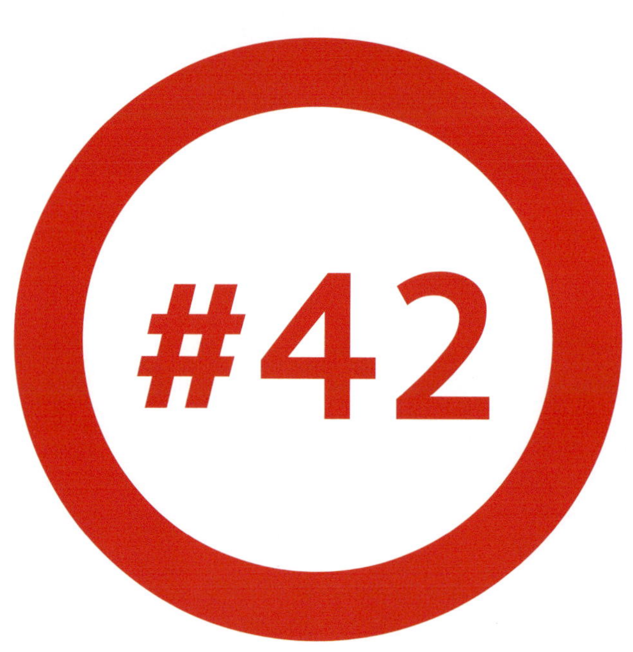

#42

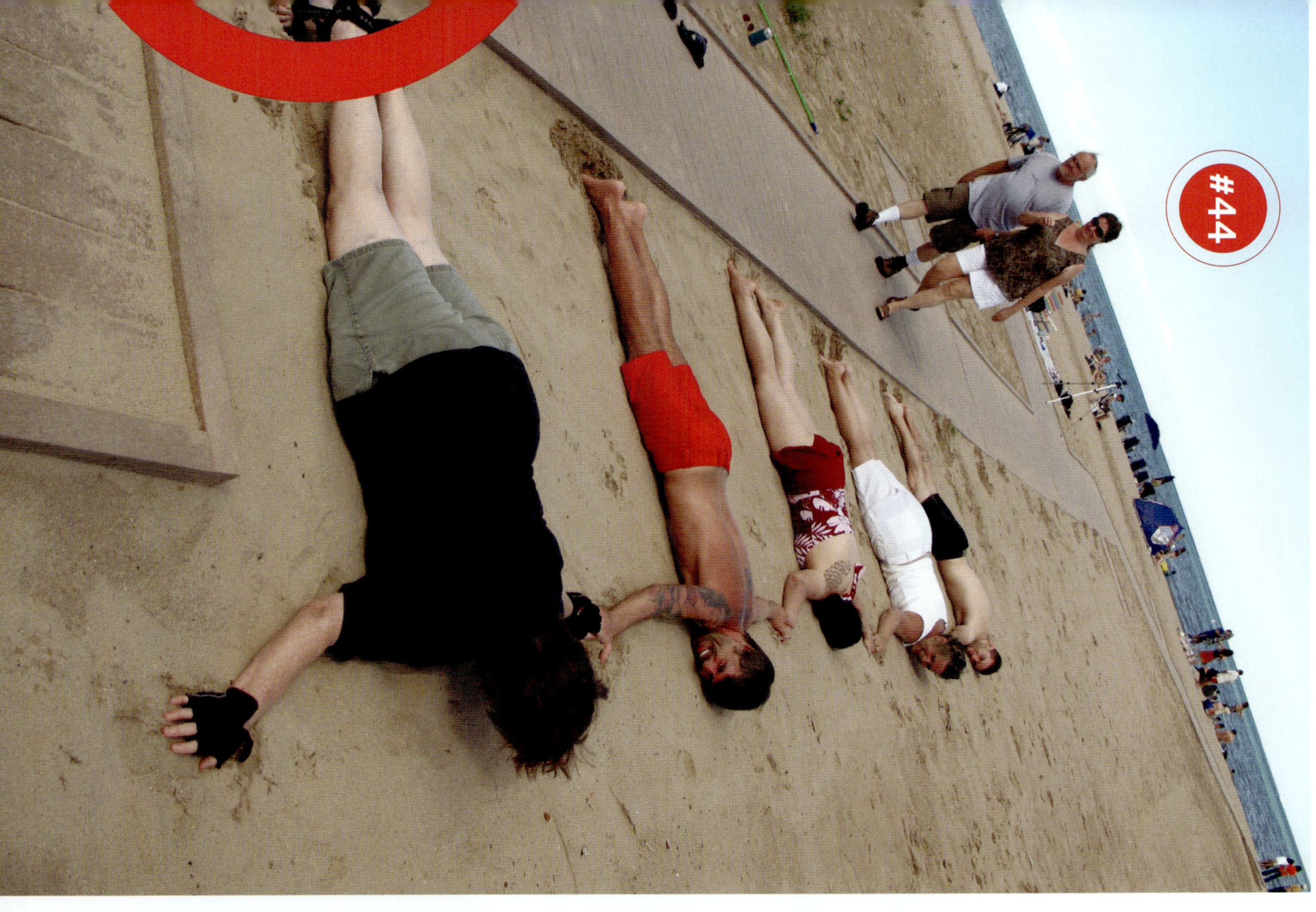

Figure 18a: Mary Patten, Josh Shores, Maggie Ananda, Nicole Garneau, and Sean Dumas make body prints in the sand for UPRISING #44. Photo by Uncle Bear.

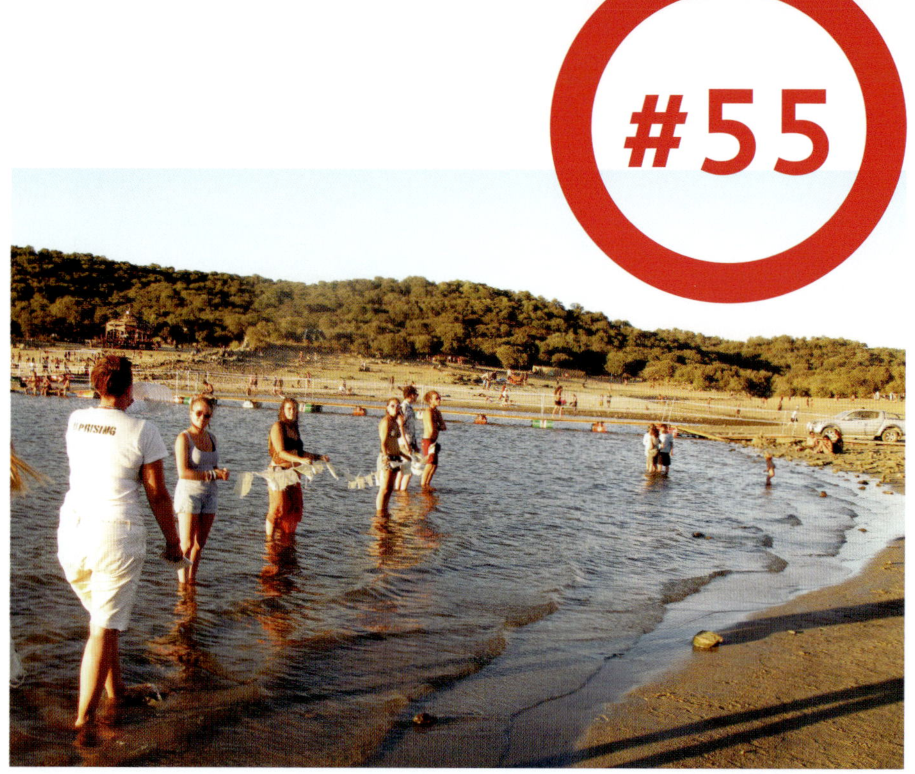

Figure 19a: Nicole Garneau and attendees of the Boom Festival in Portugal rinse flags in the lake for UPRISING #55. Photo by Liv Adda.

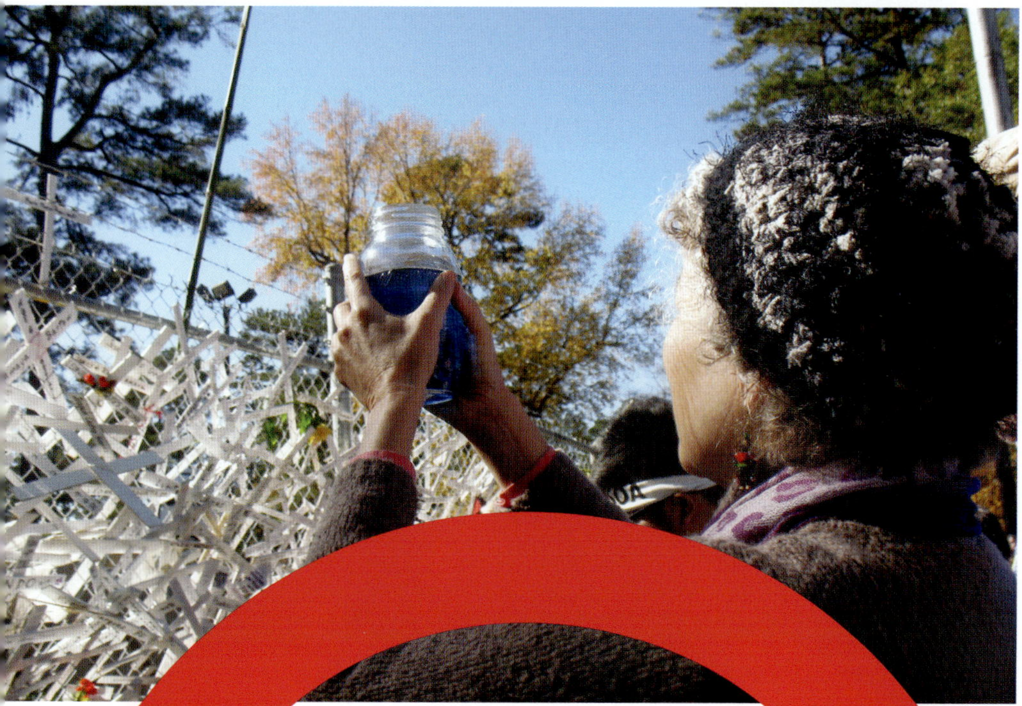

Figure 20a: Elise Witt holds up sweet water made from dissolved words on sugar cubes before pouring them out at Fort Benning, GA for UPRISING #59. Photo by Shannon Turner.

GIVE BACK TO THE GRASS ROOTS
REVOLUTIONARY PRACTICE #28

Create actions so infused with loving visions and world-building gestures, they can be commissioned as gifts in themselves. Notice the season of the hemisphere you are in, and make a ceremony that honors the people who do the arduous and often tedious work of community organizing and fundraising. Remind them of the integrity of raising money through small donations, ticket sales, and raffles. Applaud the commitment and time it takes to work together, building little by little. Send them home with grass seeds to plant.

IN ACTION: UPRISING #28
9 April 2010, 9:00pm | Links Hall, Chicago
Participants: Roell Schmidt, Nicole Garneau, and twelve other attendees at the THAW Thank-You Party
Photos: Nicole Garneau

UPRISING #28 honored the 30-member committee of volunteers that made Links Hall's THAW annual benefit a smashing success. The party was in April 2010, 40 years since the first Earth Day, a national day of grassroots demonstrations for the conservation of the earth. We worked with grass seeds and celebrated grassroots fundraising, because that is the only way to sustain the spaces, organizations, and projects we love. Participants wrote about their contributions to the event, and then were invited to thank each other while placing a handful of grass seeds on their neighbor's paper. Our bundles of gratitude were then folded, tied, and planted.

SHARE QUEER HISTORY IN QUEER SPACES
REVOLUTIONARY PRACTICE #29

Sometimes you bring your participatory performance to a fundraiser for an event you helped start years ago. You are the only person in the room who can claim that history, so you tell them stories. This is when teaching, remembering, and learning history feels like a revolutionary practice: if we do not record and publish our own histories, no one else will.

IN ACTION: UPRISING #29

28 May 2010, 11:00pm | Floupsy Tea Haus, Chicago
Participants: Mika Muñoz, Maribel, Leona, Aerin, Nicole, and dozens of Chicago
Dyke March volunteers and supporters
Photos: Nicole Garneau

UPRISING #29 was a tribute to the hardworking organizers of Chicago's 14th Annual Dyke March as well as a celebration of personal history. When I was a member of the Women's Action Coalition (WAC), we would organize a big dyke contingent for the Chicago Pride Parade, but we grew increasingly critical of the way we were treated. We experienced a lot of verbal and physical harassment along the parade route in ways that always referenced our gender expressions or supposed sexual behaviors or these things in combination with our racial and cultural markers. So we started working with the Lesbian Avengers to organize the first Chicago Dyke March. I was the designated WAC spokesperson at the first Chicago Dyke March rally, dressed in combat boots and a floor-length sheer caftan dress over a black thong.

But the Women's Action Coalition was not yet done trying to make the Gay Pride parade safer for women, so in addition to launching the Chicago Dyke March on the Saturday of pride weekend 1996, we organized an action within the Chicago Pride Parade, and we called it One Woman Marches Safely. During the parade, we created a column of people – basically a solid zone of security on either side, and we gave one person at a time the chance to march unharassed through the Pride Parade. She carried a sign that said 'One Woman Marching Safely.' To educate our community, we printed a zillion flyers explaining the action and handed them out en route. It was powerful, and I think it was the last year we even bothered to march in the Chicago Pride Parade, an event that (like many others around the United States) has grown increasingly homo-normative, apolitical, and dominated by the crassest form of corporate capitalism.

I have attended most Chicago Dyke Marches and I am proud that the Chicago Dyke March identifies as a 'grassroots mobilization and celebration of dyke, queer, and transgender resilience with a goal to bridge together communities across multiple identities' (Chicago Dyke March Collective 2016). At their benefit party in a subterranean Chicago speakeasy, I asked current Dyke March volunteers and organizers to line up in the front of the crowd. The rest of the party people lined up behind them, hands on the backs of the person in front of them, as I told them how grateful we are for their work and their leadership. I reminded them that they are not alone – they have backup. I encouraged them to look around at all of the people who have their backs. The Dyke March is kicking ass beyond our wildest dreams. Then I asked everyone else to lean forward and just speak some words of encouragement to the person in front of them, to help them understand that no one is alone.

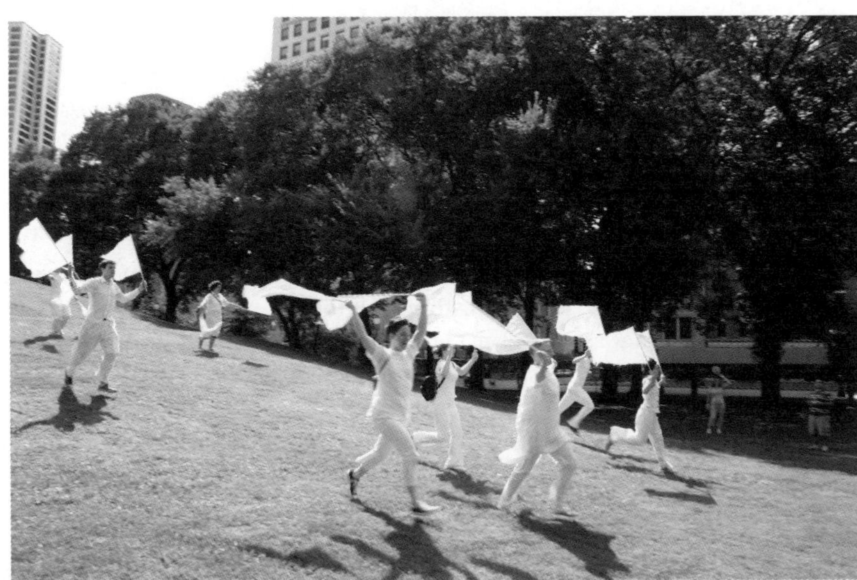

Figure 14: Running down the hill with flags in Grant Park for UPRISING #8. Photo by Tara Malik.

PUT IT ON A FLAG AND SEND IT OUT ON THE WIND
REVOLUTIONARY PRACTICE #30

Flags of states and nations represent the constructed borders we make between human beings living together on one planet. According to Dru-Gu Choegyal Rinpoche, '[Tibetan] prayer flags are messengers from the heavens to remind earth to move towards peace, harmony and happiness' (Barker 2003: 5). The flags of rebellions and demonstrations are dynamic works of art in themselves. Make kinetic and visceral representations of the ideas of liberation as a collaboration with the air. Nothing will make you appreciate a perfect breeze more than carrying a flag. Use strong arms and shoulders to draw arcs against the sky and allow other marchers a glimpse of a beautiful vision of the world. If you can do all of this in the midst of a demonstration for clean air, even better.

IN ACTION: UPRISING #30

26 June 2010, 9:00am | March for Clean Air, Good Jobs, and Justice, Detroit, MI
Participants: Nisa Joorabchi, Tanuja Jagernauth, Nicole Garneau, and healer/activists participating in the National Health and Healing Justice Coalition at the United States Social Forum
Photos & Video: Nicole Garneau

At the United States Social Forum (USSF) in Detroit, Michigan, I spent almost all of my time with the National Health and Healing Justice Coalition. We created a physical healing space in the convention center and spent many hours offering massage, reiki treatments, and other healing modalities to activists from around the world who needed our services. Health and Healing Justice was also a track at the USSF, which meant we gathered for public meetings called People's Movement Assemblies (PMA) to develop a platform for our vision of Healing, Health Justice, and Liberation. In addition to providing healing services and envisioning a liberatory health justice movement, we joined in solidarity with the March for Clean Air, Good Jobs, and Justice at the world's largest incinerator, located in Detroit, Michigan. The night before the march, UPRISING #30 volunteers created flags that incorporated the values of the Healing, Health Justice, and Liberation PMA to carry as we marched for environmental justice, sending our visions into the air we hope will sustain us.

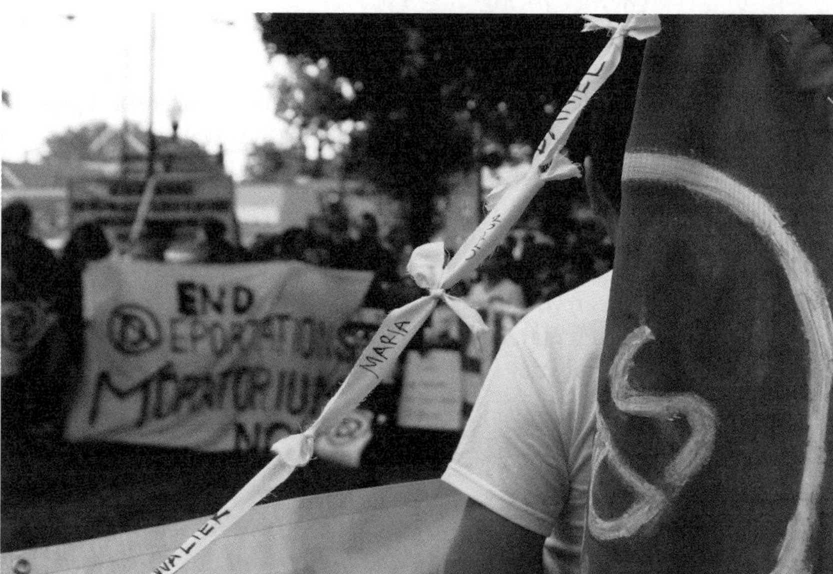

Figure 15: Rope of Humanity at UPRISING #31. Photo by Tara Malik.

BE ACTIVE IN SERVICE OF STRUGGLE
REVOLUTIONARY PRACTICE #31

Do not get stuck memorializing revolutionary history. Look around. Be in the struggles of today. Allow your work to be guided by the freedom fighters now, in your own community. Instead of being overwhelmed by what seems like a multitude of different social justice movements, choose to act in ways that you can. At the 1985 UN Decade for Women Conference in Nairobi, Australian Aboriginal artist Lilla Watson said, 'if you have come here to help me, you are wasting your time. But if you have come because your liberation is bound up with mine, then let us work together' (Leonen 2004).

Create your own public demonstrations of the possibilities for a more loving, just, and humane present and future. Develop the power and skills to manifest a peaceful, compassionate society in which everyone's basic needs are met with honor for the earth and all of its inhabitants.

IN ACTION: UPRISING #31
29 July 2010, 4:00pm | 26th & California (Cook County Criminal Court & Jail), Chicago
Participants: Anne Cushwa, Ellen Macomber, Jeannette Perkal, Daniel Benjamin, Nicole Garneau, and rally attendees/protesters
Photos: Tara Malik | Video: Ellen Macomber

Arizona's anti-illegal immigration law, SB 1070, was widely interpreted as overtly racist and unjust because it required police to check the immigration status of anyone who they 'reasonably suspected' might not be in the United States legally. The American Civil Liberties Union (2016) has fought this law on the grounds that it invites racial profiling against Latinos, Asian Americans, and others who may look or sound 'foreign.' On the day SB 1070 was to take effect, people in Illinois gathered at the location of the Cook County criminal court and jail to support the Moratorium on Deportations Campaign as a first step toward a just and humane immigration system (Moratorium on Deportations Campaign 2011). Rampant deportations of immigrants separate families and displace children. For UPRISING #31, our action was to write the first names of everyone gathered on strips of muslin and tie them together in a long rope of humanity that eventually encircled the entire demonstration. The rope was our dream for weaving our human family together regardless of borders or nationalities. That artifact traveled to my friend Nick Slie's camp on Lake Verrett, Louisiana, and then he brought it back to New Orleans for the final UPRISING and released it to the Mississippi River.

It felt empowering to enact a protest so intentionally and creatively. Asking people for their participation felt like an important way to make connections and increase the bonds of solidarity that were already formed by our shared presence. I loved the simplicity of the gesture existing alongside its powerful symbolism. Protest and performance exist at the crossroads of embodiment and resistance, and it felt so good to be there and shout together and tie our names together and share our anger and grief and to demand a better world in unison.

– Jeannette Perkal (Participant, UPRISING #31)

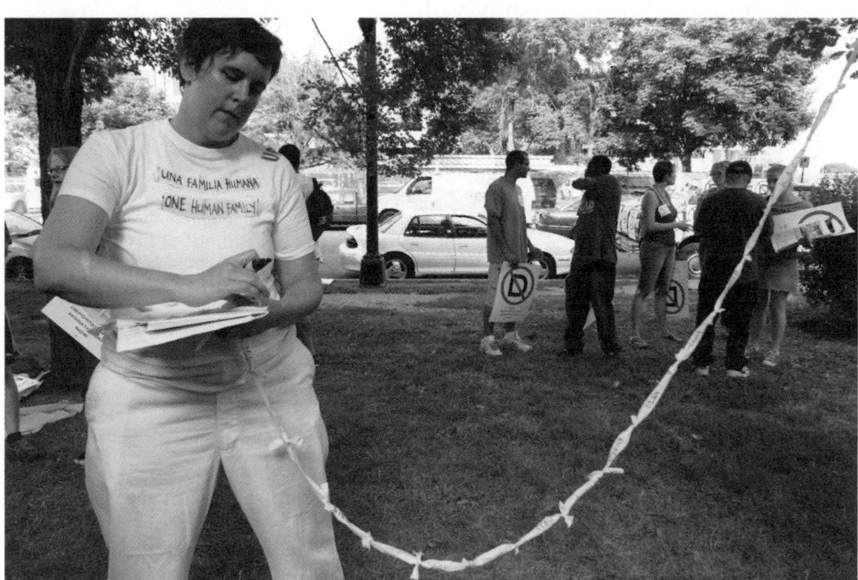

Figure 16: Nicole Garneau adds to the Rope of Humanity at UPRISING #31. Photo by Tara Malik.

Reflection on UPRISING #31

Anne Cushwa

My memories of that day: being scared to interact with strangers, and worrying about how to communicate; whether my limited ability to speak Spanish would serve me at all; and trying to stay out of the way of the rally presentations while engaging with people. Then, as reported by many other UPRISING participants, something radical happened. The fear and worry were released through the simple work of introducing myself to strangers, learning their names, writing them down on our strips of muslin fabric, offering gratitude, and smiling.

After the anxiety, moving beyond it to be open with strangers in that space, for that purpose, there was the final action of tying all of our names together to create a rope of the human family. I remember that it was longer than I thought it would be, and how we moved around, through, and past the crowd creating a new border – of solidarity, of union rather than separation – for the small park.

UPRISING #31 created a physical representation of our interconnectedness. It illuminated the specious boundaries constructed under the guise of nationalism, juxtaposing them against the reality that we are one human family.

The rope we created through conversation and courtesy, and the context of the rally revealed the work that must be done in revolution. Nicole gave me the opportunity to learn again that confronting a fear releases its physical and emotional misery, replacing it with the warmth of connection, hope, and love.

REMEMBER THE GUIDANCE OF ELDERS
REVOLUTIONARY PRACTICE #32

In our visions of the world we are trying to make, how do we conceptualize the kinds of adults we want to be? Personally, I am always on the lookout for examples of the sorts of mature freak radical elder I can see myself becoming. For those of us without traditional markers of adulthood (marriage/partnership/children), what does it mean to be grown up? Who are our role models? Unfortunately, so many of them are locked up or dead too soon. Remember the grown-ups that actually helped you. Be the elder you would have wanted. It is never too early to appreciate and start emulating them.

IN ACTION: UPRISING #32
31 August 2010, 10:00pm | The Beautiful Struggle Party at The Bar 10Door, Chicago
Participants: Nicole Garneau, Debi Moroney, Stacey Horn, and the students and supporters of UIC's graduate program in Youth Development
Photos: Nicole Garneau

The Beautiful Struggle was a monthly art and music series in Chicago that raised awareness and funds to sustain community and global initiatives, projects, social movements, organizations, radical ideas, and causes. The August 2010 Beautiful Struggle Party benefited the UIC Youth Development graduate program, which had declared itself revolutionary. I asked people at the bar to think back to their childhood and write down one really important thing an adult said or did that had a positive impact on their lives. Then we lined up with hands on each other's backs to remember how much support we have, and I read a selection of their stories out loud, reflecting back to them how much wisdom they already possess.

ENACT THE KINDS OF RELATIONSHIPS WE WANT WITH OTHER PEOPLE
REVOLUTIONARY PRACTICE #33

Whatever our own political background and ideologies, all of us have the power to encourage folks to work together on something, especially when all we really have to agree on is what action we are taking. Build community across ideological lines based on a shared practice of compassionate gestures that encourage strength. Can we all acknowledge that putting hands on someone's shoulders and whispering words of encouragement is a good thing to do? Great – let us do it. Is writing a vision of liberation on embroidered handkerchiefs a nice idea? Great – let us do it. In his essay and book *The Right to the City*, David Harvey examines our social relations in regard to urban living:

> the question of what kind of city we want cannot be divorced from the question of what kind of people we want to be, what kinds of social relations we seek, what relations to nature we cherish, what style of daily life we desire, what kinds of technologies we deem appropriate, what aesthetic values we hold. The right to the city is, therefore, far more than a right of individual access to the resources that the city embodies: it is a right to change ourselves by changing the city more after our heart's desire. The freedom to make and remake ourselves and our cities is, I want to argue, one of the most precious yet most neglected of our human rights. (2008: 1)

Many of us, especially those living in large cities, are constantly bombarded by advertising, marketing, and interactions with people who want something from us, even if just to comment on their view from behind. For that reason, try to be extra gentle and offer things in the public sphere that are loving and sincere. People might walk up and whisper, *is this some kind of protest? What are they protesting?* Create interactions with the public that are an invitation to share a dream or vision. If they are interested or curious, call that a positive encounter. Keep practicing how to ask a question or solicit feedback in a way that gives strangers permission to be honest without feeling excruciatingly self-conscious or trapped. Let them know they are truly free to go or stay.

IN ACTION: UPRISING #33
5 September 2010, 11:00am | Clear Creek Festival, Rockcastle, KY
Participants: Nicole Garneau and attendees of Clear Creek Festival
Photos: Carlton Turner | Video: Nick Slie

UPRISING #33 engaged the community of musicians, performers, and attendees of the three-day Clear Creek Festival in Rockcastle, Kentucky. The festival draws together members of the surrounding rural and urban communities along with guests from across the country with the intention of building community, promoting social change, and inspiring all of us to live more sustainably – in harmony with nature and with one another. UPRISING #33 took place during a glorious Sunday morning of song, story, and ceremony.

In such a beautiful setting, UPRISING #33 was simply an invitation to extend the lineage of UPRISING #20, #29, and #32 by resting hands on backs and shoulders and whispering words of support to the revolutionaries walking before us. I told folks in the foothills of the Appalachians about other UPRISING participants (families of men in solitary confinement, Dyke March organizers, and youth development workers), and it was almost as if we could feel that behind the last person in line in Central Kentucky were whole worlds of activists and world-builders that have our backs.

Nicole's work with the UPRISING project is a critical example of directly engaging audiences through non-traditional performances that challenge standards of venue through transgressive site-specificity and notions of impact by creating spaces where audiences witness and participate in art making. Over the past 5 years I have seen and participated in at least seven incarnations of this project from performances to rehearsal to lecture/demonstrations and have witnessed directly how the audience is taken on a journey exploring ritual, performance and creativity in making mindful and provocative gestures of how to participate fully in shaping the narrative and reality of the world around us. This is vital work in a field where institutions dominate the landscape of public performance and citizens find themselves predominantly as consumers of corporate media and disengaged from creative art practices in public space.
– Robert Martin (Participant, UPRISING #33)

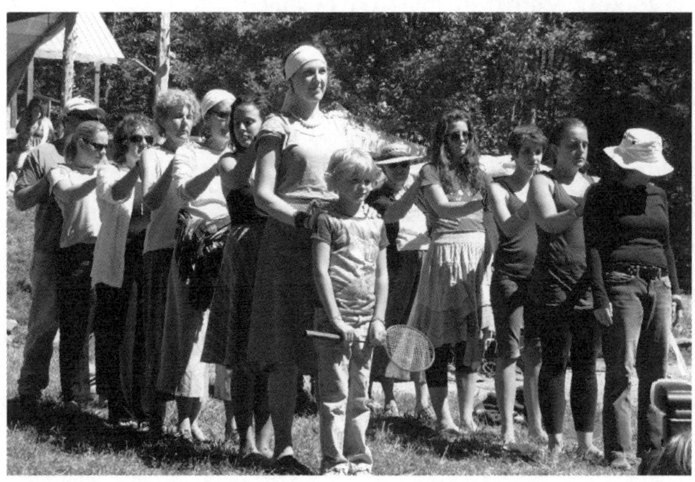

Figure 17: Sunday morning at the Clear Creek Festival for UPRISING #33. Photo by Carlton Turner.

REVOLUTIONIZE GENDER
REVOLUTIONARY PRACTICE #34

#34

Some of us are already doing the work of revolutionizing gender. Writer and organizer Mia Mingus explicitly names the political project of the queer femmes of color who surrounded her growing up:

> Their gender was about being a grounded force to end violence. Their gender was about forging dignity out of invisibility that could slice through femininity that would rather be pretty than useful. Their gender was about answering the question, what is the work you are doing to end violence and poverty, not what shoes are you wearing. Their gender was about feeding family and raising children collectively; organizing for themselves when no one else would. Their gender was a challenge to the world they lived in that was trying to erase them. (2011: n.pag.)

The trans* liberation movement is making the world safer and more possible not only for trans* and gender non-conforming people, but for all of us. It is time to reckon with the gender revolution that is already in progress. Expand your notions of what gender is and is not. Understand the layers of social and political construction that we carry as part of our gendered understandings of others and ourselves. Embrace parts of ourselves and other people that contradict our society's limited definitions of gender as a binary. These are revolutionary acts that liberate everyone from the genius-stifling and violent suppression of our full humanity.

Mark Aguhar was not only one of my favorite friends to meet on a Chicago queer dance floor, she was also a stunning artist, performer, and writer. Her 'Litanies to my Heavenly Brown Body' is a spiritual and political touchstone for me:

BLESSED ARE THE SISSIES
BLESSED ARE THE BOI DYKES
BLESSED ARE THE PEOPLE OF COLOR MY BELOVED KITH AND KIN
BLESSED ARE THE TRANS
BLESSED ARE THE HIGH FEMMES
BLESSED ARE THE SEX WORKERS
BLESSED ARE THE AUTHENTIC
BLESSED ARE THE DIS-IDENTIFIERS
BLESSED ARE THE GENDER ILLUSIONISTS
BLESSED ARE THE NON-NORMATIVE
BLESSED ARE THE GENDERQUEERS

BLESSED ARE THE KINKSTERS
BLESSED ARE THE DISABLED
BLESSED ARE THE HOT FAT GIRLS
BLESSED ARE THE WEIRDO-QUEERS
BLESSED IS THE SPECTRUM
BLESSED IS CONSENT
BLESSED IS RESPECT
BLESSED ARE THE BELOVED WHO I DIDN'T DESCRIBE, I COULDN'T
DESCRIBE, WILL LEARN TO DESCRIBE AND RESPECT AND LOVE
AMEN. (Aguhar 2012)

Try to keep up with the liberatory activism and scholarship that is radically transforming the language we use for gender. It is exploding with proliferations and terminology and an intersectional analysis that insists on honoring the humanity of those who dare to live a gender expression that feels true to themselves. Learn all the pronouns, and then learn some more. Have fun adding '*' to the word 'trans' because 'in this neologism, the * is used metaphorically to capture all the identities – from drag queen to genderqueer – that fall outside traditional gender norms' (Ryan 2014). When that symbol is no longer useful, let it go. Remember that there are always humans who you 'couldn't describe, will learn to describe and respect and love' (Aguhar 2012). Release any kind of personal attachment to another human being's gender identity or presentation. Open yourself to the rainbow of gender expressions that live inside you and everyone else. Play around. That work is healing for us and for the world.

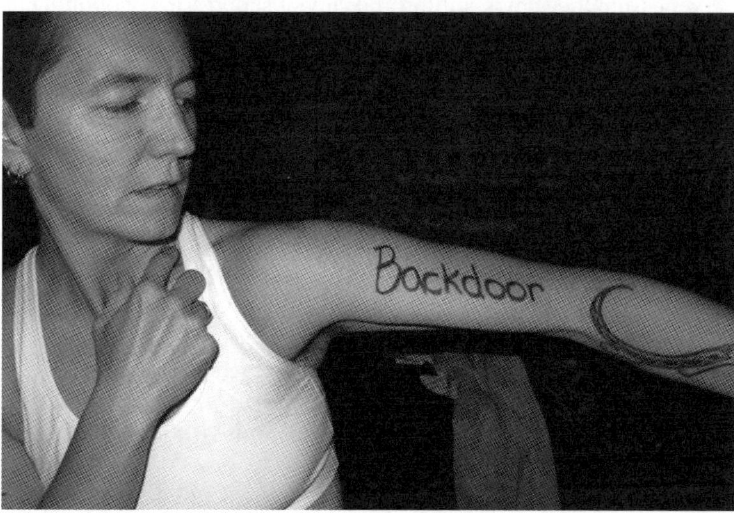

Figure 18: Ames Hawkins in UPRISING #34. Photo by Nicole Garneau.

IN ACTION: UPRISING #34

20 October 2010, 11:00pm | Parlour on Clark, Chicago
Participants: Nicole Garneau, Ames Hawkins, Uncle Bear, Anne Statton,
Maggie Ananda, Ryan Meher, Corrine Calice, and attendees of Northern
Lights party
Photos: Susan Ganem and Nicole Garneau

UPRISING #34 took place at the inaugural Northern Lights Queer Performance and Dance Party. In between raucous stiletto performances and DJ sets, UPRISING volunteers read a few sentences of some text that revolutionized their understandings of sex and/or gender. Party attendees heard selections from *Macho Sluts, Cunt: A Declaration of Independence,* and *Boots of Leather, Slippers of Gold: The History of a Lesbian Community.* Then the readers were matched up with a specific audience member to deliver a private performance of the selected text. Performer and audience member negotiated anything that happened in the space of the private performance. UPRISING #34 was part of *Come as You Are*, a series of works supported with grants from The Theater Offensive in Boston. *Come as You Are* performances celebrated diverse queer sexualities as a celebration of 40 years since the Stonewall Riots.

The ways that we're marked and unmarked by words, the ways that marking is only possible when people 'see' us: these are the things that interest me. I wanted to work with text and the transformation that occurs from when people see me with clothes on, to seeing me with clothes off – to consider the ways that the text might change. The performance turned out to be fun and sexier than I had thought because my 'audience' certainly could see me – this was, after all a queer context. I look forward to being a part of more UPRISINGs, using this as a starting point, and riffing off of the text/body/erasure ideas that this has started with.
– Ames Hawkins (Participant, UPRISING #34)

KEEP IT SILENT AND UNOBTRUSIVE
REVOLUTIONARY PRACTICE #35

Notice the occasions that desire quiet. Be sensitive to moments when calling attention to yourself would detract from actions more crucial than yours. Practice revolutionary stealth. Move gracefully and listen. Dream up gestures so gentle and inconspicuous that they disappear like the popping of so many soap bubbles. Walk humbly in the world. Make space for the rage and keening of others. Let your tiny interventions wash away with the rain.

IN ACTION: UPRISING #35

20 November 2010, 6:00pm | James R. Thompson Center, Chicago
Participant: Nicole Garneau
Photos: Nicole Garneau

International Transgender Day of Remembrance is a solemn and sacred vigil in which folks gather to remember people who have been murdered in the past year because of their real or perceived gender identity. The Transrespect Versus Transphobia project tracks these reported murders, which numbered 179 internationally and fourteen in the United States in 2010. UPRISING #35 was intentionally silent and unobtrusive. Moving quietly through the crowd and crouching on hands and knees, I drew chalk paint white flowers between the feet of the 100 mourners who gathered on the plaza in downtown Chicago to hear the names and stories of people who were during the year. My friends appreciated the gesture, but I worked not to draw too much attention to myself. In the words of Transgender Day of Remembrance Founder Gwendolyn Ann Smith, 'with so many seeking to erase transgender people – sometimes in the most brutal ways possible – it is vitally important that those we lose are remembered, and that we continue to fight for justice' (GLAAD 2016).

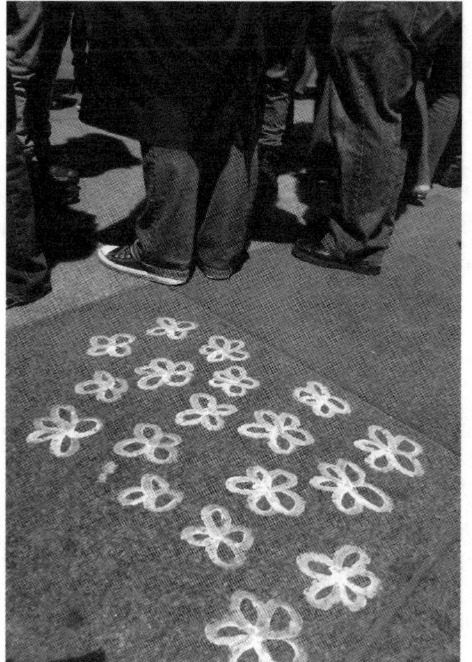

Figure 19: Chalk paint flowers in UPRISING #35. Photo by Nicole Garneau.

FACILITATE RITUALS OF RELEASE
REVOLUTIONARY PRACTICE #36

Some people believe that artists and those of us who work in the cultural realm are on the forefront of a planetary shift in consciousness, which makes ritual and ceremony a critical part of our social activism. It is a revolutionary strategy to make healing ceremonies that are relevant to our own communities, in language that our people understand, in our different contexts. How can our art be in service to a project of global spiritual transformation? Rituals of release help us let go of the things that are no longer serving us. They can be so powerful in and of themselves, and doing them at special moments with our beloved siblings in the struggle also models how anyone can invent their own simple ceremonies to meet their needs.

IN ACTION: UPRISING #36
29 and 31 December 2010, evening and afternoon | Parlour on Clark and
Pratt Beach, Chicago
Participants: Nicole Garneau and participants of Northern Lights party
Photos: Uncle Bear

Revolutionary world-builders do not need to carry any excess baggage into a new year. At the Northern Lights Queer Performance and Dance Party at Parlour on 29 December, everyone in attendance was invited to make lists of the fears, cares, and regrets they wanted to leave behind in 2010. Participants ceremoniously fed their lists into a paper shredder onstage to the cheers of the crowd, and on 31 December, I released the Northern Lights shred at Pratt Beach. Our unwanted scraps of worry swirled spectacularly in the frigid wind of Lake Michigan and undulated on the surface of the water before they disappeared under the waves.

MAKE THE ROAD BY WALKING
REVOLUTIONARY PRACTICE #37

Confession: immediately after making a commitment to the daunting task of building the world in which we want to live through a five-year series of public performances, I felt overwhelmed, anxious, and insecure. Instead of celebrating the accomplishment of each public demonstration of revolutionary practices, I mostly felt relieved that it was over and not disastrous. Eventually there was a moment when I realized that an UPRISING performance had not been preceded by a week-long sensation of panic because, as suspected from the start, we all get better at doing things with practice, which is in fact the point of the project. This sense of relaxation came as a surprise.

Allow yourself to marvel at the alchemy of: starting place + research + creative energy + site + humans + chance. Allow works to accumulate meaning from repetition and their relationship to each other. Attempt to practice some kind of 'revolutionary strategy' with others, and then find meaning in the wholeness of these strategies taken together.

IN ACTION: UPRISING #37

29 January 2011, 11:00am | Reproductive Services Providers in Chicago
Participants: Nicole Garneau, Lara Oppenheimer, Anne Statton, and Jennifer Mefford
Photos: Nicole Garneau, Anne Statton, and Jennifer Mefford

UPRISING #37 was an invitation to participate in an action of gratitude for reproductive choices made possible by the people who provide safe, legal abortions, and the ones who continually fight for that right. When I was a member of the Women's Action Coalition in Chicago, we regularly staged a counter-protest to the anti-choice 'March for Life,' a march against a woman's right to choose to have an abortion.

The end of January 2011 marked the 38th anniversary of Roe v. Wade, and anti-choice activists were holding a conference and rally in Oak Brook, Illinois. There was a caravan meeting at the University of Illinois at Chicago to go out to Oak Brook and stage a counter-protest in support of reproductive rights. I totally respect the people who organized a counter-protest, and I support anyone who felt moved to join them. I invited folks to join me in another kind of action: UPRISING #37 was a walking meditation of support for reproductive choice, and an expression of gratitude for the people who continue to provide abortion counseling and services to women.

On Saturday, 29 January, volunteers walked from their homes to an abortion provider, traveling as much as possible through alleys. When we arrived at the entrance to the building, we made a small gesture or offering of gratitude, documented our efforts, and left. The Rogers Park team walked to Planned Parenthood, and the Logan Square team walked to the American Women's Medical Center. Gratitude offerings included flowers, cards, creative talismans, and chalk drawings.

The occasion, the cause, and the call to action moved me to participate in UPRISING #37. The occasion being the 38th anniversary of the landmark Roe v. Wade decision; the cause being participation in an action to support reproductive choice, a cause that resonates deeply within me and has affected much of my short 29 years on this earth. And the call to action, which was peaceful, personal and intimate. Immediately I fell in love with the idea of a walking meditation through my own neighborhood, a place that I have resided in for a mere five months, and is virtually unknown to me.

Searching for the woman with the yellow flowers, I met Anne Statton at a coffee shop. We strolled down the boulevard, over ice, under highways, along an empty skate park and returned by way of grandiose edifices of architectural beauty. Anne introduced me to my neighborhood. She made me feel comfortable to be myself in a new city. She gave me a yellow flower. It was my gift until I gave it to the ladies at the clinic. The giving of gifts was simple: three flowers and a thank you card.

The American Women's Medical Center, which has been serving women's health care needs since 1972, allowed us to walk in without any form of security and accepted our gifts. According to Anne, the center has not been so open in the past due to a long history of anti-abortion protesters gathering out front. We did not take any photos inside to respect the center and the patients' privacy. UPRISING #37 recognized the tireless professionals who risk their lives daily to provide women with a fundamental choice. It provides families with knowledge, resources, and power to make informed decisions. This affects every day of my life. UPRISING #37 gave me the opportunity to say thank you.

My memories skipped back and forth to the strangers in my life who have provided me with choices in my most fearful moments. Now those memories include Anne Statton and that beautiful winter day when she chose to go on a walk with me.
– Jennifer Mefford (Participant, UPRISING #37)

So what was it like? Nicole sends out an invitation to honor the anniversary of Roe v. Wade and all the people who support women in their freedom of reproductive choice by taking a walk and making an offering of gratitude. That sounds nice, I thought. I would like to take a walk with intention and gratitude.

So I said yes, and the childcare fell smoothly into place so that I could do this walk with Nicole. I walked over to Nicole's place and met her – she was wearing all white and I wondered about her process and how formal this would be. She suggested getting flowers. The flower shop smelled terrific, green and fresh and we wondered which color daisies to get and settled on lavender with yellow green centers. When the flowers were paid for and getting wrapped up, I got tears in my eyes. We buy flowers for people in hospitals and when people die and when you are in love or are going to a party. What was this? Buying flowers for the Woman in a tender and vulnerable place and all the people who work fiercely and protectively to help Her choose Her own way through it.

Walking the slushy slippery icy alleys, Nicole sees we are by the old convent and takes us to a beautiful statue of Mary with a heart encircled in thorns. I thought, 'there is a suffering that men will never know, that only women know: of being pregnant, of not being pregnant, of giving birth, of not giving birth.'

Nicole remarks on the dangerous iciness of the alleys, and I imagine being pregnant, not wanting to be, trying to fall so I would have a miscarriage, throwing my body down, drinking horrible things, how I would make war on my body.

I am appreciating this walk, the talking, the thinking, imagining. We are soon at the Planned Parenthood on Broadway, so close to the Loyola University campus.

To get to the Planned Parenthood office, we have to go into an atrium with lots of green plants and sun coming warmly through the skylight. It feels nice in here, calm, an oasis. The office is closed so we decide to leave our offerings with a card:

Dear Planned Parenthood, Thank You! Love Nicole and Lara.

I have brought a packet – it is a fake pomegranate wrapped in pink linen with aqua thread, a dragonfly on the side. Blue glitter and pink sparkly stars to shake on top of the note. The pomegranate because it is Persephone's fruit. Persephone brings the seasons: she brings spring when she returns to her mother, the goddess of fecundity and the harvest, she brings fall and winter when she reassumes her throne as Queen of the Dead. She walks in both worlds. The dragonfly knows multiple worlds as well. The aqua thread and the aqua glitter signify the water element: the feminine and sexuality. I chose pink stars and pink fabric to gladden the heart with beauty, to give thanks.

Outside I suggest we do a little chalk heart and 'thank you' on their outside step. Nicole agrees and draws the heart and 'thank you.' I add circles that I think are roses but I see are really ripples. Then I add the outline of my hands. It makes me happy again. I know that people walking on the street will see this and say the words in their mind. Thank You.

I am impressed with Nicole's openness to the moment, to my suggestions. I had thought it was her thing but I see truly it was an invitation. To come along, to see what happens. I like her way of making art – not an easy action, rather an action with ease. What a gift, this invitation to walk, to think, to thank. To leave a kind mark in the world. I will ponder this walk in me for a while. It has opened the heart window a little wider.
– Lara Oppenheimer (Participant, UPRISING #37)

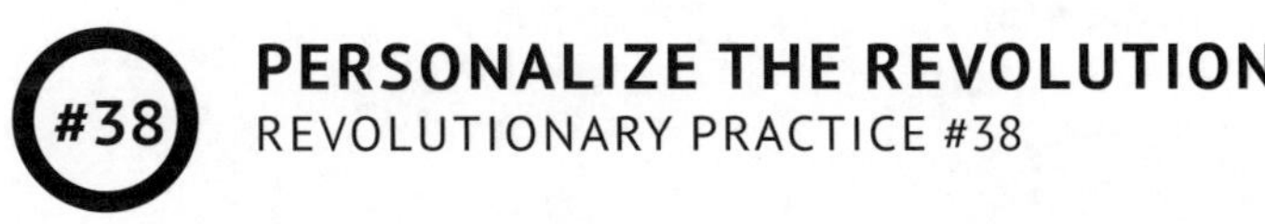

PERSONALIZE THE REVOLUTION
REVOLUTIONARY PRACTICE #38

Pay attention to current revolutionary movements, and talk to each other about them. Expand the dialogue beyond social media using simple technologies like paper and pens. Ask each other questions that anyone can answer, regardless of their background: What is my connection to this world event? How do I make it personal? Can I see myself in those streets, tears streaming down my face after being gassed by the police? What gets stirred in me when I hear stories of uprisings and leaders forced to step down? Work from the assumption that all of us are personally affected, whether we have considered it or not. Can the action of personalizing the revolution make it more possible to step into our power as positive agents of change in the world? Implicate everyone, including yourself.

IN ACTION: UPRISING #38

24 Februray 2011, 10:00pm | Quennect4 Indoor Art Fair, Wicker Well, Chicago
Participants: Nicole Garneau, Nicole Coffineau, Domenichi Morris, Jadine,
Jess Miller, Rachel Schipull, Jennifer, Raelyn Maxwell, Keyser Solze, and
party attendees
Photos: Amara Martin

UPRISING #38 explored our personal relationships to the Middle East revolutions, also known as the 'Arab Spring.' At the Wicker Well bar, 27 people were given notecards and wrote thoughtful answers to the following question: What do the revolutionary movements in Tunisia, Egypt, and Libya mean to you personally? While I read the responses from the microphone, Nicole Coffineau pulled volunteer performers in white shirts to the stage and dribbled beet juice from her mouth onto their chests. It is a revolutionary practice to pay attention to revolutionary movements and keep talking to each other about them.

> I remember engaging with people about topics I didn't know much about, but being happy to be a part of something so much bigger than myself. More than anything I remember what it was like to be a part of the performance. I remember the feeling of the beet juice being spit out onto my chest. I remember looking at the audience, making eye contact with various people who were watching. I remember not quite knowing what it all meant, but knowing it was very important.
> – (Participant, UPRISING #38)

Reflection on UPRISING #38

Nicole Coffineau

In February 2011, I interviewed Nicole Garneau, participated in UPRISING #38, and produced a short paper as a part of graduate coursework at The University of Chicago. My aims were to gain an understanding of the artist's approaches to performance throughout the series, and to contextualize her practice within the discourses surrounding contemporary, politically engaged art. Another part of my project was to document and respond critically to UPRISING #38. Extending and editing this essay in 2017 has meant attending to developments since then in the theory and history of contemporary art and activism, and, moreover, it has meant coping with Trump et al. when orienting my own perspective upon the states – or, the states of crisis – of contemporary art and politics. I have attempted not to project the urgency of the current moment onto UPRISING, and to keep a steady view of the particular arena in which it played out between 2008 and 2012, while also considering some of the discussions that have emerged since then. I thank Nicole for including my work in this book.

Nicole Garneau explained to me that the UPRISING performance series began in 2008 during a moment of revolutionary energy surrounding the 40-year anniversary of 1968. The performance's five-year duration was based upon a parallel interest in 2012. For the artist, the year's significance had to do with the end of the Mayan calendar, which, she said, many interpreted as a prediction for the end of the world. 'I'm part of a spiritual community,' she explained, 'that recognizes 2012 as significant, but not the end of the world. We do believe, though, that it's the dawn of a new age of some kind and that there is the possibility for a global shift in consciousness' (interview with Nicole Garneau, February 2011. Unless otherwise cited, all following quotations are from that interview). The year 2012 was a touchstone between the project, the Mayan calendar, and Garneau's personal beliefs. Thus, in the artist's view, UPRISING overlaid a period of five years – from January 2008 through December 2012 – marked at the beginning by the anniversary of historically scaled, massive resistance and protest, and at the end by the potential for a true rupture in our way of being on the planet. The political events of these five years – such as the US housing crisis and subsequent bank bailout, President

Obama's election and re-election, the Arab Spring, the ongoing, violent occupation of Gaza, the leaking of videos and documents known as the Iraq War Logs and Afghan War Diary by Chelsea Manning, and, of course, many, many other events and situations on global, local, and imaginary stages – were of interest to artists working within activist veins. Indeed, contemporary artists and art critics have engaged global politics with increasing seriousness since Garneau began this project in 2008 (for a discussion on contemporary art's engagement with politics since 9/11, see Belting, Buddensieg and Weibel 2013; Demos 2013; Osborne 2013; Smith 2011; Smith forthcoming; Mercer 2011). This essay will consider Garneau's methods for structuring performance to have political efficacy, and in particular it will explore the roles of imagination and participation in her approach to UPRISING. I will examine UPRISING #38, the iteration in which I participated, and the pedagogical theory of Paulo Freire, whom the artist discussed with me in an interview. My aim is to more deeply understand Garneau's approach to politically activating the space of artistic performance, and to creating artworks with political stakes and effects.

Broadly speaking, efforts within the art world in the twenty-first century to shape modes of critical, political efficacy have been made within a context that can be summarized thus:

> Since 2001, a number of unanticipated world-scale changes, notably the increasing disjunction between leading economies – each with different models of economic organization, all prioritizing national objectives, and none seeking to universalize their model – has broken the hegemonic grip of globalization. In 2008 it seemed shaky indeed [...] Acknowledging the broad outlines of the connections between art and social change, art critics, historians, curators, and theorists, have pursued an interesting set of questions. Did globalized art values spread from the modern cultural centers along with the inroads of multinational capital, intergovernmental agencies, and new technologies? Or did the globalization of contemporary art take hold in art-producing centers around the world in ways distinctive to each? In considering these questions, should we include within the overall conception of 'globalization' actions and attitudes such as anti-globalist resistance, defiant localism, critical cosmopolitanism, and evasive tangentiality? Should we see such reactions as in dialectical opposition to top-down globalization, as in continuity with previous countercurrents, or as emergent modes of living? (Smith and Mathur 2014: 164–65)

The problem highlighted here is that it is a bit unclear on practical and theoretical levels how global politics have affected art since 2001 – that is, affected art's relation to the political, ideological, economic, and discursive structures that shape the world – though it is crystal clear that these structures of 'globalized' capitalism have had major impacts upon art on many levels. This means that artists working in this century are charged with discovering, or defining the very grounds upon which artistic resistance and criticism can occur, what is at stake when we fight for political subjecthood, and the question of how we perceive and cope with the political and social subjecthood of others – others whom we actually encounter in our lives, those whom we encounter virtually, and those we simply imagine.

Known for her use of performance to develop qualities of presence and community amongst audiences, Garneau invented an UPRISING each month over the five-year period to explore situations, conversations, feelings, and actions that might lead to the revolutionary changes she was seeking. Anyone familiar with the artist or her work has heard of the importance of lovingness and gentleness to her oft-collaborative practice. As Garneau explained to me, revolution-building means using social performance to create reflective, affirmative, subversive, gentle spaces for active dialogue. She envisioned UPRISING as a series of flexible, participatory exercises in creating the potential for more loving, just, and engaged ways of being in the world. The project is intended to realize certain revolutionary qualities of relation and agency in contemporary audiences and participants. This is the politics of Garneau's work. Garneau's focus upon relationality in performance art signals her conviction that qualities of relation – of encountering and imagining others, of inhabiting the self, and of embodying political efficacy and social presence – constitute the critical intersection between contemporary art and politics that she wants her work to occupy. (I do not mean to imply a connection with the discourse known as Relational Aesthetics. The distinction between Relational Aesthetics and the relationality that I am placing at the center of my discussion of Garneau's practice is that the former imagines the aesthetic value of artworks to be within local relations in an 'artistic experience.' Relations are thus fetishized, or 'marketized,' under this theory, and lose any capacity for politics because they are subsumed under capitalist relations. Garneau, on the contrary, identifies and deploys relationality as a zone in which artworks can produce political awareness and energy by drawing attention to their qualities and encouraging participants to explore them.) The value Garneau attributes to concepts such as 'gentleness' and 'lovingness' arises from her belief that in order to enable – or even envision – political action, those qualities must be clear in our relations with one another.

The *Oxford English Dictionary* (OED) offers nine definitions of 'uprising.' A selection of relevant entries includes: 'The action of rising after a fall; Advancement in place or power, improvement in position or circumstances; An insurrection, a popular rising against authority or for some common purpose; The process or fact of coming into existence or notice; and The rising of a woman after confinement.' For Garneau, the word invokes a rising forth or an eliciting of inner strength or vision that was previously dormant or inactive. She does not use it to mean a kind of ascension or self-overcoming. While Garneau believes in the possibility of comprehensive transformation of global consciousness, as discussed above, the artist does not expect her work to constitute or enact revolution directly. I take this as a signal of her commitment to exploring the present as reality and the potential that exists to expand awareness of political and social relations through aesthetic experience and participation. Said another way, politicizing subjects as such through thoughtful and artistic intervention is the broad aim of the UPRISING series. Senses of the term 'uprising' reflected in the OED variously refer to states of agency and presence on group, individual, and abstract levels. Garneau's own meditation upon the word, and insistence that it does not mean self-overcoming, but actively self-realizing in a way that facilitates participation, combines notions of active agency – 'rising after a fall,' 'improving,' 'coming into existence' – with notions of states of being – '[in] power,' 'common [in] purpose,' 'out of confinement.' That is to say, UPRISING as an aesthetic project pursues spaces between feeling or thought and action, in which audiences become more aware of their agency and subjecthood.

In the interest of advancing a more specific, critical question about UPRISING, I posit a distinction between contemporary artworks that aim to enable the imagination of utopian alternatives to current conditions within the time and space of a performance, and those that aim to impact the real social or political structures surrounding a performance. This distinction draws a provisional theoretical line between affective aspects of political art, and concrete effects enacted by an artwork or its audience, visible in the world and distinct from the artwork itself. The payoff of parsing terms in such a way may lie in orienting an understanding of the stakes and tactics at play in politically activist art and aesthetics, a polemical task at the heart of contemporary theory and criticism. Like most theoretical dyads, its practical use probably requires setting its two sides (affective present and effective outcome of artworks) as poles of a spectrum, and claiming that most artworks lie somewhere between them. That is, all artworks with political or politicizing aims engage to a certain degree in both tactics. Fully elaborating this schema and orienting it to other examples falls outside the scope of this essay. I introduce it, however, as a model to show how Garneau's work engages audiences by creating certain qualities of relation within the space of performance, and also aims to resonate in meaningful ways after the performance is over. Both of these functions constitute the activist aesthetics of her work.

Before proceeding, however, I must describe in more detail my experience with the work. On 24 February 2011, I participated in UPRISING #38 at the Wicker Well bar in Wicker Park, Chicago, on what was apparently a big night for college basketball. The performance entailed asking patrons of the bar, none of whom Garneau had met before, to write and submit on an index card a brief account of their reactions to and feelings about the Arab Spring. The artist spoke to each person individually, face-to-face. Her prompt was simply: 'What do the revolutionary movements in Tunisia, Egypt, and Libya mean to you, personally?' She explained that the cards would be used in a performance later in the night and would be anonymous. More than 25 responses were submitted. Additionally, several people were asked to put on white shirts and have beet juice drizzled onto them. When the performance began, Garneau, standing on a small platform at the back of the bar, read the cards over a microphone while I led eight white-shirted participants by the hand to a visible area in front of her, where they stood facing the audience and holding hands. Garneau continued reading while I pressed my lips to each person's left shoulder and deposited a mouthful of beet juice onto their white shirts, which bled outward from the point of contact and dripped down the fronts of their shirts, down their arms, and onto the floor. When Garneau finished reading, I spat juice onto her shoulder, then she onto mine. The performance ended with ten beet-juiced performers facing the bar room and holding hands. As a participant, linked in a chain with others, I felt vulnerable, but also present to the moment. Though we appeared to be wounded – the dripping, spreading beet stains resembled fresh, fuchsia blood – we visually symbolized the collective voice embodied in the statements Garneau had read from the cards.

I was struck by how willingly people participated without knowing the artist or expecting to participate in a performance that night. Nearly everyone whom was asked agreed to make a card, and Garneau's genuine and charismatic presence was an important facilitator of this openness. Moreover, the nature of the question, punctuated at the end by the word 'personally,' was such that the scope and depth of responses did not really matter; there was no fear of getting it wrong. What seemed to be on offer was simply discussion that was artistically moderated, but not censored. Garneau's interventions transformed the bar as a public space into a place characterized by a heightened sense of communality, presence, and inclusion. As a participant, my own agency was manifest both in my theatrical performance and in my real, sincere interactions with others. Walking across the bar, taking people by the hand, I was visible as myself, but it was also clear that what I was doing was scripted, part of a planned, artistic performance. Rather than being contradictory, this dualism was empowering – my presence and actions were felt by others and affected the immediate environment. Whether the audience learned something crucial about the Arab Spring during the performance was doubtful. I believe that the revolutionary lesson we were meant to take was that our collective awareness of, response to, and active presence in the world could be seen and heard and mattered. And it is upon this point that I see an aesthetics of contemporary political art at play: feelings of agency within a gathered community, even if that community was temporary, allowed me to imagine myself as a political being whose actions affect reality. This feeling was on the one hand utopian because it allowed me, within a specific and temporarily artistically charged space, to imagine an alternative mode of identity that might condition better social relations. On the other hand, that feeling was real, concretely changed my relations with those around me, and disrupted my expectations regarding the possibility of discussing global topics with strangers in a bar.

UPRISING helps make clear that contemporary artworks may be affectively political by bringing critical attention to the ways that life on a local scale relates to global movements and currents, making way for an aesthetics of sustained awareness of things in the world beyond specific experience. T. J. Demos suggests this more broadly when he writes of activist art: 'The most compelling artistic models, in my view, join the aesthetic dimension of experiential and perceptual engagement with commitment to praxis, and do so with sustained attention to how local activities interact with global formations' (2016: 12). Édouard Glissant describes what he calls the 'poetics of relation' in a book of the same title (2006). He outlines the development of a modern/contemporary meaning of relation, claiming that because we can imagine the whole planet as such, and vast diversities of people upon it, important ethical and artistic questions center upon how we relate to things in the world, and not upon merely discovering the existence of diversity and otherness. The term poetics, within this conceptual structure, suggests a consciousness of the qualities and textures of relation, or inspiring awareness of the subtleties and nuances of the dynamic set of relations we may hold or imagine with other beings (Glissant 2006). Asking participants to think about a global current event, while at the same time transforming their relations to and within a familiar, social space, in UPRISING #38 Garneau infused the space of the bar with sustained attention to a discussion about other people in another part of the world – bringing our modes of relation to place and to each other into view by interrupting them. Glissant's understanding of poetics of relation includes both an aesthetics of the imagination and an ethical interest in real situations. He notes that the concept of relation does not imply stability, equality, or commensurability, but rather refers to a quality of subjective awareness of real connections and orientations to the world and parts of it beyond immediate experience. Its significance for contemporary art is in its description of the potential to at the same time understand oneself as a part of the world, and to be critically aware of one's relations to it and to relations within it. Glissant writes of 'aesthetics of interruption and connection' to describe an aesthetics that comprises a feeling of awareness of, for him, the planet as system, and a feeling of disruption from normal, or automatic, routine experience (2006). Along the lines of his poetics of relation, we can ask how, or to what extent, Garneau's performances oblige their participants to think about the humanness of other people living under different circumstances in distant parts of the world, and about their personal relations to political and social events in other countries and cultures. Without the imperative that UPRISING directly affects global politics, but with the goal of assessing the qualities of relations they produce, another question to posit about #38, is: what exactly might its participants be made conscious of related to the uprisings in Egypt at the time, and what are the political and artistic qualities and values of that consciousness?

It is not possible to speculate upon the complexity of the audience's understanding of the events of the Arab Spring, nor upon their political orientations to it. Indeed, this kind of insight was never the point of UPRISING #38. Instead, its critical significance lies in the artist's methods of constructing an environment with certain qualities of presence, communication, and relation. In Garneau's terms, the qualities are firstly gentle, loving, safe, and open. They are also self-conscious, imaginative, and communal. To the extent that the location of UPRISING #38 was arbitrary – the bar and the basketball game had little to do with the Arab Spring, and the Wicker Well is not an art space – the performance's primary operation was interruption and augmentation, adding to the participants' expectations and changing the trajectories of their experiences. I would argue that Garneau's strategy has to do with altering or intensifying certain qualities of relation within the contexts of her performances. UPRISING intervenes in ways that create change, but does not specify exactly what form those changes must take. Participants had neither to imagine a certain outcome of the Arab Spring, to share in a political perspective, nor to engage in activism during or after the fact. Rather, the potential of contact and communication – the potential of people hearing each other and thinking about things happening on the planet, beyond direct experience – within a group that only ever intended to drink and watch basketball, might initiate the kinds of re-orientations to consciousness and subjecthood that Garneau situates at the heart of her sense of revolutionary potential. Moreover, UPRISING #38's delicate admixture of affect, imagination, and effective re-orientation to immediate experience and to world events participates in several ways in the emergent aesthetics of political contemporary art.

As a final point of discussion, I found it significant that the artist spoke with me about pedagogical theorist Paulo Freire's idea of praxis, or the combination of action and reflection. Freire (1921–97) is a Brazilian teacher and theorist best known for his book, *The Pedagogy of the Oppressed*. He links education with revolution and liberation, in that the capacity for the latter pair is engendered systematically through the former. Freire notes the importance of developing a sense of presence to objective reality in tandem with subjective awareness and acknowledgment of broader situations and situatedness. This means being truly awake to one's situation and desires relative to material and social realities, including structures of oppression and trends of what Freire identifies as dehumanization. He also maintains that the dichotomy of oppressor and oppressed must be overcome – both groups must be liberated – through a self-lifting of the oppressed instigated by humanization and critical intervention. Garneau spoke about learning 'revolutionary skills,' and 'mental structures that can be altered' over time. Public demonstrations of revolutionary practices cultivate or catalyze a collective atmosphere of critical reflection upon the prospect of revolution, the possibility of utopian alternative, and/or the nature of subjective relations to the material and social world. A level of sensitivity to and awareness of world events, local events, private events, social events, other people, and oneself are vital roots of the revolutionary potentials and behaviors sought in Garneau's work. In referencing Freire's pedagogical theory, Garneau indicated that she aims to motivate political and social agency with her work, rather than advance a particular vision. Freire writes, 'To surmount oppression [...] the oppressed must confront reality critically, simultaneously objectifying and acting upon that reality [...] action is human only when it is not merely an occupation but also a preoccupation, that is, when it is not dichotomized from reflection' (1993: 32). This means, for Freire, that the type of education that can enable revolutionary praxis and the rejection of oppressive structures is dialogic, and empowers subjects to realize and pursue human relation through self-reflection combined with action. What I believe Garneau takes from Freire is the imperative to open dialogues that allow participants to reflect upon their subjective situations relative to broader historical, political, or social realities. Furthermore, Garneau's insistence upon vocabulary such as 'loving' and 'gentle,' is, to me, similar to Freire's assertion that a human relation must be consciously realized, pursued, fought for, and offered universally in order to transform structures of oppression. In Freire's model, as in Garneau's, revolution means the liberation of people not as individuals, but as subjects in Freire's sense: critically conscious of themselves and of others.

In this essay, I look back upon an experience I had interviewing an artist and participating in her artistic performance. With an understanding of certain problems in contemporary art, theory, and criticism – those of art's methods of political action and efficacy, and the possibility of an aesthetics of contemporary, political art – I considered the ways in which participating in the work affected me in the moment. It was clear to me in speaking with Garneau, and in observing and participating in her work, that how people relate to each other in a social space transformed by an artist, how people relate to world events and other, unknown people via personal discussion, and how such experiences might subtly affect a person to maintain new or different kinds of awareness after the performance was over were the major inquiries of her practice. I see these concerns as foundational to the problem of art's political efficacy – how it works, and from where and when an artwork's value derives. It would be far too strong to say that Garneau's practice defines or epitomizes this polemic, let alone offers a solution to it. Her work does, however, significantly demonstrate productive tensions between the experience of the here-and-now, and imaginative relations with the world more broadly.

SEW IT BY HAND
REVOLUTIONARY PRACTICE #39

International Women's Day, 8 March, is a labor holiday that originated in the United States, even though it is mostly celebrated in other countries. Its origin was the global reaction to the devastating Triangle Shirtwaist Factory Fire of 1911. Remember the Triangle Fire Coalition (2016) has done a lot of work not only to teach the history of this tragic and influential episode in US labor history, but also to align that work with current labor struggles. Sewing-related actions bring generations of (young, mostly female) needle workers into the present day. In an age of mass production of fabrics and machine embroidery, it is good to remember just how labor intensive it is to stitch with fingers, needle, and thread. Hand-sewing a triangle onto someone else's clothes requires us to ask for consent, and then be in close proximity to another person's body for a conversation about who makes our clothes.

IN ACTION: UPRISING #39
25 March 2011, 7:30pm | *To Art and Profit* Benefit at Defibrillator in Chicago
Participants: Silvita Diaz, Lani Montreal, Nicole Garneau, and party attendees
Photos: Maria Hadden

UPRISING #39 commemorated the 100-year anniversary of the Triangle Shirtwaist Factory Fire, the landmark industrial disaster that killed 146 of the New York factory's 500 employees, most of them young immigrant women and girls of Italian and European Jewish descent. When fire broke out on 25 March 1911, workers found exit doors locked and ran to the fire escape, which collapsed and sent them to their deaths. While New Yorkers on the street watched in horror, scores of young women jumped out of the windows and landed on the street below. After the incident, the factory owners, long known for their anti-union activities, were indicted for manslaughter. But the pair was acquitted after less than two hours of deliberation. The fire became a rallying cry for the international labor movement. The tragedy sparked a nationwide debate about workers' rights, representation, and safety (Remember the Triangle Fire Coalition 2016).

UPRISING #39 was performed at Defibrillator in Chicago at a benefit event for the performance series, *To Art and Profit*. We surveyed the clothing labels of the folks in attendance, and read back to the crowd a list of all the places our clothing was made. One by one, we hand-sewed white triangles to the clothing of participants while talking to them about the Triangle Shirtwaist Factory Fire, in an intimate gesture of solidarity with garment workers everywhere.

RE-ENACT REVOLUTIONARY HISTORY
REVOLUTIONARY PRACTICE #40

When someone in your town has organized a clever and cheeky work of revolutionary theater, sometimes you just want to be in the mix. There is no need to come up with a better idea. Help that comrade by recruiting a few more volunteers and then show up and do what needs to be done. Participate in someone else's public demonstration of revolutionary practices, and learn a thing or two. If there is an afterparty in the pub, all the better.

IN ACTION: UPRISING #40
30 April 2011, 3:00pm | Site of the Haymarket Riot: Randolph & Halsted, Chicago
Participants: Linda Horwitz, Sally Kolin, Amy Partridge, Nicole Garneau,
and hundreds of other re-enactors
Photos: Nicole Garneau

Sometimes the best way to engage in revolutionary practice is to join in the efforts of someone else. At UPRISING #40, volunteers and I participated in Paul Durica's large-scale re-enactment of the Haymarket Riots, which took place in Chicago in 1886 (Pocket Guide to Hell 2011). The re-enactment itself was a methodology for teaching Chicago radical history and making the events and speeches come to life. On that day more than 125 years ago, workers gathered to demand an eight-hour workday. Police shot several demonstrators and a bomb went off. There was a riot, and whether labor leaders or the police were the bombers has never been proven one way or the other. The police, government, and corporate powers were out to crush the labor movement at the time. Labor activists were railroaded and sentenced to death.

This late April Saturday in 2011 was the kind of sunny spring day that creates ecstasy in Chicagoans who have been cooped up all winter. The atmosphere of the re-enactment was euphoric and celebratory. UPRISING volunteers donned police uniforms and waited for our cue to march down the street portraying the police force that marched in to break up the labor demonstration. We joyfully listened to the speeches from the actor playing Ida B. Wells and music from Jon Langford as himself. Our revolutionary strategy was to do our part in remembering the forgotten history of labor organizing in Chicago.

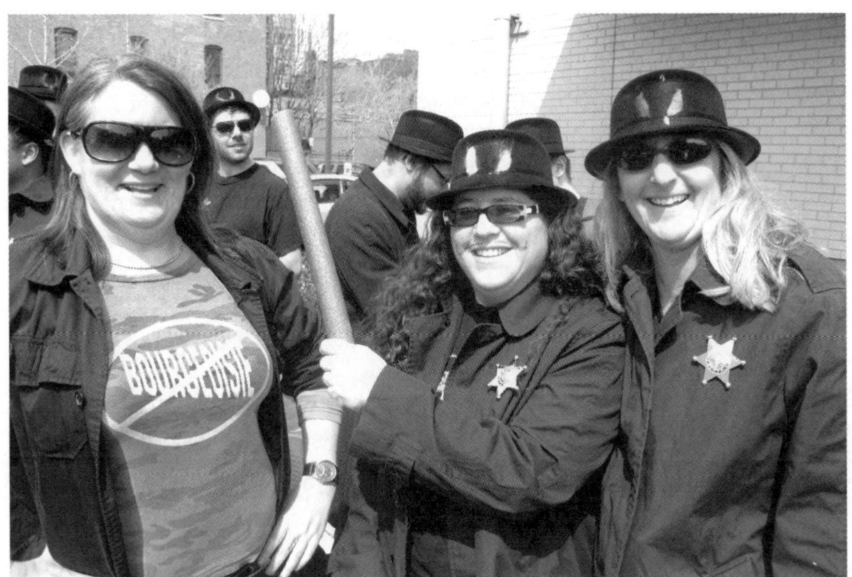

Figure 20: Amy Partridge, Linda Horwitz, and Sally Kolin dressed up for UPRISING #40. Photo by Nicole Garneau.

#41 UNDERSTAND THAT WE WILL NEVER FIT IN ONE BOX
REVOLUTIONARY PRACTICE #41

In an attempt to gather resources in order to use art for practicing revolutionary skills, or to legitimize our work to institutions of culture, artists encounter moments that require the marking of a box to designate a genre for the work. We fill out a lot of application forms. How often do these boxes accurately contain what we are doing now or want to do in the future? The box designers serve the capitalist art market and are always and forever behind the times. Don't be constrained by the boxes. Let's set our own terms and reframe as needed. A great example of the tension around genres, activism, and capitalism appears in Ben Davis' piece from the *International Socialist Review*, 'A critique of social practice art: What does it mean to be a political artist?':

> 'Social practice' as a genre has been around in one form or another
> for a long time, though it hasn't always had that label, or been quite
> so lauded. With the creative activism of the Occupy movement on one
> side and the sheer nauseating decadence of the commercial art world
> on the other, the idea of charging art with a concrete social mission is

having a bit of a moment. A recent article on the phenomenon in the *New York Times* explained the vogue for 'social practice' like this: [I]ts practitioners freely blur the lines among object making, performance, political activism, community organizing, environmentalism and investigative journalism, creating a deeply participatory art that often flourishes outside the gallery and museum system. And in so doing, they push an old question – 'Why is it art?' – as close to the breaking point as contemporary art ever has. (2013a: n.pag.)

IN ACTION: UPRISING #41

18 May 2011, 8:00pm | Home of Bill Ayers and Bernardine Dohrn, Chicago
Participants: Iveliz Orellano, Esteban del Valle, Michael Johnson, Bill Ayers, Nicole Garneau, and two 'young comrades' of Bill Ayers
Photos: Nicole Garneau

An important revolutionary practice is intergenerational dialogue and solidarity-building, and when presented with the opportunity to bring three friends for dinner at the home of Bill Ayers and Bernardine Dohrn, the evening became UPRISING #41. As a former member of a radical left revolutionary organization, Bill Ayers has unique wisdom and perspectives on contemporary culture and activism. Bernardine was out of town, so Bill cooked a delicious meal and used the occasion of the UPRISING to invite some friends to join us at the table.

Iveliz Orellano was one of my students in my Making and Unmaking Whiteness Class at Columbia College Chicago. She had since enrolled in a graduate law program at UIC and has a great deal of interest in social justice. The other person I invited was Michael Johnson, an undergraduate who was in the Columbia College Art + Activism student organization for which I was the faculty advisor. Iveliz brought her friend Esteban del Valle, an artist who was in Chicago to help his father Miguel del Valle run a mayoral campaign. Over sautéed fiddlehead ferns and stuffed peppers, this small community of artists, activists, educators, students, and children from ages 2 to 67 analyzed the 2011 mayoral election, dissected Chicago political movements, and explored the revolutionary possibilities of gathering together for a meal.

Hello Bill,

I was the lucky winner of the dinner with Bill & Bernadine at the AREA Wants & Needs Auction. So I'd like to start talking about scheduling, and also clue you in on how having dinner with you & Bernardine might dovetail with a project I'm doing.

First of all, we're all busy people and I regularly schedule things pretty far in advance, so I'll throw some dates out to get us rolling...

Second, I'm in the 4th year of a 5-year art project exploring practices of revolution. I started in 2008, and I'll finish in 2012. The project is called UPRISING, and it consists of monthly, mostly public 'performances' created by a cast of volunteers and me. Sometimes these UPRISINGs really look like performances, and sometimes they are totally task-based or gestural (like last month when a crew of women made walking pilgrimages through the alleys of our neighborhoods to leave offerings of gratitude at abortion clinics.)

I think a really important revolutionary practice is intergenerational dialogue and solidarity building, so I would like to consider our dinner to be an UPRISING. That doesn't mean I'm going to perform! It just means that I'd be intentional about that dialogue and be curious to talk to everyone about revolution. We could figure out together how to document it. I'd also be intentional about who else I invite. I'm 40, so I'd definitely like to reach out to some of my younger comrades.

I look forward to meeting with you and breaking bread.

Sincerely,
Nicole

Love love love it!

Let's have an UPRISING in some wonderful form.

You won dinner for 4? You bring 4, and I'll bring 4 – BD and me and 2 of our young comrades. OK?

xxx Bill

CONSTRUCT METAPHORS OF COMMUNITY REPAIR
REVOLUTIONARY PRACTICE #42

The forces of market capitalism routinely destroy communities in stunningly ingenious ways. The lives of actual people are wrecked by greed, alienation from the planet, and profound disconnection from other human beings. But cultural workers will win the contest of imagination. In *The Reenchantment of Art*, Suzi Gablik quotes the painter Ciel Bergman:

> Negative images have a way of coming alive just as positive images have. If we project images of beauty, hope, healing, courage, survival, cooperation, interrelatedness, serenity, imagination and harmony, this will have a positive effect. Imagine what artists could do if they became committed to the long-term good of the planet. The possibilities are beyond imagination. If all artists would ever pull together for the survival of humankind, it would be a power such as the world has never known. (1992: 155)

Fueled by generosity, love, and reverence for the earth, we will dream up and demonstrate ways to knit together the fractured bits of our neighborhoods and our lives. We will practice in metaphors until we have the skills to do it in real life. We will heal and be stronger in our broken places.

IN ACTION: UPRISING #42

26 June 2011, 2:00pm | ROOTS Fest 2011: Many Communities, One Voice.
West Baltimore, MD
Participants: Ashley Sparks, Natalya Brusilovsky, Saint 43, Shannon Turner, Carlton Turner, Adam Tourek, Nicole Garneau, and about 50 attendees of ROOTS Fest 2011
Photos: Nicole Garneau

ROOTS Fest 2011: Many Communities, One Voice was a music, arts, and community festival seeking to heal, empower, and unite Baltimore through the celebration of arts and culture. The festival took place over the 'Highway to Nowhere' in West Baltimore – a road-building project that bulldozed a thriving African American community 40 years ago, splitting it into two halves. The road was never finished, but lives on as a decaying scar and a reminder of the relationship between racial oppression and urban development. UPRISING #42 enacted a metaphor of healing communities: participants stretched out along 100 feet of white rope, recruiting participants to hold on as we paraded from the highway overpass to the newly cleaned and re-dedicated Hidden Stream Park. Along the way, we anointed the rope with community healing transmitted through our hands.

> Nicole's work physically connected us with the space we were in, and this connection created an opportunity to engage with people who otherwise would have been strangers swimming about in the public otherness. My dog even joined in the walk through the festival site and I got to meet several people who I recognized but had never talked to. Who knew!!? Such a beautiful ceremonial act – sacred but formal and simple.
>
> Sometimes the most bold and innovative ideas are the simplest ones. The act of grabbing onto a rope and winding our way through the streets of Baltimore sounds simple – but then when you do it, and you watch young children grab hold and strangers opening up to each other, you realize that the simple act of connection gives people a reason to belong.
> **– Saint 43 (Participant, UPRISING #42)**
>
> I remember Baltimore and moving through a crowd of hundreds of people. We were joined together by a rope – written with love notes or aspirations or dreams or forgivenesses. But we walked with intention, smiling at strangers, and left it somewhere special. I think there were 40 of us holding the rope – different ages and races. I was limping a little with a sprained ankle. I was grateful to be holding on to a rope that felt like connective tissue to my community and the people that keep me standing and enable me to walk strong.
> **– Ashley Sparks (Participant, UPRISING #42)**

RECHARGE HEARTS WHILE PROTESTING TORTURE
REVOLUTIONARY PRACTICE #43

The problems we are trying to solve often seem insurmountable. We are devastated to learn of the harms inflicted upon the bodies and psyches of people deemed disposable. The space of witnessing and formulating strategies for activism can be overly rational and cerebral as we try to protect or avoid tender emotions. It is a revolutionary practice to continually invite our hearts to re-engage: to make space for softening in the midst of so much hardness. There is no one task that will open the heart of every person, but offering simple moments of connection and contemplation can be profound. In Mary Oliver's poem 'Lead,' she writes: 'I tell you this / to break your heart, / by which I mean only / that it break open and never close again / to the rest of the world' (Oliver 2005). Remember that the task is not only to open the heart, but to fill it with sweet feelings of solidarity and courage. Toward the end of his life, Wendell Berry's character Jayber Crow recalls that 'there are moments when the heart is generous, and then it knows that for better or for worse our lives are woven together here, one with one another and with the place and all the living things' (2000: 210). Recharge empathy and compassion for all living things.

IN ACTION: UPRISING #43

28 June 2011, 8:00pm | Chicago Torture Justice Memorials Project launch,
Hull House Museum, Chicago
Participants: 100+ activists, concerned citizens, and former prisoners
Photos: Prudence Browne

The goal of the Chicago Torture Justice Memorials Project is to memorialize the Chicago Police torture cases and honor the survivors of torture, their family members, and the (mostly) South Side African American communities affected by specific histories of torture in Chicago. I was invited by Amy Partridge and the committee planning this event to offer a creative ceremony at the launch of the project. They were specifically interested in a group ritual that would unite folks and engage their hearts. Amy Partridge asked for 'a sort of on-the-spot collective memorial to simultaneously make concrete and demystify the process of collective memorialization but also to add the artistic gravitas to a political activist line-up.'

At the end of their launch event, over 100 folks circled the room, and everyone was given a piece of black ribbon. We took a moment in silence to allow the information presented about torture to sink into our hearts, and then blow that feeling into the ribbon. In pairs, we told one other person what our personal world-changing gift is: what we uniquely bring to the struggle. Then, in a gesture of mutual accountability, we tied the ribbons to each other's wrists. We closed with the song 'Woyaya' ('We Are Going'), a song written by the Ghanaian pop group Osibisa that I learned from Elise Witt of Alternate ROOTS.

Leading this song at the Chicago Torture Justice Memorials Project launch was directly influenced by my experience in West Baltimore for ROOTS Fest 2011, where I had performed UPRISING #42. One of my amazing singing teachers is Elise Witt, who makes her home in Pine Lake, Georgia, but tours as a musician and song leader. Elise not only teaches movement songs and directs pop-up community choirs, she also challenges us to learn songs and teach them in our communities. It is a revolutionary skill to take up the challenges of our mentors, so for UPRISING #43, I taught the group a movement song because I believe that singing together energizes our heart spaces. I reflected back to my teacher:

Elise,

Thank you so much for all of the music and instruction you provided for the Alternate ROOTS National Learning Exchange, birthday party, and festival. The choir during the 35th birthday party was so beautiful. I wanted you to know I *heard* your challenge to learn songs and teach them in our communities. This has been a struggle for me, where my Chicago Left community is often so... cerebral? Cynical? Analytical? They have a hard time understanding the importance of something like singing. But I can see that as I keep bringing songs, people are getting used to it, and even getting into it! Anyway on Tuesday/29 right after ROOTS Fest I led a ceremony as part of the launch of a project to memorialize victims of torture by Chicago police. A year ago we had a major conviction of a police chief who tortured men into confessing crimes and also led a whole torture operation. I taught Woyaya and we sang it and it was really nice. Thank goodness I had some other singers in the room too. This photo features the words projected on the screen!

I just want you to know I consider you to be a mentor and I don't take your challenges lightly. I really appreciate you and your work in the world.

Love,
Nicole

Dear Nicole,

Thank you for this beautiful note. I am thrilled to hear how the music gets passed along and has new life in each community where it is re-born.

Hooray for you for having the courage to midwife the birth of singing in your community!!!! Do keep me posted on further developments. This is balm for my soul – to know that the ripples keep extending. I have had such wonderful teachers and mentors too. I hope to sing with you again soon.

Peace with harmony,
oxoxoxoox
Elise

USE YOUR BODY TO REMEMBER MURDERED BODIES
REVOLUTIONARY PRACTICE #44

The New Orleans Radical Faeries introduced me to James Broughton's 'Shaman Psalm.' Broughton was a poet of the San Francisco Radical Faeries, a member of the Sisters of Perpetual Indulgence, and a devotee of divine embodiment:

> Only through the body can
> you clasp the divine
> Only through the body can
> you dance with god
> In every man's hand
> the gift of compassion
> In every man's hand
> the beloved connection
> Trust one another
> or drown (1990: 166)

There is something about working in the physical present that is essential to revolutionary movement building. It is critically important to work face-to-face, on the ground with folks. Work that we call performance is very useful in demonstrating the ways our culture enacts oppression on people's bodies: bodies are raped; shot running across the border; imprisoned and tortured; legislated, displaced, invaded, occupied, and bombed. If we look at the evidence of who can be murdered by police with impunity and whose lives are rewarded with every possible societal advantage, we see that certain bodies are considered more human and more valuable than others. The artist Carolee Schneeman emphasizes the importance of working in the corporeal realm: 'Artists are increasingly going online, but with virtuality there's the loss of materiality, of feeling in your flesh. I would recommend activism instead. We're on the edge of blowing up everything that makes our history go forward. It's time for resistance' (Smith 2016: n.pag.). When we work in our bodies, all kinds of physical sensuality and pleasure can be harnessed as revolutionary forces. Embodiment can concretize the courage of people who put themselves in harm's way in the fight for justice.

IN ACTION: UPRISING #44

21 August 2011, 1:00pm | Hollywood Beach, Chicago
Participants: Uncle Bear, Maggie Barrack, Mary Patten, Barbara Egel, Josh Shores, Joseph Varisco, Sean Doumas, Nicole Garneau, Adam and two others
Photos: Uncle Bear | Video: Joe Varisco

In August of 1964, the bodies of murdered civil rights activists James Chaney, Andrew Goodman, and Michael Schwerner were found, six weeks after their lynching in Mississippi, where they had been participating in the Freedom Summer voter registration drive. There are so many brave comrades that have come before us and who walk alongside us every day. 47 years later, I wandered among the sunbathers at Chicago's Hollywood Beach in my white uniform, stopping occasionally at someone's blanket to ask them if they would like to come over and make body prints to remember fallen revolutionaries. I recruited five more participants on the spot. For UPRISING #44, we created a 'shadow' chain of comrades by making body prints in the sand all along the boardwalk to Lake Michigan. We dedicated this action to someone who gave their life to the struggle, imprinted our bodies on the beach and then rinsed off in the lake.

> My belt left a definitive imprint. I wear that belt a lot (am wearing it now) and think about its imprint in the sand often. I make art of a more permanent sort, and it was really intriguing to be part of a project that was so painstaking to make and so ephemeral. I've since moved to a building right on the beach, and I can see the place we were from my window. There is no trace of us or the intent of the UPRISING left except in memory and a few photos. I think it's the memory part that's most important.
> **– Barbara Egel (Participant, UPRISING #44)**

NAME YOUR GIFTS TO THE WORLD
REVOLUTIONARY PRACTICE #45

There is a sacred 'naming' practice in the Pachakuti Mesa Tradition of don Oscar Miro-Quesada. At the beginning of a ceremony, each person is called upon to say their name and also to identify their 'medicine gift to the world.' This can be a confounding and emotional experience for those of us whose internalized oppression has prevented us from recognizing and believing that we have something of value to offer the planet. Naming our gifts out loud in front of other people requires incredible courage. It also builds systems of community accountability. We each possess a unique medicine that is essential for healing the earth, our communities, and ourselves.

IN ACTION: UPRISING #45
4 September 2011, 12:30pm | Clear Creek Festival, Rockcastle, KY
Participants: Ashley Sparks, Nick Slie, Will MacAdams, Shannon Turner,
Philip Gilbert, Kathy, Andri Kukas, Nicole Garneau, and the artists and audience
of the Clear Creek Festival
Photos: Jeremy Brady

When I first attended the Clear Creek Festival in August 2010 and performed UPRISING #33 there, I was stunned by the exquisite beauty of this piece of land in the foothills of the Appalachian Mountains. I could not believe the sweetness of the music or the warmth of the people. I returned in August 2011 with UPRISING #45 because the whole project of the festival is infused with revolutionary ethics of care for land, water, food, and community in order to build the world in which we want to live. For the closing ceremony of the festival, UPRISING #45 called on audience members and participants to name their unique, world-building talent and then witness others naming their gifts. To mark this action and remind folks of their gifts, we tied sections of white rope to each other's wrists. The rope we used had traveled from UPRISING #42 in Baltimore, where it had been part of an action for community repair.

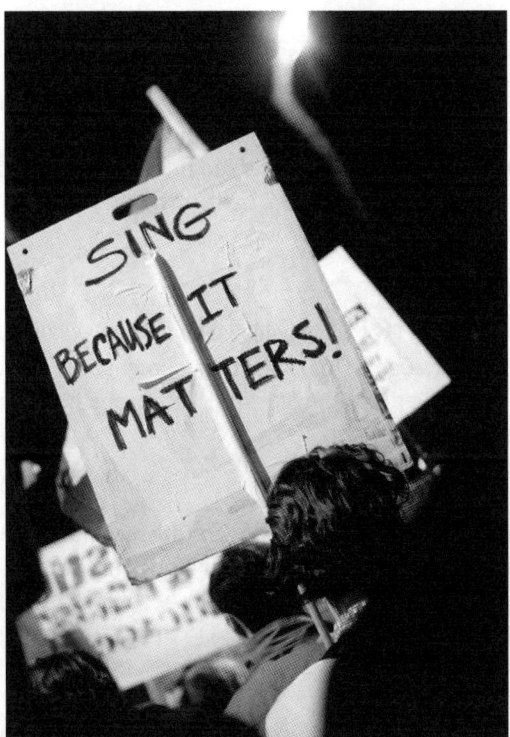

Figure 21: Nicole Garneau carries song lyrics in an Occupy Chicago march for UPRISING #46. Photo by Sarah Jane Rhee.

#46 WHEN A YOUTH-LED, LIBERATORY, ANTI-CAPITALIST REVOLUTIONARY MOVEMENT STARTS, JOIN IMMEDIATELY

REVOLUTIONARY PRACTICE #46

The Occupy movement began in September of 2011 in New York with Occupy Wall Street and within a month, Occupy protests had taken place in 95 cities across 82 countries, including over 600 communities in the United States (Wikipedia 2016c). This was an invigorating moment of action and discourse about social change, spurred by the urgency and seriousness of real-world events. As Bill Talen, a.k.a. Reverend Billy, says in his introduction to *Revolution for the Hell of It,* 'We must ask ourselves, what is the thing that we do that releases Peace? It still remains within us. How does the architecture of power become no longer monumental, how do these deadly official policies lose their skin of ads and show their absurdities? We have an emergency. People are dying as I type. We have to start over now' (Hoffman 2005: xxii).

What are the world-building gestures we can create inside of political demonstrations? Offer opportunities for people to engage in transformative, visionary activities even within the space of the protest. The American left has failed to articulate a coherent and positive vision of the world we are trying to build. We are good at tearing down and critiquing the aspects of our society that we hate. Where is the intellectual, emotional, and creative investment in naming what we are *fighting for*? Invite folks to practice peaceful actions in our bodies and our social relations.

IN ACTION: UPRISING #46

22 October 2011, 11:00pm | Occupy Chicago demonstration in Grant Park, Chicago
Participants: Joseph Varisco, Tom Slazinski, Sarah Jane Rhee, Nicole Garneau, and Occupy Chicago demonstrators
Photos: Sarah Jane Rhee

Due to police interference, the Occupy movement in Chicago was never able to establish an encampment like the one in Zucotti Park in New York and in other cities around the world. Multiple attempts to set up tents for overnight occupation were broken up by the Chicago police. UPRISING #46 took place during an Occupy Chicago march on the evening of 22 October 2011, which was also the second attempt at establishing a more stable encampment.

The arts and culture working group of Occupy Chicago had called on participants to bring more songs to the Occupy demonstrations. UPRISING #46 took up that challenge. One of the cherished understandings of the UPRISING project is that all historic revolutionary movements have had songs. I carried a large easel paper sign in the Occupy march that read, 'Sing Because it Matters,' with lyrics attached for spontaneous song circles during the march and rally afterward. I carried lyrics to songs that are fun to sing, like 'I Will Survive,' and 'We Will Rock You.' As police moved in on the Occupy encampment and loaded 130 people into wagons, we did not even need lyrics. I started singing 'This Little Light of Mine,' and the crowd around me joined right in.

> I remember sitting in a circle just after the rally had started with a group of folks singing songs while holding hands. Most of the people I met there were strangers to me – strangers for a moment until we found ourselves laughing, harmonizing and holding one another's hands. As much as Occupy created a kinship among various folk, this UPRISING experience did something that specifically connected us more deeply.

'Never go to a rally in the winter without liquor,' is one of the best pieces of advice I ever received via Daddy Garneau. It was so cold. We kept getting separated from one another while singing and walking a line after the police showed up to make us leave. When I would catch a familiar face from our earlier singing circle it was such a relief. The panic of being lost and found again and again.
– Joe Varisco (Participant, UPRISING #46)

In this space there was an incredible opportunity for interaction. It was a chance to see whom among those we know hold similar views and values about our society, and that makes for a stronger bond. That same bond made it easier to converse with total strangers too.

The song 'This Little Light of Mine' emphasized the impact an individual is able to have. At the heart of the Occupy movement I felt that value was placed on the individual – how individual spirit is of greater value than a corporation and how individuals have a responsibility to each other to build a functional society.
– Tom Slazinski (Participant, UPRISING #46)

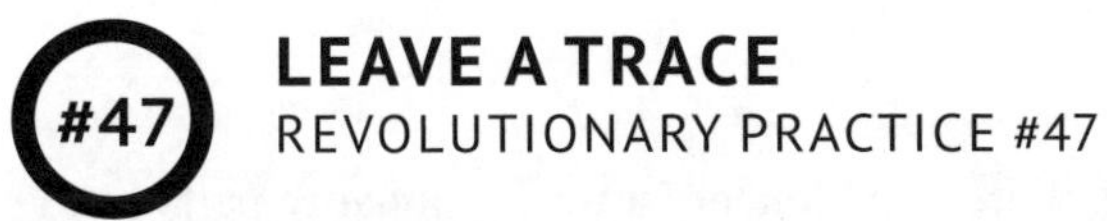

LEAVE A TRACE
REVOLUTIONARY PRACTICE #47

In our cities, every surface seems covered by an advertisement or warning label. In the face of the erasure of our struggles and our stories, rebel against invisibility. Take a page from artist-educator-troublemaker Indi McCasey and remind folks that there was a person on that spot. Let people wonder at the mystery of it. Create things for people to find. Scribble graffiti poems. Leave notes on handmade paper. Leave body tracings or imprints of your belt in the sand. Leave chalk paint flowers on pavement. Leave manifestos painted on the sidewalk in beet juice. Notice the interaction between our bodies and the earth, and the feelings that come up for us in the process of doing it. Leave gentle marks intended to hurt no one.

IN ACTION: UPRISING #47

20 November 2011, 6:30pm | Transgender Day of Remembrance,
Center on Halsted, Chicago
Participants: Demonstrators/readers at Transgender Day of Remembrance event
Photos: Nicole Garneau

Transgender Day of Remembrance, 20 November, began in 1998 to memorialize our transgender friends and allies who lost their lives because of who they were or who they were perceived to be. At the time of this writing, the lives of trans* people are systematically devalued and destroyed around the world. Trans* women of color are especially targeted for violence. Too many of my own beloved trans* siblings take their own lives, unable to survive in a world that will not love their revolutionary brilliance. Returning to this event with UPRISING #47 felt like an important reminder of how much work is to be done. Chicago's 2011 Day of Remembrance included a candlelit vigil at the Center on Halsted, and a reading of the names and causes of death of murdered transgender people around the world. Before the reading began, participants in UPRISING #47 quietly made body tracings in white chalk on the pavement at the entrance to the Center. Those outlines bore silent witness to stories such as that of Paulinha Cesar de Oliveira, age 31, who died in Campos Gerais, Brazil, of multiple stab wounds.

TAP INTO PARTIES AS SITES OF RESISTANCE
REVOLUTIONARY PRACTICE #48

After the 2016 massacre of 49 people gathered for a queer Latinx night dance party at the Pulse nightclub in Orlando, Florida, there was a re-emergence of writing on the importance of queer clubs as sacred spaces: particularly, about the importance of parties explicitly designed to create a safe space for queer/trans* people of color to gather and find healing through community and dancing. As my Northern Lights collaborator Erik Roldan wrote after the Pulse nightclub shooting, 'queer people escape our daily lives under the cover of night to dance beneath a sparkling spotlight. These fleeting hours in a club or at a queer night might be the only time during the week where we are as free as we want to be – as freely as we should be' (2016: n.pag.).

Protect the spaces that are public, accessible, openly queer and anti-racist. Tap into the ancient power of Bacchanalia, ecstatic Roman festivals to Bacchus, God of Wine. Make radical politics explicit. Inject unexpected content into social spaces. Deepen community connections by offering ways to interact around ideas. Help folks find each other in the sexiness of solidarity. Dance and sweat the night away. Roll a taste of freedom around on your tongue.

IN ACTION: UPRISING #48

31 December 2011, 10:30pm | Northern Lights Queer Performance and Dance Party at Parlour on Clark, Chicago
Participants: DJ Erik Roldan, Nicole Garneau, and the Northern Lights party attendees
Photos: Nicole Garneau | Video: Joe Varisco

Chicago taught me everything I know about being an activist. I needed to say that before I left the city, and I wanted to say it in the radical space of the Northern Lights Queer Performance and Dance Party. Chicago's revolutionaries still terrify and thrill me. To say goodbye to the assembled community, I distributed white three-day candles in glasses and asked everyone to look not at me, but at each other. I shared words and song while they tried to stay present with each other. Because, when everything else falls away, there are just our communities and us. Tonight I might want your hands, mouth, body, but for right now I will love your eyes. I will make my eyes available to you and look in yours, and know everything I need to know.

Be the Touch You Want to Feel: Prefiguring Intimacy in a Time of Deformed Social Relations

Daniel Tucker

> [W]e have lost the pleasure of being together. Thirty years of precariousness and competition have destroyed social solidarity. Media virtualization has destroyed empathy among bodies, the pleasure of touching each other, and the pleasure of living in urban spaces. We have lost the pleasure of love, because too much time is devoted to work and virtual exchange. (Berardi and Lovink 2011: n.pag.)

Grappling with the technical aspects of the capitalist economic order, people seem, inevitably, to find their way to describing social relations in an attempt to map their analysis onto lived experience. There is a lot of talk about the fragmentation of social life and our bubbles and sorting. Whether 'bowling alone' or competing with others, it is undeniable that economics impact our relationships beyond simple workplace dynamics.

On three separate occasions between 2008 and 2011, I touched a stranger. I do not remember their names or the color of their clothing or the texture of their skin. But I did feel their warmth and their vulnerability as they let me put my hands on them. Each occasion was different and unique – each time invoked a temporary unity amidst the splintered disunity of modern social life through one of Nicole Garneau's UPRISING performances.

At Garneau's UPRISING #12, I held one person's right hand and another person's left hand while a circle of people (attendees of a local non-profit organization's gathering) formed with everyone holding hands, facing inward. We sang so-called revolutionary and personally relevant songs with/for others. Lots of classic labor, socialist, civil rights, and counterculture songs were shared, with a clear generational divide expressing itself through who had committed which lyrics to heart. Disrupting others' expectations, Garneau successfully encouraged a third of the 80 people in the circle to step out of their comfort zones and sing alone. After the singing, there was a palpable sense that the UPRISING had changed our expectations of what this kind of event could be. Within the wider cultural context in which 'events' are overproduced, the disruptive act of togetherness cut through the indistinguishable haze of receptions, lectures, and parties. Singing made a mark.

Nine months later, I was in attendance at a party to support a local prison policy reform initiative, and there was Nicole, again conjuring a profound social encounter into being as UPRISING #21. UPRISING was set once more within an already meaningful situation, but with an added layer of intentionality and dramatic flare that seem to come about uniquely from an outsider rather than the event organizers. From the balcony of the large room, Nicole donned her iconic white outfit and gave directions to a room of the incarcerated men's families, policy-makers, and activists. She told us we were to put our hands on the shoulders of the person in front of us and share a word of encouragement. I did the act, as someone else did from behind me, and a thrill of collectivity ran through me (and I suspect through others, given the smiles and glowing faces all around in the immediate aftermath).

Finally, at UPRISING #43, nearly two years after my previous meeting with Nicole, I heard her shouting out a new proposal, an opportunity for a gathering to participate in some unfamiliar forms of interaction. This time we met at the launch event for an ambitious effort to publicly recognize and memorialize the torture of Chicago residents by a former police commander and his officers (their systemic, criminal cruelty took place from 1972–91). A diverse constellation of people hailing from distinct communities and subcultures found themselves together under the auspices of an event that could only be deemed successful if it reached beyond the communities of interest and geography that often segregate our lives and work. Garneau offered an invitation to have a social exchange with a stranger in this particular circumstance. She asked us to find someone we did not know, to tell them about our plans to change the world, and to tie a ribbon around their arm to remember the encounter.

A few questions emerge from describing my experiences in UPRISING: Besides touching strangers, what do these events have in common? What is the significance of having this series of special feelings? What is the relationship between intimate contact and the kind of revolutionary politics that Garneau references in the framing of her work?

Each environment in which I participated in UPRISING was charged with the convergence of many people's energies toward a common goal. There is a kind of opportunism in the way the artist chose to site her work in the previously scheduled meetings and special gatherings of these groups. It represents a simultaneous celebration of the work of others, and a conscious recognition that the production of yet another separate event will stretch our networks and communities further. The necessity of collaboration is deeply important to Garneau and indicates a commitment to weaving the art experience into other meaningful life experiences. Embedding the work in different social projects pushes the form into contact with content.

The conclusion of numerous psychological studies released since the 1986 publication of Ashley Montagu's hugely popular *Touching: The Human Significance of Skin* is that touching other humans literally keeps us sane and alive. The relevance of this kind of bodily stimulation for artistic and political practices can be seen if the personal and private question of an individual surviving, much less feeling good, is re-formulated as a social problem requiring a social solution. The socialization of concerns typically residing on an intimate scale is fundamental to the concept of a political left.

As Ivan Illich notes, 'The transition to socialism cannot be effected without an inversion of our present institutions and the substitution of convivial for industrial tools' (1973: 12). Illich's choice of the term 'conviviality' proposes a distinctly nonindustrial form of exchange and interdependence. And while it has potential relevance for politics in the sense Hannah Arendt defines, 'Politics deals with the coexistence and association of different men,' it is also about the larger project of being human (2005: 93). The political philosopher Anthony Bogues continues with this lens on the political when he says, 'The creativity of human freedom is about constructing forms of human association (common association) [...] The work of the radical imagination [is] to imagine anew what human life could be like' (2012: 45). This treatment of the political as a human evolutionary project can be seen nowhere better than in the work of Grace Lee and Jimmy Boggs in Detroit.

In her 2008 introduction to the reprinting of the 1974 book, *Revolution and Evolution in the 20th Century*, Grace Lee Boggs writes:

> Thus the American revolution at this stage in our history, and in the evolution of technology and of the human race, is not about jobs or universal health insurance or fighting inequality or making it possible for more people to realize the American Dream of upward mobility. It is about creating a new American Dream whose goal is a higher humanity instead of the higher standard of living that is dependent upon empire. It is about acknowledging that we Americans have enjoyed upward mobility and middle class comforts and conveniences at the expense of other peoples all over the world. It is about living the kind of lives that will end the galloping inequality both inside this country and between the global North and South, and also slow down global warming. About practicing a new, more active, global and participatory concept of citizenship. About becoming the change we want to see in the world. (2008: xxxi)

Boggs' invocation of the Ghandian prefigurative ethos, 'be the change you want to see' is central to an understanding of the performance work of Nicole Garneau.

Two months into her UPRISING project, I invited Nicole to be part of a round-table interview called Town Hall Talks. The series was co-organized with Nato Thompson from Creative Time and was focused on documenting the work of 100 socially engaged artists from five cities in their own words. One of Nicole's responses in the interview has stuck with me over the years:

> At the risk of stating the obvious, I'm trying to practice getting over my fear of being corny. I just wanted to put out there that what I'm really going for is a whole world in which justice prevails. We have love and respect for humanity and we live in harmony with the earth. If democracy is a means to that end, then by all means let's go for it. Otherwise, we don't need it. I really think of myself as participating in world transformation in a different way, through energy. I'm working the energy. I'm working the energy of my body. I'm working the energy of this room. I'm working the energy of the earth. I'm trying to let the earth work through me. I'm going all the way there. I'm just straight up going all the way there. I'm calling on my ancestors. I'm calling on my guides. All of your ancestors, all of your guides (LAUGHTER). The guides of whoever is in the room. I'm asking for everybody's help. I'm inviting all the spirits to check right in to the work and help us transform this whole earth. It's a spiritual choice and a spiritual practice, but it is not separated from me, from what I'm doing out when I'm doing these things in public. Because it's creating neural pathways. Practicing being in public space. Practicing being out on the street. Practicing engaging with people in a loving and respectful way. People who you don't know. People who are different from you. Just going ahead and practicing that and getting good at it. Because it's a skill that we can learn and that we can get good at. I think it's a revolutionary skill. (Garneau in Thompson and Tucker 2008: 164–65)

Where are we supposed to find that engaging contact? Some lucky people achieve it in their romantic lives, but what about the public touch and socialization of human physical stimulation? No other artist better embodies this spirit than Mierle Laderman Ukeles, who theorized and performed the daily reproductive (childcare and cleaning) work required to upkeep a home, a cultural institution, and a city in her five-decade career exploring 'Maintenance Art.' Not unlike Garneau's significant coordination across years of activity for UPRISING, Ukeles' seminal work *Touch Sanitation Performance* (lasting from 24 July 1979 to 26 June 1980) required the artist to manage, in her words, 'daunting administrative tasks that came with this year-long endeavor, including writing daily telexes, coordinating the work of ten photographers' and other responsibilities in order to complete the work: shaking the hands of 8,500 New York City sanitation workers while saying 'Thank you for keeping New York City alive.' The artist had to create an elaborate schedule with multiple shifts to realize the work within the set time frame. In her fascinating and entertaining epic catalogue essay surveying Ukeles' work, author Patricia Phillips quotes the artist: 'I felt I had absorbed eighty-five hundred volts of electricity through my right hand from shaking that many hands, and the energy was residing inside of me. I needed to pass it along. I needed to send the energy back out to the people because it was always for them.' As Phillips elaborates,

> If the repeating handshake was the nucleus and catalyst, there were many other coexisting, often fortuitous or improvisational, spheres of interactivity [...] Ukeles frequently asked children about their neighborhood and encouraged them to wave at the sanitation workers and thank them for their important service. With Touch Sanitation Performance Ukeles provided a vital and animating transfusion of attention and compassion to an immense organization in critical condition due to fiscal crisis and a degraded culture of work and morale. (2016: 97–99)

Another artist operating in a similar vein from a different continent was the Brazilian Lygia Clark (1920–88). Clark produced a series of *Objetos Sensoriais,* which required the audience to come into deep and intimate contact with another audience or participant. One such work, *Dialogue of Goggles* (1968), required two participants to put on eye pieces that forced each to look into the eyes of the other. A contemporary of Ukeles, Clark was invested in the relationship between art and therapy, which eventually led to a near-abandonment of her individual art practice, and she worked collaboratively to develop 'Cuerpo Colectivo (Collective Body), a collective therapeutic experience through artistic means' (Hoffman and Jonas 2005: 111). In letters exchanged with artist Hélio Oiticica, Clark wrote that 'The Object for me has lost its significance, and if I still use it, it is so that it becomes a mediator for participation.' In a later reply, Oiticica shared some of his writings on her work in which he described her cell-inspired practice: 'From person to person, this is an improvised corporal dialogue that can expand into a total chain creating something of an all-encompassing biological entity [...] The idea of creating such relations goes beyond that of a facile participation, such as in the manipulation of objects: there is the search for what could be described as a biological ritual [...] an interpersonal practice that leads towards a truly open communication: a me-you relation, rapid, brief as the actual act' (Clark and Oiticica 2006: 110–15).

Ukeles and Clark provide prehistories to Garneau's engagement with the intimate touch as something with social and political consequences. I don't know that I can convincingly argue that touch and intimate-scale relationships are a serious political gesture. But I do see a link relating that which we are deprived of in our current life and that which I believe we will find integral to our future life. As the anti-establishment sentiments of the 2016 US Presidential election suggest, there is a general disenchantment with government and bureaucracy. The localist impulse in economics and ecology may suggest a desire for more intimate control over one's life. I have cited examples above of artists and thinkers willing to make an explicit connection between touch, love, human association, and the political. These exist in contrast with rigid and technocratic conceptions of politics, such as German philosopher Carl Schmitt's formulation of politics as essentially being about the Friend/Enemy dichotomy (Schmitt 2007). These examples concede that there is a cultural dimension to the political that happens when people get together – echoing Arendt's and Bogues' emphasis on 'association' referenced above. Against the backdrop of debates about what defines politics and being human, in dialogue with precedents from art history, and in the midst of social movements organized around torture, prison, and numerous other sensorial, intense, and depriving ways that humans treat one another, Nicole Garneau's UPRISING thrusts participants into intimate physical communication. On three separate occasions between 2008 and 2011, I touched a stranger. What it accomplished, I do not know. If they were uncomfortable, I do not know. But from my vantage point, on the intimate scale of my body, I felt a form of connection to other people that fed me. It made me aware of how little contact with others I had and how much more I would need to have if I was ever going to be serious about the political challenge of transforming the deformed social relations of the present into something better and more human.

SERVE HOT TEA TO COLD STRANGERS
REVOLUTIONARY PRACTICE #49

Make hospitality a revolutionary act. Generously feed and nourish others. Counteract the disposable cup culture. Hearken back to Soviet-era vending machines serving soda, *kvass*, or sparkling water out of one small, communal glass that got filled, used, and left behind. Experiment in offering something. Make a stone soup in a giant cauldron; fry corn cakes over an open fire; season pots of beans with honey and apple cider vinegar. Be happy when someone accepts, and do not take it personally when someone refuses because they suspect you are selling them Jesus, and they're not buying.

IN ACTION: UPRISING #49
30 January 2012, 3:00pm | Hans Knudsens Plads, Copenhagen, Denmark
Participants: Marge Whiteford, Laura Georgescu, Joss Allen, Melissa Turner, Marion Preez, Dragoș Ivaneț, Marina Mussapi, Anna Kautenburger, Isabella Martin, Nicole Garneau, and Michael Vienne
Photos: Bailey Ferguson | Video: David Granskog

In January 2012, I joined eleven other artists and architects in Copenhagen, Denmark, to work on creative solutions to urban problems as part of the 'Living Copenhagen' artist residency. UPRISING #49 was our first attempt to meet the people of the community. We worked in a plaza that a Danish urban planner described as 'the single ugliest urban space in all of Copenhagen.' So we made a big batch of hot tea, brought it outside in soup pots, and poured it into white ceramic mugs. We offered hot tea to Copenhagen residents coming home from work, changing buses, and stopping their bikes for the traffic light. We tried to have conversations over tea. We discovered that this kind of public interaction with strangers is very unusual to native Danes, but a lot of folks who told us they came from somewhere else were more than willing to talk and drink tea from our mugs.

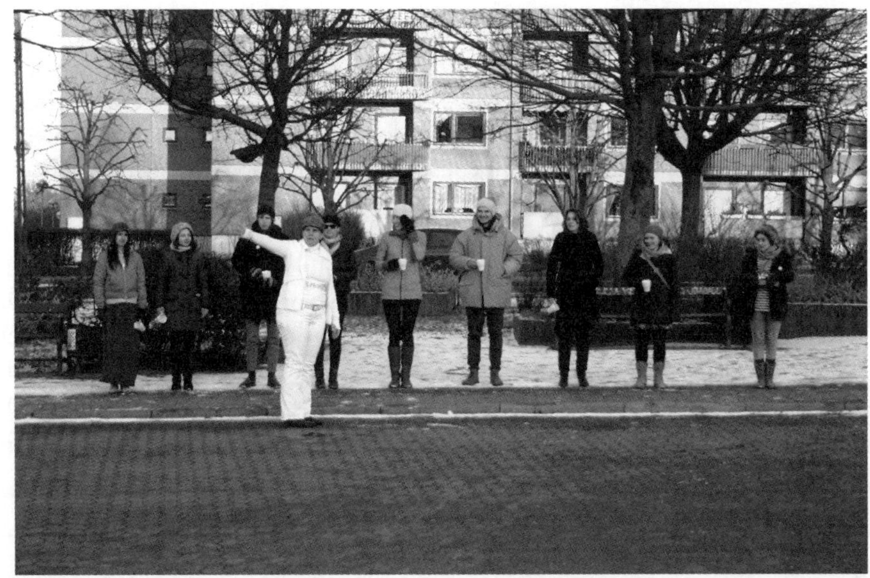

Figure 22: Serving hot tea to cold strangers in Copenhagen for UPRISING #49. Photo by Bailey Ferguson.

#50 RECALL MOMENTS WHEN YOU BELIEVED THE WORLD MIGHT ACTUALLY CHANGE FOR THE BETTER

REVOLUTIONARY PRACTICE #50

Have you had such a moment? When was it? Was it in the middle of a protest or demonstration? Have you been carried away by the ecstasy of feeling that what was happening was actually good for the world? Have you ever thought: 'This injustice cannot possibly continue. This is when we win!' Did you win? Were you crushed by defeat? When you are honest with yourself, are you surprised by how complicated your feelings were? Have you ever had a glimpse at your deeply loving commitment to the systems that oppress you?

IN ACTION: UPRISING #50

25 February 2012, midnight | (in)Xclusion 24-hour Live Art Occupation, Leeds, UK
Participants: Nicole Garneau and festival attendees
Photos: Kara Lloyd

The Occupy movement continued into 2012. While I was in the midst of the Living Copenhagen artist residency, I answered a call for performers to participate in an event initiated as a direct response to the Occupy movement. The organizers of the 24-hour (in)Xclusion Live Art Occupation described it as 'an occupation of solidarity [...] artists and audience alike share space for 24 hours and explore the principles of unconditional love, generosity and hope for a better future' (Live Art Leeds 2012). The 24-hour Occupation of Live Art took place at Patrick Studios in Leeds, UK, and featured work from over 40 artists.

For a few hours around midnight of (in)Xclusion, UPRISING #50 engaged participants in questioning the possibility of actual world transformation. I shredded beets into my lap while explaining that during an Occupy Chicago demonstration, I entertained the real possibility of the demise of capitalism. I confessed that a feeling of sheer terror immediately followed that thought. Our complicity in oppressive systems is painfully real. I asked others for stories of the moments when they thought the world might actually change, and then fed them shredded beets from my lap. We finished by learning and practicing the song 'Bread and Roses', the lyrics to which were written on a sheet on the floor, which became increasingly stained with beet juice and flesh as the night went on.

OFFER FEATHERS AND POEMS TO THE WIND
REVOLUTIONARY PRACTICE #51

Wind is the element of air, often associated with wisdom, spirits, and ancestral guidance. Tall buildings offer us views that help us see the largeness of the world, and the smallness of ourselves. Sometimes our precious loves join the ancestors after attempting flight. The air also receives our gifts of poems. Feel the pull of a wind so strong that all you have to do is loosen your grip on a feather and it is snatched from your hand.

IN ACTION: UPRISING #51

31 March 2012, 3:00pm | Kollektivhuset Rooftop, Copenhagen, Denmark
Participants: Leanne, Marge Whiteford, Anna Kautenburger, Laura Georgescu, Marion Preez, Angus, Joss Allen, David Granskog, Nicole Garneau, and Bailey Ferguson
Photos: Bailey Ferguson | Video: David Granskog

'Poetry isn't a revolution, but a way of knowing why it must come' (Rich 2016: 685). The death of the American poet Adrienne Rich was a moment to share her revolutionary words with collaborators in Copenhagen. Through tears, Marge Whiteford read aloud 'Diving into the Wreck,' which was personally meaningful to her:

> We are, I am, you are
> by cowardice or courage

the one who find our way
back to this scene
carrying a knife, a camera
a book of myths
in which
our names do not appear.
(Rich 2016: 370)

The eleventh floor of Kollektivhuset, the Copenhagen building where twelve of us were living communally, was once the home (and perhaps final resting place) of people who needed iron lungs. The 11th floor also had an open-air patio, probably to provide fresh air to the terminally ill patients who lived up there. Folks in the neighborhood told us that a number of people had killed themselves by jumping from our deck, which was the tallest building in the area. After scaffolding was erected for ongoing remodeling projects, our building also became a semi-famous urban playground for adventurous climbers. When they made it up to our floor, we invited them in for tea and a warm-up. On the day of UPRISING #51, we offered poems and white feathers from the rooftop. That day, all we had to do was blow our prayers into the feathers and then release our fingers – gusts carried our feathers immediately, swirling over Copenhagen below.

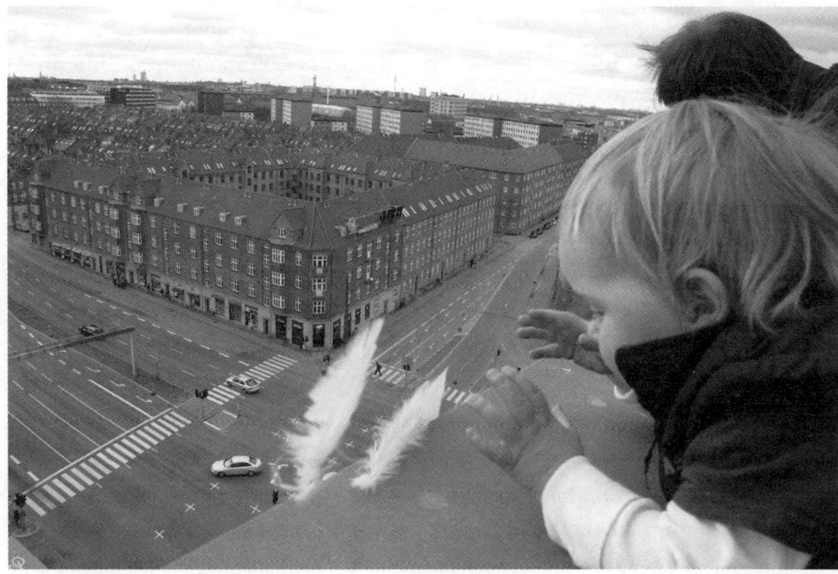

Figure 23: Angus releases feathers from the rooftop of Kollektivhuset for UPRISING #51. Photo by Bailey Ferguson.

SPEAK ALOUD THE PLACES WHERE OUR CLOTHES WERE MADE
REVOLUTIONARY PRACTICE #52

Part of marking important revolutionary moments in the garment industry is connecting that history to present-day labor struggles. As a strategy for generating dialogue and content around the issue of garment worker exploitation, ask people where their clothes were made. This requires them to read their clothing labels or those of their neighbors. The gesture of checking clothing labels makes participation simple and accessible because in public, everyone is wearing clothes, and everyone is wearing something with a label that says where it was made. A person can do it without leaving their seat, and it makes space for the easy social interaction of helping others read their tags. Sometimes people start out defensively, because they think they are going to be judged for how they shop or accused of supporting sweatshop labor. But in this transaction, it does not matter whether the shirt was purchased new or second-hand; that garment was made by someone somewhere, and we are curious about who and where.

Gather this information into one long list and have someone read the list aloud. The list of countries sounds like a poem. It makes those workers just a little bit present in the room. Naming the places our clothes are made does not organize workers or accomplish labor reform. But it might serve to remind us of the human hands that have touched our bodies: from Sri Lanka, Mauritania, or the Dominican Republic. Maybe our shirt was made in Bangladesh, the country that pays the lowest wages among the top five exporters of garments to the United States (*New York Times* 2012), where garment workers have been openly rebelling, and where the collapse of an eight-story commercial building in April 2013 killed more than 1000 workers in what is considered the deadliest garment-factory accident in history (Yardley 2013).

IN ACTION: UPRISING #52
21 April 2012, 9:00pm | Live Art Salon of Ellen and Henrik Vestergaard, Copenhagen, Denmark
Participants: Nicole Garneau, Ellen Vestergaard, Henrik Vestergaard, and attendees of Live Art Salon
Photos: Solveig Thimm

Ellen and Henrik Vestergaard support, document, and analyze the live art scene in Copenhagen through their *Samtalekøkken* series of curated performances. UPRISING #52 took place at a Salon in their home. We checked our tags to find out where our

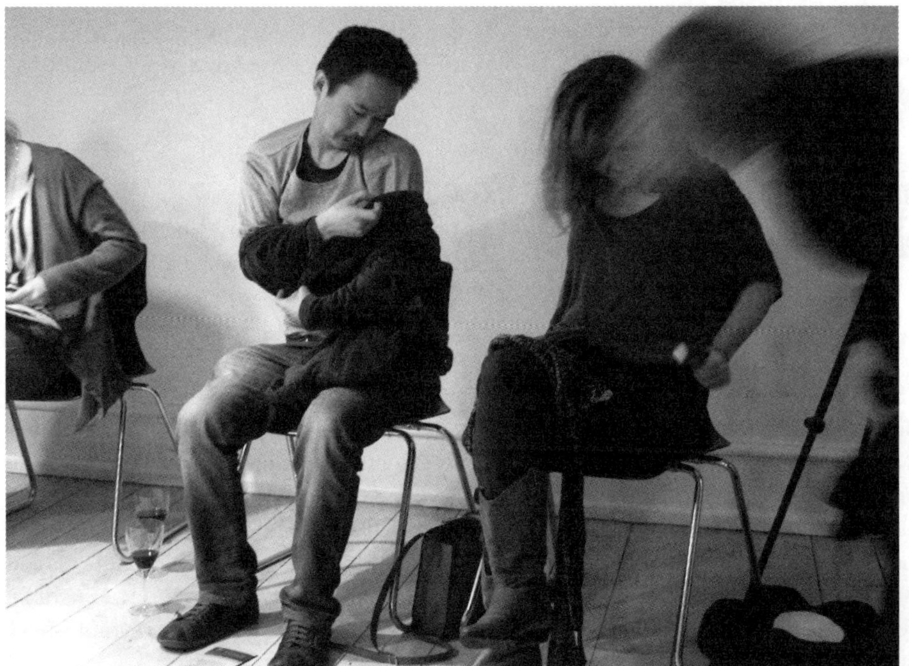

clothes were made while discussing the 100-year anniversary of the Lawrence Textile Workers Strike, also known as the 'Bread and Roses Strike.' Everyone was given a slice of beet to hold in the Vestergaard's immaculate white living room. There was something appropriately Scandinavian about the small, subtle beet stains appearing on the fingertips of participants as we all sang together: 'No more the drudge and idler / Ten that toil while one reposes / But a sharing of life's glories / Bread and Roses, Bread and Roses' (Oppenheim [1912] 1964: 195–96).

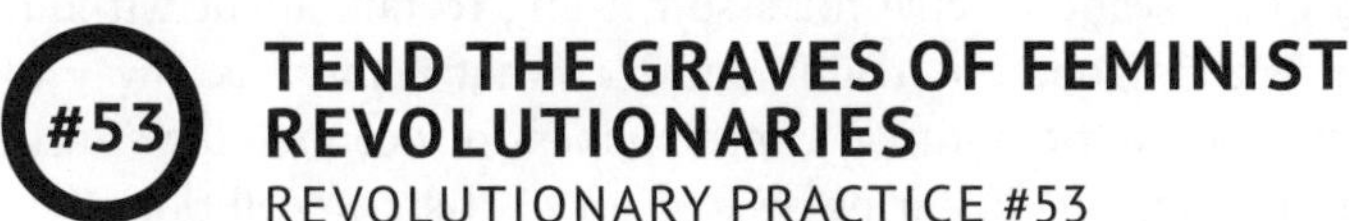

(#53) TEND THE GRAVES OF FEMINIST REVOLUTIONARIES
REVOLUTIONARY PRACTICE #53

Taking care of gravesites is sacred work, and visiting them is a form of paying respects to the people whose remains are buried there. It feels especially important if the gravesite has been neglected. Cemeteries usually have a map of gravesites. Use it to locate the gravestone of the feminist revolutionary. Sweep the dead leaves away. Pick up fallen flower arrangements and banners. Make new offerings. Leave fresh flowers. Give thanks for her work.

IN ACTION: UPRISING #53

22 May 2012, 1:00pm | Novodevichy Cemetery and Convent, Moscow, Russia
Participants: Karina Dimont, Irina Sushina, Valeryi Romanovich Beliakovich, and Nicole Garneau
Photos: Nicole Garneau

UPRISING #53 finished at the grave of Russian Communist revolutionary Alexandra Kollontai (1872–1952), but it took place over seven days with friends in Moscow during heated discussions of her philosophy regarding the place of women, and her notion of 'free love,' which Tina Braun describes as Kollontai's interest in love and sexual relations liberated from bourgeois possessiveness (1998). I asked my friends what Kollontai's work means in their contemporary Russian lives and relationships. These conversations led to a visit to Kollontai's grave in the Novodevichy Cemetery with my friend Ira Sushina, where I cleaned up and made offerings of gratitude for someone I consider a revolutionary feminist heroine.

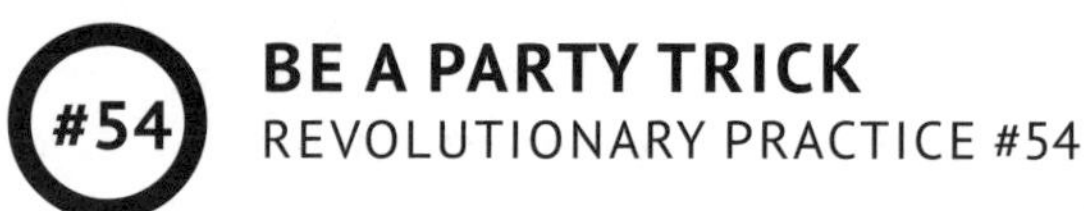

BE A PARTY TRICK
REVOLUTIONARY PRACTICE #54

Speaking as a self-defined party technologist, I have attended some soirées that could have benefitted from revolutionary performance art. How can we ensure that groups of adults who do not know each other very well can enjoy social space together? I knew some young actors who had a small business hiring themselves out to parties of rich people and causing enough of a scene to give folks something to talk about without destroying the entire vibe. That is good entertainment, but what if there is a way to invite folks into a moment of authentic political consciousness or deep feeling? Party throwers: make your gathering legendary by hiring performance artists. Revolutionaries: understand that parties, too, are spaces of transformational possibility. Dare to be the force that disrupts the social order, all while maintaining a commitment to the heart of the work.

IN ACTION: UPRISING #54

16 June 2012, 9:00pm | Home of Theis Molin, Copenhagen, Denmark
Participants: Nicole Garneau, Theis Molin, and Lars Mørch
Photos: Jørn Eichhorn

Revolutionary practices can also be party tricks. UPRISING #54 was a present for Danish filmmaker Theis Molin, commissioned for him by the artist Maria Bruun Eichhorn. At his birthday party, the crowd of sophisticated Danes rolled their eyes as I moved through the space, quietly gathering a list of the countries where everyone's clothing was made. When it was time to surprise Molin with his performance art present, I gathered a volunteer to read aloud the list of country names, explained the 1912 Lawrence Textile Workers Strike, gave Theis Molin a jar of beet juice, laid down on a tarp on his balcony, and told him to show no mercy. Lars Mørch read aloud the list of places where people made our clothes. While I struggled to sing 'Bread and Roses,' Theis stood over me pouring beet juice in my mouth.

Afterward, the hosts let me use their shower, and I re-joined the party. Now that folks had seen the entire action, they were done rolling their eyes. Theis' girlfriend made a special effort to clean up a few stray drops of beet juice that had gone over the ledge of the balcony onto the white leather of the boat floating in the canal below. Theis told me he felt his task was cruel, and it moved him to tears.

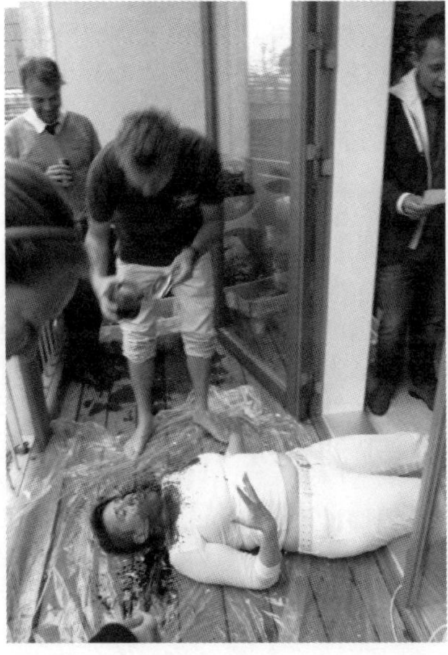

Figure 25: Theis Molin pours beet juice into Nicole Garneau's mouth for UPRISING #54. Photo by Jørn Eichhorn.

FIND A SHADED SPOT AND LISTEN TO STORIES OF ECONOMIC CRISIS

REVOLUTIONARY PRACTICE #55

Occupying a shady patch of carpet nailed into the ground under some trees might be the single most important enticement to participation in a public demonstration of revolutionary practices during the afternoon heat of a Portugal desert. Consider the ways in which comfortable accommodations and weather conditions provide incentives to participate. Discover that asking questions about financial meltdown leads to answers that are intensely personal.

IN ACTION: UPRISING #55

27 July 2012–1 August 2012, daily in the late afternoon | Boom Festival, Idanha-a-Nova, Portugal
Participants: 53 festivalgoers from twelve different countries
Photos: Liv Adda and Archie | Video by: Massi

In the spring and summer of 2012, the Portuguese economic crisis was all over the news. As an American performer in Europe, I wanted to structure the UPRISING at the Boom Festival in Portugal as a way to learn more about European financial crises. Every afternoon of Boom, I sat in a shady spot in front of a banner that read, 'Tell me a story about economic crisis.' Folks came by and did some level of investigation before they decided to sit down. I explained that in this project, I was trying to learn something about their experiences. Then I chose a word from their story and painted it with milk on a small flag of white fabric.

I spent the festival embroidering those words on top of the dried milk while I listened to more stories. The flags were displayed near the banner, accumulating as the week went on. The last day of the festival, I strung all of the embroidered word-flags together and made a performance of reading all the words, and naming the people and the twelve countries from which they came. A lovely group of students from the University of Leeds documented and rinsed the milky flags in the lake, sending the words into the water. I laid the wet flags on a tarp on the beach and offered them as gifts to anyone walking by.

The people who sat down on the blanket and told me stories about economic crisis were: Bizjak, Khashayar, Hugo, Maria, Marta, Matt, Ina, Dan, Ali, Yasha, Light, Han, Samuel, Dan, Jordan, Amali, Sharon, Valeryi, Loren, Ines, Pierre, Sophie, Fabio, Josh, Maia, Hugo, Omi, Toni, Kutner, Tim, and Nicolas. They were from: Slovenia, Iran, Sweden, France, Portugal, United Kingdom, Germany, the Netherlands, Israel, United States, Brazil, Russia, Belgium,

Turkey, Mexico, and Austria. The words from their stories that were painted in milk and embroidered: Labor, Water, Leaders, Love, Art, Family, Illusion, Bankers, Trust, Skew, Independent, Humility, Tumor, Let Go, Waterfall, Mountain, Friends, Freemasons, Milk, Challenge, Gold, Lucky, Heart, Shanty, Rage, Values, and Catalyze.

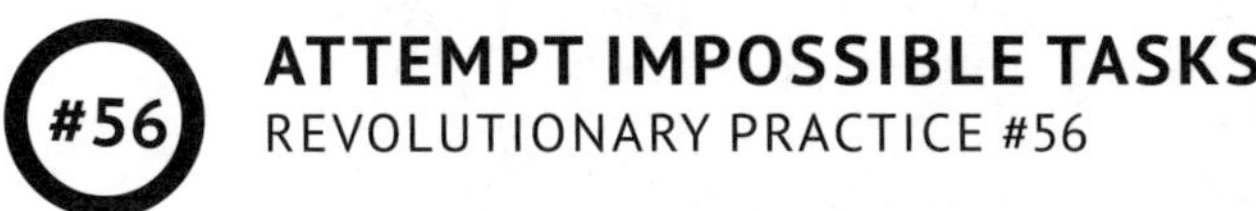

ATTEMPT IMPOSSIBLE TASKS
REVOLUTIONARY PRACTICE #56

What happens to an audience witnessing a performer straining against impossible odds? Your expressions of fierceness are a gift, especially when they are presented live and unmitigated by scripts and video editors. Let the effort be part of the experience. Refuse to make it look easy just so that viewers will be more comfortable. Who knows what might be stirred in the emotional center of someone who sees us push against the edges of our own tolerance for hardship?

Earnestly try to accomplish something, even if it is not possible. Should someone worry about your physical safety, allow yourself to feel the contradictions between that concern for the integrity of your (racialized, gendered, loved) body as contrasted with the rampant lack of concern for other (racialized, gendered, loved) bodies, whose murders are captured on video phones. Notice that feeling. Consider the possibility that your visible labor might inspire others. Do not be deterred by the seeming insurmountability of the task. No one said revolution was going to be easy or painless. My friend Kim Crutcher once told me that we who are doing the really big work are going to have to take some hits. Embody that audacious metaphor for revolutionary change: The Beautiful Struggle. Let them see you sweat.

IN ACTION: UPRISING #56
18 August 2012, 2:00pm | Beacon Festival, Skipton, UK
Participants: Adam Young, Joanne Stafford, Becki Griffiths, Nicole Garneau, and festivalgoers
Photos: Joanne Stafford

The Beacon Festival in Yorkshire, UK, is primarily an outdoor music festival where Brits camp and carouse for the weekend, but I managed to sneak in an UPRISING performance, thanks to my friends from Indivisible performance ensemble in Leeds. On the afternoon of 18 August, the rain stopped for a couple of hours and from my spot at the performance shed, I asked festivalgoers where their clothes were made. I reminded them of the struggles of women textile laborers in the Yorkshire region and drew connections between local

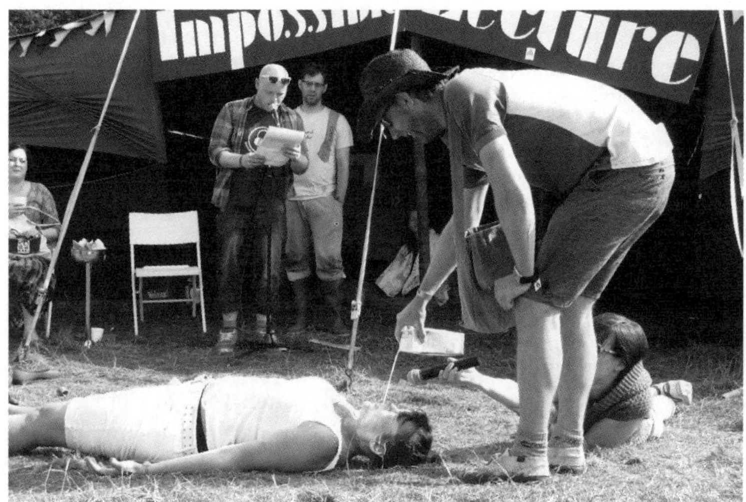

Figure 26: Pouring milk into Nicole Garneau's mouth for UPRISING #56. Photo by Joanne Stafford.

activism and the 1912 Lawrence Textile Workers Strike. I recruited one volunteer, Adam Young, to read aloud the list of the places where our clothes were made, and another volunteer to stand over me and pour milk into my mouth while I lay in the grass trying to sing 'Bread and Roses.' Nearby, Indivisible friends had set up the 'Impossible Lecture' tent, where they were drawing performance tasks from a bucket and creating a 72-hour endurance work. I wrote out instructions for UPRISING #56 and left them a carton of shelf-stable milk. The performance was repeated without me in the wee hours of the morning.

SHARE LIFE'S GLORIES: BREAD AND ROSES
REVOLUTIONARY PRACTICE #57

The poem 'Bread and Roses' (Oppenheim [1912] 2004) is a quintessential praxis text. It speaks to the absolute necessity for art and culture in human lives. It celebrates the idea that demanding beauty is something folks 'go marching' for. Far from being something extra that we layer on if we are economically privileged, art and culture are fundamental needs that we all possess, and all deserve. Revolutionary art projects feed urgent longings in the world!

> Our lives shall not be sweated
> From birth until life closes;

Hearts starve as well as bodies:
Give us bread, but give us roses!

As we go marching, marching,
Unnumbered women dead
Go crying through our singing,
Their ancient cry for bread.
Small art and love and beauty
Their drudging spirits knew.
Yes, it is bread we fight for,
But we fight for roses too! (Oppenheim [1912] 2004)

IN ACTION: UPRISING #57

2 September 2012, 11:00am | Clear Creek Festival, Rockcastle, KY
Participants: Nicole Garneau, Kathie deNobriga, Philip Gilbert, Susanna Lein,
Nick Slie, Bob Martin, Carrie Brunk, and attendees of the Clear Creek Festival
Photos: Shannon Turner

I landed softly back in the United States via the foothills of the Appalachian Mountains.
The 2012 UPRISING tour continued at the Clear Creek Festival, where attendees gather
for music, community, healing, and transformation. Participants used the task of checking
each other's clothing tags as an excuse for embrace and connection as we built a list of
the countries where people sewed our clothes. By total coincidence, Jack Herranen and
Chelsea Elizabeth had already installed a public altar on the festival grounds to honor
labor movement leaders, songwriters, and singers. I told stories of the Lawrence Textile
Workers Strike, sang 'Bread and Roses,' and enjoyed Sunday morning hugs.

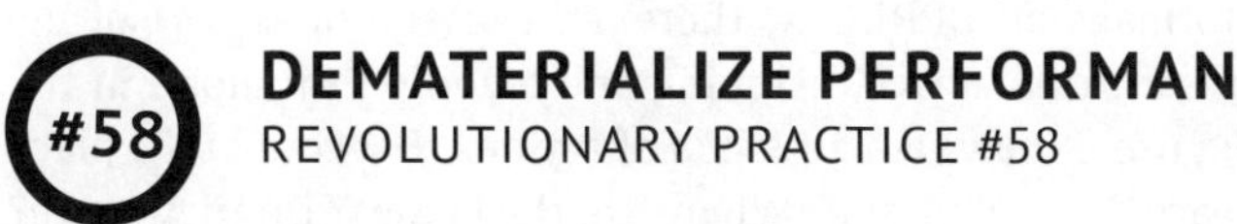

DEMATERIALIZE PERFORMANCE
REVOLUTIONARY PRACTICE #58

Making objects is wonderful, but unless you are an artist with a large studio in which to store/
archive these objects, they are a burden to manage. It also begs the question: does the earth
need more stuff? Including art stuff? Lucy Lippard points out that this resistance to being
encumbered by art objects has been around since the mid-60s. She says, 'at that time such
"looking around" was the product of a rejection of art as precious objects, as more stuff filling

up the world. The idea was to look at what was already in the world and transform it into art by the process of seeing – naming and pointing out – rather than producing' (1996: 126).

Cultural work that takes place live can be light and portable. When it is time to move on, it should not end up in a landfill. Work with the real tension between creating material artifacts and ephemerality. Materials are helpful for facilitating interactions with audiences, but think ahead about what will be left over: it might feel like excess baggage. Keep it light.

IN ACTION: UPRISING #58

28 October 2012, 7:00am | Pine Mountain Settlement School, Harlan County, KY
Participants: Nicole Garneau, Gerald Stropnicky, Bob Martin, and attendees at
NET Microfest Appalachia
Photos: Nicole Garneau

Pine Mountain Settlement School was founded in 1913 as a school for children in the mountains of Appalachia in Harlan County, Kentucky. The notion that the children of coal miners deserved an education was a radical idea 100 years ago. We stayed there during the Network of Ensemble Theater's Microfest in Appalachia.

My friend Bob Martin told me that when he and his partner Carrie Brunk were looking for a beautiful mountainous spot in Kentucky for their commitment ceremony, they had visited the chapel at the Pine Mountain Settlement School and heard an amazing story. When the rolling, forested land that provides the lovely view from the Pine Mountain chapel was threatened with strip-mining, a legal battle ensued. The mining company was legally prevented from mining that land on the basis that it would destroy the view from the chapel. Since the view was so important to the divinity and majesty of the site, and since so many weddings and other ceremonies had been conducted there, the view itself was deemed worthy of legal protection.

Bob and I were fascinated by that story, since we both believe that repeated ceremonies on a piece of land enhance its sacred charge. When I got to Pine Mountain, I headed for the chapel to figure out how to make an UPRISING there. As I often do, as part of my performance research, I simply sat in the space, listening and feeling. I sat alone in the dark, on a pew worn glossy from use. I imagined all kinds of actions that could take place there. I tried to see bodies in space. I asked myself: Where are the bodies? Do they move? From where do they enter? How does it start? How does it end? What is the action? Do we sing? Do we tell stories? All of these are my usual questions, but this time I had no answers. None of my ideas felt right.

The next morning, I rose before dawn and spent my first waking hour on the land as the sun was rising. I thought that this miracle might be very beautiful to witness from inside the chapel. I invited everyone at the conference to join me for an hour of silence on

Sunday morning, starting at 7:00am and ending at 8:00am. I asked theater professionals from all over the United States to participate in a performance of sitting in silence and watching the light change for an hour. The UPRISING had a life of its own, and I was there to facilitate, even if what it wanted was to evaporate like the dew. That morning, the turning of the earth itself was an UPRISING, and eight of us sat quietly noticing it.

'Sure,' I said. 'I'll join you in the chapel for a sunrise ceremony. What's it about?' There wasn't an answer, except to come to the Chapel at Pine Mountain Settlement, with some others, very early, and watch the sun rise. 'OK.' The Chapel is a beautiful structure, tucked into in those stunning Kentucky hills. It was a beautiful, cool morning. Still. Quiet. A time for meditation. Nothing happened. Everything happened as it should. Monks and nuns have done this for millennia – they still do today. Aaron Copeland wrote Appalachian Spring for a time and place like this, though this was Fall, not Spring. Quiet. Perfect. The sun rose, the Chapel filled, ever so slowly with the light of day. And then we went for breakfast, having shared something, feeling somehow full already. Here's the thing about ceremony. Since that morning, every time I see a sunrise, my spirit returns to that Kentucky morning. That morning, that experience, made each morning full, if I permit it to be.
– Gerald Stropnicky (Participant, UPRISING #58)

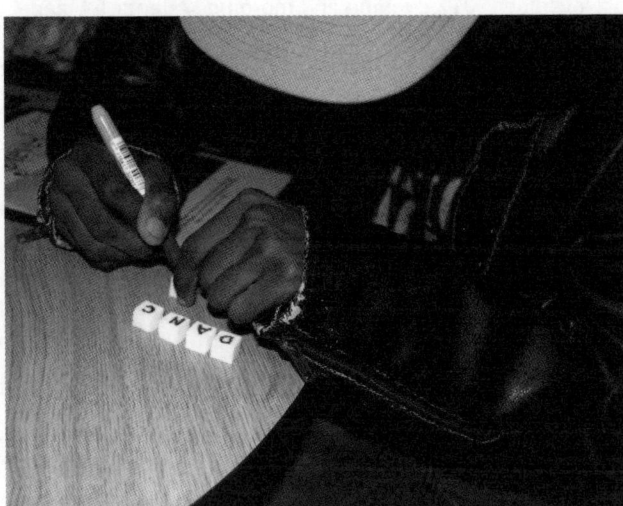

Figure 27: Taye Beasley writes new subjects of study for the School of the Americas on sugar cubes for UPRISING #59. Photo by Nicole Garneau.

CHOOSE HONESTY AND SINCERITY AS AESTHETIC AND REVOLUTIONARY STRATEGIES. AVOID ART JARGON. SPEAK PLAINLY
REVOLUTIONARY PRACTICE #59

If engaging with strangers is the way the art gets made, refine a simple and heartfelt explanation for what is happening and why you are approaching them. Interact with the public in the most sincere way possible. Avoid art jargon or other language that might make people feel unable to participate. Use everyday gestures, words, and materials. You will know the work is accessible when people are not really sure it is art, and they feel free to come up and ask, 'What is that? What are you doing?' rather than turning away from something they do not feel qualified to penetrate. These choices are not only about the process for creating the work: they are hopes for the relationships we might cultivate in a more humane world.

Honesty is an important value because it relates to the ways we perform our revolutionary selves in public. Go for plain talk and simple tasks or gestures. There is so much cynicism, trickery, and dishonesty in our current culture! The only way we can even hope to solicit a genuine response from someone we do not know is to peel away layers of artifice and try to be totally real. We must learn to embody a trustworthy integrity if we are enacting post-revolutionary or transformed social relationships.

IN ACTION: UPRISING #59
15 and 17 November 2012, evening and morning | Atlanta, GA, and
Fort Benning, GA
Participants: Elise Witt, Taye Beasley, Omari Fox, Nicole Garneau, and SOA Watch
benefit concert attendees
Photo: Robert Watkins

The School of the Americas (SOA) Watch is dedicated to closing the US Army's School of the Americas at Fort Benning in Georgia, which trains Latin American military and paramilitary in techniques of torture and assassination. People trained at Fort Benning are responsible for decades of disappearances, torture, and unspeakable atrocities against Latin American civilians and activists. At a benefit concert for SOA Watch, participants were invited to imagine subjects they would rather see taught at the school. Folks used blue markers to spell out their wishes on sugar cubes, which were collected in a jar and passed on to Atlanta-based musician Elise Witt. During a weekend vigil for peace at Fort Benning in Georgia, Elise shared the story of the UPRISING with Father Roy Bourgeois, founder of SOA Watch. Elise added water to dissolve our collective visions of humanity and love, making a sky-colored 'sweet water' that she poured out at the base of the fence surrounding Fort Benning, with prayers that the US military will stop training torturers and assassins there.

RELEASE MATERIAL BURDENS. CLEAN UP AFTER OURSELVES
REVOLUTIONARY PRACTICE #60

Ceremonial teachings emphasize the importance of how we dispose of things we have put to sacred use. If the materials left over can be recycled or reused, do that. Beet juice, milk, chalk, and cookies return easily to the earth. Ropes can be used repeatedly and stay in rotation as a ceremonial item. White clothes can be stained with beet juice, laundered, and reused for years. Give ample space for closure. Capture meaning through thoughtful reflection. Practice revolutionary clean-up: wrap things up, deconstruct them, and release them with intention.

IN ACTION: UPRISING #60

2 December 2012, 11:00am | The End of the World, New Orleans, LA
Participants: Bonnie Gabel, Jezebel, Heidi, Mat Schwarzman, Myron Blaine, Scotty Heron, Donovan Caesar, Clay Thomas, Nikki Thanos, Hannah Pepper-Cunningham, Will Bowling, Ashley Sparks, Nick Slie, Louisa Sargent, Kathy Randels, Maurice Turner, and Nicole Garneau
Photos: Melisa Cardona

There was a moment at the end of 2011 when my friends and I realized we were approaching the fifth and final year of the UPRISING project. We marveled at the journey. My friend and collaborator Ashley Sparks wanted to know if I had a plan for the final UPRISING. She suggested it take place in her home of New Orleans, among a community of artist-activist beloveds down there at the bottom of the Mississippi River. Ashley felt a strong pull toward a hair-cutting ritual, so I worked that into the UPRISING.

We gathered on a patch of land known as The End of the World in the Bywater neighborhood, where the Mississippi River meets the Industrial Canal. Since 2 December is the anniversary of the 1859 hanging of abolitionist John Brown, and the United Nations International Day for the Abolition of Slavery, participants were invited to publicly state their commitment to racial and social justice while cutting some (or all) of their hair. We used the hair cuttings to furnish a birdhouse in the hopes that our prayers for love, justice, and humanity would weave into warm nests and travel the world on bird wings.

My experience at the last UPRISING was beautiful. The weather was so nice and the people were really into the ceremony, so you couldn't help but be enthused. My big surprise was when Jezebel cut their big chunk of hair off. I think everyone else was a bit surprised too. They cut off the most.

The part where we had to talk about how we are participating in our lives to bring about change was powerful. You could tell that some people do it more than others, but that everyone had something to say. There was harmony and balance to the ceremony, as well as a bit of humor.
– Clay Thomas (Participant, UPRISING #60)

I remember cutting my hair on the levee at the End of the World in New Orleans, being invited again to let something go, to speak in front of others about what I mean when I say revolution. I remember feeling self aware, being challenged to be better and say more. A lot of times, it has been the feeling of unease that has been the best for me at an UPRISING, as it reminds me of how far I have to go in my own practice.
– Nick Slie (Participant, UPRISING #60)

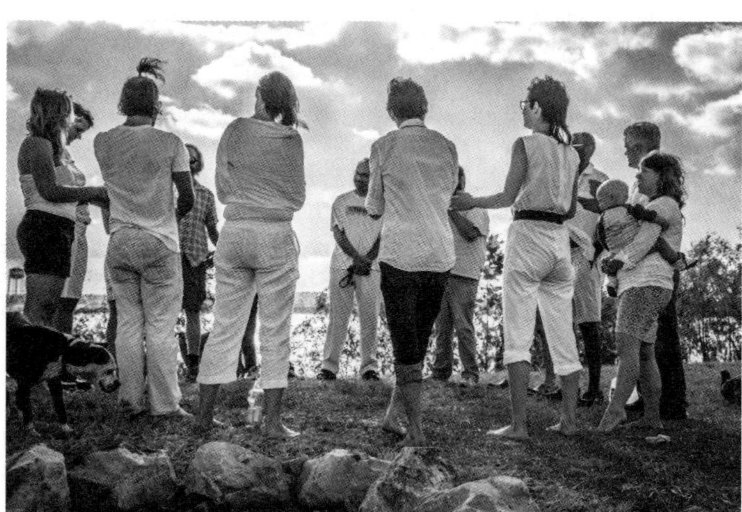

Figure 28: Gathering at the End of the World for UPRISING #60. Photo by Melisa Cardona.

Appendix: Where I'm From

SpiritHouse Inc. is a Durham, North Carolina-based cultural arts organization that works to uncover and uproot the systemic barriers to long-term self-sufficiency. As part of their Harm Free Zone training, they lead a simple but incredibly powerful exercise called 'Where I'm From.' This is also the name of a poem written in 1993 by George Ella Lyon, the 2015–16 Poet Laureate of Kentucky. It opens a space for people to name the places, people, and experiences that shaped their lives and work, bringing them to the here and now. This exercise touches me because it directly and poetically addresses the erased and contested places people come from, especially when the people are women, queer, people of color, poor folks, workers, or otherwise marginalized. 'Where I'm From' lets us celebrate the teachers without degrees, the stories never recorded in history, and the artists whose work was never legitimized by institutions. It invites us to claim the smells of our grandmother's kitchen and the hidden wounds we carry as origin points that are just as valid as what goes on a CV.

- I'm from backstage rooms crammed with 100 tiny dancers in sequined tutus while the burgundy-haired ballerina Yvonne Brown squeezed among us repeating 'Merde!' and blessing our foreheads with her saliva-wet thumb.
- I'm from elementary school gymnasium productions of *Puff the Magic Dragon* conjured by Penny Choice's belly laughs, and from the diaphanous gown caressing my teen sexuality as I played Titania in Carolyn Thomas Davidoff's *A Midsummer Night's Dream* at the Children's Theater of Western Springs.
- I'm from long white robes and electric-candelabra rituals outlined in a small purple cloth-bound book, processing through Masonic Temples with a dozen other Daughters of Job singing 'Onward Christian Soldiers.'
- I'm from Jane Siberry playing on my Walkman after dark, on streets lined with old-money mansions, dreaming of the day I could join the

chaotic urban existence from which Hinsdale was determined to protect me.

- I'm from the narcissistic anglophile director of my high-school theater program who taught me how to read and perform Shakespeare, and a lot of other valuable things about acting, but whose demented misogyny took years to unpack, and whose disgustingly explicit commentary on our young bodies and lives can never be unheard.
- I'm from Reverend Martin Deppe's Methodist Church sermons against South African Apartheid that sent me running to the library to learn more, where being feminist, queer-loving, anti-war, and in solidarity with poor and oppressed people was what one should do to be most like Jesus.
- I'm from the African-American Studies Department at University of Illinois at Chicago, where I went seeking to fill a hole in my education before I even understood how deep and wide that hole was.
- I'm from a grandmother who sent me a handwritten letter thanking me for taking an overnight bus to Washington, DC, to a Reproductive Rights March because birth control and abortion are worth defending. This letter described my great-grandmother's anguish and suffering over having more children than she could handle.
- I'm from a mother who took her own journey to understand what it meant to have a queer daughter and turned that into decades of activism and support for families of LGBTQ people.
- I'm from decades marching through city streets chanting some version of 'No Blood for Oil!'
- I'm from the small university theater program where students and professors fell in love with a Russian theater company on its first tour outside the Soviet Union, only a few years after Sting (1985) sang, 'I hope the Russians love their children too.'
- I'm from the fog-machine clouds and tight columns of overhead light in the Theatre of Moscow South-West, listening to the psychedelically colorful мат (profanity) of Valery Romanovich Beliakovich (1950–2016).
- I'm from ten years of weekly Russian language lessons at the dining room table of Alla Dekhtyar, doyen of the Chicago Soviet Expat Literary Intelligentsia.
- I'm from the direct action feminist organization I joined in order to make out with hot, politically engaged lesbians.

- I'm from delivering newspapers at age 10, a reputation as a babysitter with a special talent for hellions, and awareness of the extreme privilege of being able to be under-employed by choice for a few years in order to make art and write this book.
- I'm from the Interdisciplinary Arts Program at Columbia College Chicago, where Suzanne Cohan-Lange declared that ideas are airborne; Nana Shineflug insisted that non-dancers make interesting movement; Jenny Magnus suggested one breath on stage before and after the piece; Sherry Antonini modeled the most loving and challenging writing feedback; and Joan Dickinson lifted up menstrual theorists. Jeff Abell told me 1970s feminists had already said everything that needed to be said about menstruation, and years later he knelt on Michigan Avenue with a handkerchief, dabbing my beet-juice-splattered face.
- I'm from the creaky wood floors and clanging radiators of the Rogers Park church that housed Insight Arts, where I found the space to make artwork that was difficult and stimulating, hold weekly drum rehearsals, produce annual Women's Performance Jams, and understand that artists are essential to movements for social change.
- I'm from earth-based Goddess spirituality that promotes reclamation of the divine feminine as a strategy for healing the destructive ravages of heteropatriarchy. I'm from percussive, eclectic, feminist Euro-Pagan Equinox and Solstice celebrations created by Uncle Bear, Alice Lowenstein, Anne Statton, and Jane Haldiman.
- I'm from the day in my 31st year when I almost bled to death on an operating table, and woke up without a uterus.
- I'm from the Mikao Usui lineage of practitioners of Reiki, a Japanese form of energetic therapy. I'm from the effervescent healing and transmissions of my teachers Ruth Robbins, Geryll Robinson, and Jane Fresne.
- I'm from the morning that Ruth rearranged the elements on my home altar and began my initiation into the cross-cultural Pachakuti Mesa tradition created by don Oscar Miro-Quesada Solevo, through the guidance of his teachers don Celso Rojas Palomino and don Benito Corihuamán Vargas of Peru. I sit in circles in rooms filled with Palo Santo smoke and Agua Florida, praying, learning, rebuilding, and wrestling with ancient teachings outside of my cultural tradition.

- I'm from the dance floor of the Wednesday-night queer performance party that provided a brief monthly respite from an epically broken heart.
- I'm from friends who offered unconditional support for the decision to uproot my home, quit a really plum job, release many material possessions, and take my act on the road.
- I'm from four beloved niblings who call me Ms Nicole and bring unmeasurable joy to my life as their aunt.

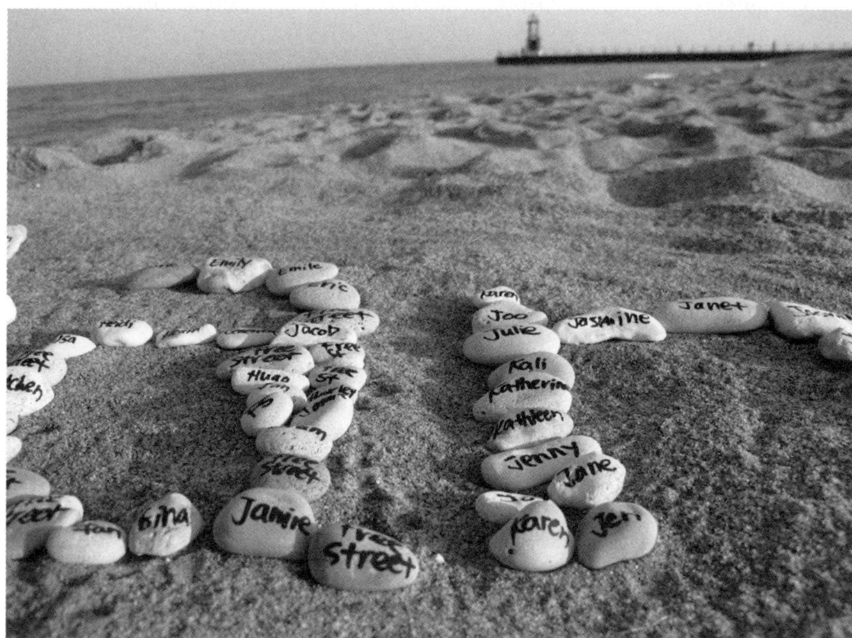

Figure 29: The names of UPRISING participants to date written on stones for UPRISING #23. Photo by Uncle Bear.

Notes on Contributors

Nicole Coffineau is a Ph.D. candidate in the history of art and architecture at the University of Pittsburgh, and Kress Fellow at the Bibliotheca Hertziana – Max Planck Institute for Art History in Rome, Italy. Her dissertation considers photography in Italy before World War I and relations amongst collecting practices, social thought, aesthetic philosophy, modernity, and the artistic avant-garde. Nicole is also a critic and curator focusing upon photography, portraiture, theories and histories of contemporary art, and intersections of art, politics, and activism. Nicole received her MA from the University of Chicago in 2011, and currently lives and works in Los Angeles and Rome.

Anne Cushwa received her Ph.D. in art history from the University of Iowa. Her doctoral dissertation focused on the work of Félix González-Torres. She was a founding member of Category 5 Artists' Collective, formed after Hurricane Katrina. Category 5 worked primarily with installation and earth art, focusing on participation from the public and the ephemeral nature of installations. Anne has worked as a visiting assistant professor in the Department of Art at St. Mary's College in South Bend, Indiana; as assistant professor and director of Ameen Art Gallery at Nicholls State University in Thibodaux, Louisiana; and as an adjunct professor at the University of Rochester, leading their study abroad program in Arezzo, Italy. She also worked as the assistant to the director of the Heriard-Cimino Gallery in New Orleans.

Nicole Garneau is an interdisciplinary artist making site-specific performance and project art that is directly political, critically conscious, and community engaged. *Performing Revolutionary: Art, Action, Activism* is her first book. Nicole is on the executive committee of Alternate ROOTS, an organization of artists and activists who center their work in the US South. She holds a BA in theater from the University of Illinois at Chicago and an MA in interdisciplinary art from Columbia College Chicago. She has taught in Cultural Studies and Women and Gender Studies at Columbia College Chicago, DePaul University, and Eastern Kentucky University. She also makes ceremonies, facilitates meetings, throws parties, and does healing work. Website: http://nicolegarneau.com/.

Daniel Tucker works as an artist, writer and organizer, developing documentaries, publications, exhibitions, and events inspired by his interest in social movements and the people and places from which they emerge. His writings and lectures on the intersections of art and politics and his collaborative art projects have been published and presented widely. Tucker recently completed the feature-length video essay *Future Perfect: Time Capsules in Reagan Country* and curated the exhibition and event series *Organize Your Own: The Politics and Poetics of Self-Determination Movements*. He earned his MFA from the University of Illinois at Chicago and BFA from the School of the Art Institute of Chicago, and is an assistant professor and founding graduate program director in social and studio practices at Moore College of Art & Design in Philadelphia. Website: https://miscprojects.com/.

Bibliography

350.org. (2009), 'The science', https://350.org/about/science/. Accessed 4 November 2016.

Aguhar, M. (2011), 'Litanies to My Heavenly Brown Body', *Cultural Disruptions*, http://culturaldisruptions.blogspot.com/2012/03/litanies-to-my-heavenly-brown-body.html. Accessed 26 March 2017.

Allan, H. (2007), 'Interrogating dissent: Coco Fusco on the art and politics of terror', *Bitch Magazine,* 37, pp. 64–67, 94.

American Civil Liberties Union (2016), 'Arizona's SB 1070', https://www.aclu.org/feature/arizonas-sb-1070. Accessed 13 November 2016.

Arendt, H. (2005), *The Promise of Politics*, New York: Schocken Books.

Barker, D. (2003), *Tibetan Prayer Flags: Send Your Blessings on the Breeze*, London: Connections.

Beaven, K. (2012), 'Performance art 101: The Happening, Allan Kaprow', Tate Blog, http://www.tate.org.uk/context-comment/blogs/performance-art-101-happening-allan-kaprow. Accessed 26 March 2017.

Belting, H. and Buddensieg, A. (eds) (2009), *The Global Art World: Audiences, Markets, and Museums*, Ostfildern: Hatje Cantz.

Belting, H., Buddensieg, A. and Weibel, P. (2013), *The Global Contemporary and the Rise of New Worlds*, Cambridge: The MIT Press for ZKM, Karlsruhe.

Benedetti, M. (1983), *Why Do We Sing?*, http://collectiveliberation.org/wp-content/uploads/2013/01/Benedetti-Why-do-we-sing.pdf. Accessed 26 March 2017.

Berardi, F. and Lovink, G. (2011), 'A call to the army of love and the army of software', http://networkcultures.org/geert/2011/10/12/franco-berardi-geert-lovink-a-call-to-the-army-of-love-and-to-the-army-of-software/. Accessed 3 November 2016.

Berry, W. (2000), *Jayber Crow: A Novel*, Washington, DC: Counterpoint.

——— (2013), 'The commerce of violence', *The Progressive*, http://progressive.org/dispatches/commerce-violence/. Accessed 26 March 2017.

Bey, H. ([1991] 2003), *T.A.Z.: The Temporary Autonomous Zone, Ontological Anarchy, Poetic Terrorism*, New York: Autonomedia.

Bishop, C. (2006), *Participation,* London: Whitechapel.

—— (2012), *Artificial Hells: Participatory Art and the Politics of Spectatorship*, New York: Verso Books.

Boal, A. (1995), *The Rainbow of Desire: The Boal Method of Theatre and Therapy*, London: Routledge.

Boggs, G. L. and Boggs, J. (2008), *Revolution and Evolution in the 20th Century*, 2nd ed., New York: Monthly Review Press.

Bogues, A. (2012), 'And what about the human? Freedom, emancipation and the power of the radical imagination', *boundary 2,* 39:3, pp. 30–46.

Bourriaud, N. (2002), *Relational Aesthetics*, Dijon: Les Presses du réel.

Braun, T. (1998), 'Peace profile: Alexandra Kollontai', *Peace Review,* 10:2, pp. 295–300.

Broude, N., Garrard, M. D. and Brodsky, J. K. (1994), *The Power of Feminist Art: The American Movement of the 1970s, History and Impact,* New York: H. N. Abrams.

Broughton, J. (1990), *Special Deliveries: New and Selected Poems,* Seattle: Broken Moon Press.

Busch, K. (2008), 'Scholars talk academic freedom at DePaul', *The Chicago Maroon*, 5 February, https://www.chicagomaroon.com/2008/02/05/scholars-talk-academic-freedom-at-depaul/. Accessed 10 November 2016.

Butler, J. (2004), *Precarious Life: The Powers of Mourning and Violence*, London: Verso.

Caute, D. (1988), *The Year of the Barricades: A Journey through 1968*, New York: Harper & Row.

Chicago Dyke March Collective (2016), 'About us', https://chicagodykemarch.wordpress.com/about-2/. Accessed 4 November 2016.

Chicago, J. (1996), *Beyond the Flower: The Autobiography of a Feminist Artist*, New York: Viking.

Chris Hedges: War Is a Force that Gives Us Meaning (2006), Janis Shields, PRX, US, 1 November, https://beta.prx.org/stories/7562/details. Accessed 26 March 2017.

Clark, L. and Oiticica, H. (2006), 'Letters', in C. Bishop (ed.), *Participation*, Cambridge: The MIT Press, pp. 110–116.

Columbia Strike Committee (1968), *Why We Strike,* New York: Columbia Strike Coordinating Committee.

Conwill Màjozo, E. (1996), 'To search for the good and make it matter', in S. Lacy (ed.), *Mapping the Terrain: New Genre Public Art*, Seattle: Bay Press, pp. 88–93.

Cromidas, R. (2015), 'Evidence of the corporatization of pride parade, in one pie chart', *Chicagoist,* 6 July, http://chicagoist.com/2015/07/06/evidence_of_the_corporatization_of.php#_jmp0_. Accessed 27 March 2017.

Davis, B. (2013a), 'A critique of social practice art: What does it mean to be a political artist?', *International Socialist Review*, http://isreview.org/issue/90/critique-social-practice-art#_jmp0_. Accessed 26 March 2017.

——— (2013b), 'Ben Davis responds', http://www.abladeofgrass.org/growing-dialogue/ben-davis-responds/. Accessed 26 March 2017.

Democracy Now! (2016), 'A moral giant: A Democracy Now! Special on the life & legacy of Father Daniel Berrigan', https://www.democracynow.org/2016/5/3/a_democracy_now_special_on_the. Accessed 26 March 2017.

Demos, T. J. (2013), *The Migrant Image: The Art and Politics of Documentary during Global Crisis*, Durham and London: Duke University Press.

——— (2016), *Decolonizing Nature: Contemporary Art and the Politics of Ecology*, Berlin: Sternberg Press.

Eisenstein, C. (2016), 'The election: Of hate, grief, and a new story', http://charleseisenstein.net/hategriefandanewstory/. Accessed 10 November 2016.

Felshin, N. (1994), *But is it Art? The Spirit of Art as Activism*, Seattle: Bay Press.

Fisher, M. and Berardi, F. (n.d.), 'Give me shelter: Franco "Bifo" Berardi and Mark Fisher discuss exhaustion, the financial crisis, aesthetic resistance and the "slow cancellation of the future"', Frieze.com, https://frieze.com/article/give-me-shelter-mark-fisher. Accessed 26 March 2017.

Freire, P. (1970), *Pedagogy of the Oppressed*, New York: Herder and Herder.

——— (1993), *The Pedagogy of the Oppressed,* rev. ed., New York: The Continuum Publishing Company.

Fusco, C. (2008), *A Field Guide for Female Interrogators*, New York: Seven Stories Press.

Gablik, S. (1992), *The Reenchantment of Art*, New York: Thames and Hudson.

——— (2002), *Living the Magical Life: An Oracular Adventure,* Grand Rapids: Phanes Press.

Gardner-Huggett, J. (2007), 'The women artists' cooperative space as a site for social change: Artemisia Gallery, Chicago (1973–1979)', *Social Justice*, 34:1, pp. 28–43.

——— (2012), 'Artemisia challenges the elders: How a women artists' cooperative created a community for feminism and art made by women', *Frontiers: A Journal of Women Studies*, 33:2, pp. 55–75.

Garneau, N. (2007), 'Conference report: Engaging through place at *Imagining America*', https://web.archive.org/web/20070524225043/http://www.communityarts.net/readingroom/archivefiles/2007/03/conference_repo.php. Accessed 27 March 2017.

——— (2011), interviewed by Nicole Coffineau, 19 February, Sheffield's Bar, Chicago.

Giroux, H. (2013), 'The violence of organized forgetting', *Truthout*, http://www.truth-out.org/opinion/item/17647-the-violence-of-organized-forgetting#. Accessed 26 March 2017.

GLAAD (2016), 'Transgender day of remembrance #TDOR – November 20', https://www.glaad.org/tdor. Accessed 4 November 2016.

Glass-Coffin, B. and Miro-Quesada, O. (2013), *Lessons in Courage: Peruvian Shamanic Wisdom for Everyday Life*, Garden City Park: Square One Publishers.

Glissant, É. (2006), *Poetics of Relation* (trans. B. Wing), Ann Arbor: University of Michigan Press.

Goldberg, R. (1998), *Performance: Live Art Since 1960*, New York: Harry N. Abrams.

Gómez-Peña, G. and Sifuentes, R. (2011), *Exercises for Rebel Artists: Radical Performance Pedagogy*, London: Routledge.

Gopnik, A. (2014), 'Christopher Michael-Martinez's father gets it right', *The New Yorker*, http://www.newyorker.com/news/news-desk/christopher-michael-martinezs-father-gets-it-right. Accessed 26 March 2017.

Guerrilla Girls (2011), 'Guide to behaving badly, which you have to do most of the time in the world as we know it', lecture delivered at Feminist Panel, *College Art Association Annual Conference*, New York City, US, 8 February.

Halifax, J. (1993), *The Fruitful Darkness: Reconnecting with the Body of the Earth*, San Francisco: HarperSanFrancisco.

Harshaw, C. (2012), Facebook post, 22 December, https://www.facebook.com/craig.harshaw.3/posts/10151299242543704?comment_id=25391859¬if_t=mentions_comment. Accessed 26 March 2017.

Harvey, D. (2008), 'The right to the city', https://davidharvey.org/media/righttothecity.pdf. Accessed 26 March 2017.

Heart of the Healer (2016), 'Pachakuti Mesa tradition lineage', http://heartofthehealer.org/shamanism-pachakuti-mesa-tradition/. Accessed 4 November 2016.

Hedges, C. (2002), *War Is a Force that Gives Us Meaning*, New York: PublicAffairs.

—— (2010), 'Hope will only come now when we physically defy the violence of the state', speech delivered at an anti-war rally at the White House gates, Washington, DC, 16 December.

Hennessy, K. (2013), '10th anniversary of the war & occupation of Iraq (I tried to stop the war)', http://circozero.org/writing-rants/2013/04/10th-anniversary-of-war-occupation-of.html. Accessed 27 March 2017.

Hoffman, A. (2005), *Revolution for the Hell of It: The Book That Earned Abbie Hoffman a Five-Year Prison Term at the Chicago Conspiracy Trial*, Boston: DaCapo Press.

Hoffmann, J. and Jonas, J. (2005), *Perform*, London: Thames & Hudson.

hooks, b. (1994), *Teaching to Transgress: Education as the Practice of Freedom*, New York: Routledge.

—— (1995), 'Performance practice as a site of resistance', in C. Ugwu (ed.), *Let's Get It On: The Politics of Black Performance*, London: Institute of Contemporary Arts.

hooks, b. and Mesa-Bains, A. (2006), *Homegrown: Engaged Cultural Criticism*, Cambridge: South End Press.

Illich, I. (1973), *Tools for Conviviality*, New York: HarperCollins.

Iron & Wine (2009), 'Peng! 33', single, Seattle: Sub Pop Records.

Isakovsky, M. (1938), 'Катюша' ('Katyusha'), https://www.marxists.org/history/ussr/sounds/lyrics/katyusha.htm. Accessed 5 November 2016.

Jensen, D. (2006), 'Excerpt from *Endgame*: Premises', http://www.derrickjensen.org/endgame/premises/. Accessed 26 March 2017.

Johnstone, S. (2008), *The Everyday*, London: Whitechapel.

Joravsky, B. (2007), 'Will the games displace their games?: Quigley the brave', http://www.chicagoreader.com/chicago/will-the-games-displace-their-gamesquigley-the-brave/Content?oid=924969. Accessed 5 November 2016.

Juno, A. and Vale, V. (1991), *Angry Women*, San Francisco: RE/Search Publications.

Kawasaki, G. and Welch, S. (2013), *APE: Author, Publisher, Entrepreneur*, Palo Alto, CA: Nononina Press.

Keehn, D. (2011), *Eco Amazons: 20 Women Who Are Transforming the World*, Brooklyn: PowerHouse Books.

Kizer, C. (2001), *Cool, Calm & Collected: Poems, 1960-2000*, Port Townsend: Copper Canyon Press.

Koplevsky, I. (2006), 'Катюша' ('Katyusha'), https://www.marxists.org/history/ussr/sounds/lyrics/katyusha.htm. Accessed 5 November 2016.

Kwon, M. (2004), *One Place after Another: Site-Specific Art and Locational Identity*, 1st paperback ed., Cambridge and London: The MIT Press.

Lacy, S. (1995), *Mapping the Terrain: New Genre Public Art*, Seattle: Bay Press.

Langlois, J. (n.d.), 'Methodologies of failure: Evaluation practices for socially engaged art', http://justinlanglois.com/writing/methodologies-of-failure-evaluation-practices-for-socially-engaged-art/. Accessed 26 March 2017.

Leonen, M. (2004), 'Etiquette for activists', *yes! magazine*, http://www.yesmagazine.org/issues/a-conspiracy-of-hope/etiquette-for-activists. Accessed 5 November 2016.

Lerner, B. (2012), 'A note on the human microphone', *Critical Quarterly*, 54, pp. 66–8.

Lippard, L. (1995), 'Looking around: Where we are, where we could be', in S. Lacy (ed.), *Mapping the Terrain: New Genre Public Art*, Seattle: Bay Press, p. 126.

Live Art Leeds (2012), '(in)Xclusion', http://www.liveartleeds.com/inxclusion. Accessed 10 November 2016.

Lorde, A. (1984), *Sister Outsider: Essays and Speeches*, Trumansburg: Crossing Press.

March, A. (2005), *The Che Reader,* Cape Verde: Ocean Press.

Mercer, K. (2011), 'The cross-cultural and the contemporary', in M. Wallace (ed.), *21st Century: Art in the First Decade*, Brisbane: Queensland Art Gallery/Gallery of Modern Art, pp. 194–201.

Michaels, A. (2009), *The Winter Vault*, New York: Alfred A. Knopf.

Miejan, T. (2012), 'Birth 2012: An interview with Barbara Marx Hubbard', *The Edge Magazine*, http://www.edgemagazine.net/2012/11/birth-2012/. Accessed 14 November 2016.

Milevska, S. (2006), 'Participatory art: A paradigm shift from objects to subjects', *SpringerIn*, http://www.springerin.at/dyn/heft_text.php?textid=1761&lang=en. Accessed 26 March 2017.

Miller, M. (2017), 'Ta-Nehisi Coates: "Chicago is the capital of Black America"', *Chicago Tonight*, http://chicagotonight.wttw.com/2017/02/01/ta-nehisi-coates-chicago-capital-black-america. Accessed 26 March 2017.

Miller, R. (2012), 'Reactivating the social body in insurrectionary times: A dialogue with Franco "Bifo" Berardi', *Berkeley Planning Journal: The Urban Fringe blog*, http://ced.berkeley.edu/bpj/2012/09/reactivating-the-social-body-in-insurrectionary-times-a-dialogue-with-franco-bifo-berardi/. Accessed 26 March 2017.

Mingus, M. (2011), 'Moving toward the ugly: A politic beyond desirability', *Leaving Evidence*, https://leavingevidence.wordpress.com/2011/08/22/moving-toward-the-ugly-a-politic-beyond-desirability/. Accessed 26 March 2017.

Montagu, A. (1986), *Touching: The Human Significance of the Skin*, New York: William Morrow Paperbacks.

Moraine, S. (2011), '"Mic check!": #occupy, technology & the amplified voice', *The Society Pages*, https://thesocietypages.org/cyborgology/2011/10/06/mic-check-occupy-technology-the-amplified-voice/. Accessed 3 November 2016.

Moratorium on Deportations Campaign (2011), 'Why we march? ¿Porque Marchamos?', https://moratoriumondeportations.org/march-10-2011/why-we-march/. Accessed 4 November 2016.

Mouffe, C. (2012), 'Strategies of radical politics and aesthetic resistance', http://truth.steirischerherbst.at/texts/?p=19. Accessed 26 March 2017.

Movement for Black Lives (2016), 'Platform', https://policy.m4bl.org/invest-divest/. Accessed 9 November 2016.

New Millennium Essences (2011), 'Beetroot flower essence', http://www.nmessences.com/essences/beetroot.html. Accessed 4 November 2016.

New York Times (2012), 'Wages and poverty among top apparel exporters', http://www.nytimes.com/interactive/2012/08/23/world/asia/Wages-and-Poverty-Among-Top-Apparel-Exporters.html?ref=asia&_r=3&. Accessed 4 November 2016.

Oliver, M. (2005), 'Lead', in M. Oliver, *New and Selected Poems*, vol. 2, https://www.neopoet.com/kailashana/blog/840-am-2-jun-2011. Accessed 26 March 2017.

Omi, M. and Winant, H. (1994), *Racial Formation in the United States: From the 1960s to the 1990s*, New York: Routledge.

Oppenheim, J. ([1912] 1964), 'Bread and Roses: Poem by James Oppenheim – 1912', in Joyce L. Kornbluh (ed.), *Rebel Voices: An I.W.W. Anthology*, Ann Arbor: University of Michigan Press.

Osborne, P. (2013), *Anywhere or Not at All: Philosophy of Contemporary Art*, London: Verso.

Page, C. (2010), 'Reflections from Detroit: Transforming wellness & wholeness', INCITE! blog, https://inciteblog.wordpress.com/2010/08/05/reflections-from-detroit-transforming-wellness-wholeness/. Accessed 4 November 2016.

Pareles, J. (2014), 'Pete Seeger, champion of folk music and social change, dies at 94', http://www.nytimes.com/2014/01/29/arts/music/pete-seeger-songwriter-and-champion-of-folk-music-dies-at-94.html?_r=1. Accessed 3 November 2016.

Phillips, P. (2016), *Mierle Laderman Ukeles: Maintenance Art*, New York: Prestel.

Pinchbeck, D. (2006), *2012: The Return of Quetzalcoatl*, New York: Jeremy Tarcher and Penguin.

Pocket Guide to Hell (2011), 'The Haymarket reenactment', https://pocketguidetohell.com/the-haymarket-reenactment/. Accessed 5 November 2016.

Rage against the Machine (1992), *Rage against the Machine*, album, New York: Epic Associated.

Reardon, P. (2008), '3 weeks later, literary shrine still just fine', *Chicago Tribune*, http://articles.chicagotribune.com/2008-11-08/news/0811070318_1_shrine-sojourner-truth-bookcase. Accessed 26 March 2017.

Remember the Triangle Fire (2016), 'History & mission', http://rememberthetrianglefire.org/about-2/about/. Accessed 4 November 2016.

Reynolds, L. (2009), *Not a Bystander*, event program, Chicago: Tamms Year 10 Campaign.

——— (2013), 'Tamms is torture: The campaign to close an Illinois Supermax Prison', http://creativetimereports.org/2013/05/06/tamms-is-torture-campaign-close-illinois-supermax-prison-solitary-confinement/. Accessed 4 November 2016.

Rich, A. (2016), *Collected Poems, 1950–2012*, New York: W.W. Norton.

Robertson, J. and McDaniel, C. (2005), *Themes of Contemporary Art: Visual Art after 1980*, Oxford: Oxford University Press.

Roldan, E. (2016), 'En Casa: Finding home at Latin night', http://www.mtv.com/news/2893695/en-casa-finding-home-at-latin-night/. Accessed 4 November 2016.

Rothenberg, P. S. (2012), *White Privilege: Essential Readings on the Other Side of Racism*, New York: Worth Publishers.

Ryan, H. (2014), 'What does trans* mean, and where did it come from?', Outward: Expanding the LGBTQ conversation, http://www.slate.com/blogs/outward/2014/01/10/trans_what_does_it_mean_and_where_did_it_come_from.html#_jmp0. Accessed 4 November 2016.

Said, E. (1994), *Representations of the Intellectual: The 1993 Reith Lectures*, New York: Pantheon Books.

Sandoval-Sánchez, A. and Saporta Sternbach, N. (2001), 'Rehearsing transculturation: A theory for U.S. Latina Theater and solo performance', in A. Sandoval-Sánchez and N. Saporta Sternbach, *Stages of Life: Transcultural Performance & Identity in U.S. Latina Theater*, Tucson: University of AZ Press.

Schmitt, C. (2007), *The Concept of the Political: Expanded Edition*, Chicago: The University of Chicago Press.

Sholette, G. (1999), 'News from nowhere: Activist art and after, a report from New York City', *Third Text #45*, 3, http://www.gregorysholette.com/wp-content/uploads/2011/04/13_newsfrom1.pdf. Accessed 26 March 2017.

—— (2008), 'Gifts of resistance', http://www.gregorysholette.com/wp-content/uploads/2011/04/GiftsOfResistance.Perifieric.1.pdf. Accessed 26 March 2017.

Sloan, P. F. and McGuire, B. (1965), 'Eve of Destruction', single, New York: RCA Records.

Smith, I. (2016), 'Carolee Schneemann on feminism, activism and ageing', *OnAnother*, http://www.anothermag.com/art-photography/8462/carolee-schneemann-on-feminism-activism-and-ageing. Accessed 26 March 2017.

Smith, M. (2015), 'Abolish the police. Instead, let's have full social, economic, and political equality', *The Nation*, https://www.thenation.com/article/abolish-police-instead-lets-have-full-social-economic-and-political-equality/. Accessed 26 March 2017.

Smith, T. (2011), *Contemporary Art: World Currents*, London: Laurence King.

—— (forthcoming), *Art to Come*, Durham: Duke University Press.

Smith, T. and Mathur, S. (2014), 'Interview: Contemporary art: World currents in transition beyond globalization', *Contemporaneity: Historical Presence in Contemporary Culture*, 3:1, https://contemporaneity.pitt.edu/ojs/index.php/contemporaneity/article/view/112/110. Accessed 17 March 2017.

SpiritHouse Inc. (2016), 'Who we are', http://www.spirithouse-nc.org. Accessed 8 November 2016.

Starhawk (2009), 'Winter Solstice, 2009', http://starhawk.org/winter-solstice-2009/. Accessed 15 November 2016.

Sting (1985), *The Dream of the Blue Turtles*, album, Los Angeles: A & M Records.

Stoltenberg, J. (1984), 'Refusing to be a man', *Women's Studies International Forum*, 7, pp. 25—7.

Sundiata, S. (2006), '51st (dream) state: Creativity, collaboration and student learning', presentation at The Ohio State University, Columbus, OH, 7 October.

Thompson, N. (2012), *Living as Form: Socially Engaged Art from 1991-2011*, Cambridge: The MIT Press.

Thompson, N. and Tucker, D. (2008), *Democracy in America*, Chicago: Creative Time, https://never-the-same.org/5-questions/question-5/. Accessed 7 November 2016.

Thompson, N., Sholette, G., Thompson, J., Mirzoeff, N., Chavoya, C. O. and Noordeman, A. (2004), *The Interventionists: Users' Manual for the Creative Disruption of Everyday Life*, North Adams: MASS MoCA.

Transrespect versus Transphobia Worldwide (2015), 'TvT research project: Trans murder monitoring', http://transrespect.org/en/research/trans-murder-monitoring/. Accessed 3 November 2016.

Tucker, D. (2011), 'Interview with Nicole Garneau', in *Never the Same: Conversations About Art Transforming Politics & Community in Chicago & Beyond*, https://never-the-same. org/interviews/nicole-garneau/. Accessed 27 March 2017.

TRUNEWS (2016) 'Sarah Palin: "Donald J. Trump is that revolutionary!"', YouTube, 14 March, https://www.youtube.com/watch?v=F9-S-oTY5oY. Accessed 3 November 2016.

Unknown (1998), *Nelson Algren Memorial Fountain*, Chicago: Milwaukee/Division/Ashland, Sculpture.

'Uprising' (1926), *Oxford English Dictionary*, Oxford: Oxford University Press, http://www. oed.com.pitt.idm.oclc.org/view/Entry/220099?result=1&rskey=heLroh&. Accessed 2 May 2016.

Wikipedia (2016a), 'Arab Spring', http://en.wikipedia.org/wiki/Arab_Spring. Accessed 3 November 2016.

———— (2016b), 'Days of rage', https://en.wikipedia.org/wiki/Days_of_Rage. Accessed 3 November 2016.

———— (2016c), 'Occupy movement', https://en.wikipedia.org/wiki/Occupy_movement. Accessed 3 November 2016.

Yardley, J. (2013), 'Report on deadly factory collapse in Bangladesh finds widespread blame', *New York Times,* http://www.nytimes.com/2013/05/23/world/asia/report-on-bangla-desh-building-collapse-finds-widespread-blame.html. Accessed 3 November 2016.

Zorach, R. (2008), '68/08 Introduction', *AREA: Chicago Art, Research, Education, Activism*, 7, http://areachicago.org/6808-introduction/. Accessed 9 November 2016.

Index